Haynes
Restoration
Manual

Land Rover 90, 110 and Defender

Lindsay Porter

First published in 1999
Reprinted 2002, 2004, 2006, 2009, 2010, 2011 and 2012

A catalogue record for this book is available from the British Library

ISBN 978 1 85960 600 1

Library of Congress catalog card no. 98-74169

Published by Haynes Publishing,
Sparkford, Yeovil, Somerset BA22 7JJ, UK

Tel. 01963 442030 Fax 01963 440001
Int. tel. +44 1963 442030 Fax +44 1963 440001
E-mail: sales@haynes.co.uk
Website: www.haynes.co.uk

Haynes North America Inc.,
861 Lawrence Drive, Newbury Park,
California 91320, USA.

Printed and bound in the USA

Contents

Introduction and Acknowledgements

Land Rover owners can, and do, go on at considerable length about what makes their vehicles great. So, for the uninitiated, let's go through a list of all the things that help to make the Land Rover 90, 110 and Defender the ideal vehicles for restoration:

– *They're vehicles with character that can still be used on an everyday basis in a modern environment.* (Tick)

– *They're easy to work on.* (Tick)

– *There's almost one hundred percent parts availability . . .* (Tick)

– *. . . with a choice of manufacturers or less-expensive, good quality non-original parts.* (Tick)

– *Versions can be adapted to run on unleaded fuel.* (Tick)

– *There's an ample source of restoration information.* (Tick - Now that this book is written!)

Which brings me neatly to the next point because, without the day-to-day expertise of certain key specialists, this book would not have been half as comprehensive as I believe it to be. **Liveridge British 4x4** deal with literally hundreds of 90s, 110s and Defenders each year and their knowledge of what can go wrong, what does go wrong, and how to put it right is very good.

Another company that was extremely helpful is **PWB Replacement Motor Parts Ltd**, now known as SPI Distribution Europe Ltd. This company makes Land Rover body panels which won't break the bank to buy. You can't buy them direct because they only supply the trade. However, if you're worried that the quality is not going to be good enough just bear this one in mind:

As any 'fule noe', if you put a piece of aluminium next to a piece of steel, and then let water wash over the joint as it comes down the insides of the doors, corrosion is bound to occur sooner or later - it's called electrolytic reaction. PWB (as they were then) developed their own range of doors which attempts to keep the two metals entirely apart and may reduce dramatically, if not totally eliminate the corrosion problem.

In my office, Zoë Palmer has put an enormous amount of support work into this project and without her, I fear that Haynes would have had an even longer wait for the finished book to appear!

I hope you enjoy this book and, above all, that you enjoy your Land Rover. It's not difficult!

Lindsay Porter
Bromyard

SAFETY NOTE: Please be sure to read **Chapter 2 - Preparation and Essential Safety** before carrying out any work on your vehicle.

Chapter 1

Heritage and Buying

The original Land Rover project began in the spring of 1947 after much study of the Jeep design by the Rover Company's Managing Director, Spencer Wilks and his design engineer brother, Maurice. In fact a Jeep chassis was used for the first prototype which was completed that summer with the first 25 trial vehicles ready for testing by the autumn.

The model was launched at the Amsterdam Motor Show in April 1948. It had an 80in (2,032mm) wheelbase, pick-up body and 1595cc Rover 'P3' type four-cylinder engine, permanent four-wheel drive and a freewheel facility in the front drive line. It was spartan, and was priced at £450.

Forty-eight of these vehicles were produced, with the real production run starting in July 1948 – at the same price but with better fittings! In October, a light-alloy panelled station wagon was introduced at a price of £959. This style was built until 1951.

In 1950 an alternative top was offered, so that both metal and canvas were available. Also, the freewheel feature was discontinued, and the transmission had optional four-wheel or rear-wheel drive with cockpit control of the transfer gearbox.

From the beginning of 1952 the engine was bored out to 1997cc, and in 1954 the wheelbase was increased from 80in to 86in (2,184mm). A long-wheelbase version (107in/2,718mm) was produced with an extra 41in (1,041mm) of loading platform. In 1956, the

▲ H1. Everything about the Series I Land Rover speaks of function and practicality. This 1951 80in model was owned and lightly restored by the author after having led a very sheltered life. It was said to have been used by a farmer with a small dairy herd. Each day, it had been driven a couple of miles to the milking parlour, powered the milking machines, then trundled the farmer back home again. This was typical of the use to which the original designers had expected the vehicle to be put.

wheelbase of each version was extended to 88in (2,235mm) and 109in (2,769mm) respectively, to take new engines, both diesel and petrol. These measurements were to remain standard for about 30 years with the station wagon remaining at 107in until September 1958.

The 2052cc diesel engine with overhead valves was introduced in June 1957 and was very quickly available for the export market.

SERIES II AND IIA
In April 1958 the Series II Land Rover replaced all previous models. The chassis remained unchanged, but wheel tracks were increased, while front wheel lock and

turning circles were reduced. There was a new style which included 'barrel' body sides and panels beneath the doors. The tenth anniversary of the Land Rover also saw a new petrol engine of 2286cc announced, again, with overhead valves.

An important milestone was reached in November 1959 when, eleven years after the Land Rover had been launched, a total of 250,000 vehicles was recorded.

Series IIA Land Rovers replaced the previous models in 1961. The main mechanical difference was that the diesel engine was increased to 2286cc, with the same bore and stroke as the petrol engine.

A big change was accomplished with the introduction of the forward-control vehicle, based on the 109-in frame but

▲ *H2. This Series IIA was also owned by the author and his wife. It had spent most of the years of its life on a country estate, being used for shooting parties – again typical of a lightly-used Land Rover.*

'FORWARD CONTROL' AND SERIES III

In October 1971, the forward-control Land Rovers became described as Series IIB, and Series III replaced the Series IIA normal-control machines. Series III vehicles had a synchromesh gearbox, newly styled grilles and instrument panels, and added comfort. Wheelbases remained at 88in and 109in with the same choice of engines, petrol and diesel.

The Commercial Vehicle Show in London in September 1972 saw the introduction of a new specialised military Land Rover, the 101-in (2,565mm) wheelbase machine, produced for the British forces only. It was produced in 1974 and used the Range Rover's V8 3528cc engine with permanent four-wheel drive central transmission on a new chassis. The cab and pick-up body was simple, and there was a rear power take-off drive for the hitching up of trailers, providing a 6x6 combination.

Civilian forward-control Land Rovers ceased production after the last export order in 1973 but in August 1974 an optional Fairey overdrive was announced, for the transfer box of all types of Land Rovers.

with a new overframe, adapted cab, and 1,525kg (3,363lb) payload, (1,270kg/2,800lb when driving over rough country). The 2286cc petrol engine became standard, with no option of diesel.

Although it had taken eleven years to produce the first 250,000 vehicles, the next 250,000 were achieved in only 6½ years, to April 1966. In September that year the suspension was modified, and the wheelbase of the forward-control extended to 110in (2,794mm). There was now a choice of three engines, 2286cc petrol, 2286cc diesel and (for the first time) 2625cc six-cylinder petrol. Wheeltracks were enlarged by 2½in (63mm) to improve stability and roadholding.

The following year the 2625cc six-cylinder engine was produced on the 109-in chassis normal control Series IIA Land Rovers. Also, some internal improvements were made with more comfortable seat padding provided.

After 20 years of the original styling, some modifications were made in the headlight position for the export market – they were now mounted on the front wings. (This style was introduced into the UK market in February 1969.)

In September 1968 a special heavy-duty '1 ton' version was produced, using the 109-in chassis and the six-cylinder 2625

cc engine, and also around this time, the 'Rover 1' or 'half-ton' was produced, but only available for the Army. It had a standard 88-in chassis, but a lightweight body (lighter than the standard Army Land Rover, but still heavier than the civilian version). This variant was introduced for ease of transportation.

In June 1971 the 750,000th Land Rover was completed.

▼ *H3. The Series III Land Rover was the last of the leaf-sprung vehicles and, although larger and rather more practical, it was identical in concept and execution to the very first vehicles.*

June 1976 saw the millionth Land Rover produced and this was presented to the British Motor Industry Heritage Trust collection, to join R.01, the original pilot vehicle.

It had been hoped to have doubled the Solihull based production by this time, but Leyland's financial problems delayed these plans until the end of 1978. By 1980 an investment cost of £280 million was made for new projects.

ONE TEN AND NINETY

At the 1983 Geneva Motor Show came the beginning of the end for the old 'series' Land Rovers when the One Ten was introduced – the most dramatically revised Land Rover in 35 years of production. By now, the world's best selling four-wheel-drive vehicle was no longer a Land Rover but the Toyota Land Cruiser. Land Rover were pinning their hopes on the new One Ten – hopes of regaining ground that was lost in the 1970s and of reversing their trend of a sliding market share.

The big news about the One Ten was that it used the helicoidal coil-spring suspension first seen on the Range Rover, the long suspension travel provided by this set-up giving a comfortable ride both on

▲ H5. CWK 30Y was the prototype Land Rover 90 disguised to look not too different from a Series III. There are no 'eyebrows' round the wheelarches, there is an imitation split windscreen and, under the skin, there is a shortened 110 chassis with a wheelbase of exactly 90in.

and off the road. To implement this system on the Land Rover though, its chassis had to be *completely* redesigned. Several ease-of-servicing ideas were introduced at the same time, such as a bolt-on crossmember below the gearbox to make removal and maintenance that much easier. Disc brakes were added to the front wheels, and servo-assistance became standard. Power steering was also available for the first time ever on a Land Rover. Along with the chassis changes came an increase in wheelbase to 110 inches (2,794mm) – obviously the source of the new model's name!

All three engines used in the existing Series III Land Rovers were carried over

into the One Ten, albeit in higher states of tune. The 2¼-litre diesel and petrol engines were both enlarged to 2.5 litres and now developed 60hp and 74bhp respectively, while output from the 3.5-litre V8 was now up to 114bhp at 4,000 rpm. Five-speed gearboxes became available on the four-cylinder versions, with the same option to follow for the V8s in due course.

Styling was similar to that of the 109-in V8s, although a one-piece windscreen and deformable wheelarch guards made the One Ten instantly recognisable. The interior was also redesigned, with a functional but fresh and modern feel to it and, for the first time ever, the option of factory-fitted air-conditioning.

With the One Ten came the usual variety of different body styles available to the customer, from the full tilt pick-up to the station wagon, still available in County trim, even in this form.

It was only a matter of time before the 'One Ten treatment' was applied to the short wheelbase Land Rovers too, this happening in 1984 with the launch of the Ninety. Like the One Ten, it appeared with the usual choice of body styles, although engine choice was limited to just two – the 2¼-litre petrol unit and a new 2.5-litre diesel engine that similarly found its way into the One Ten the same year.

In many ways, the Ninety looked just like a shortened version of the One Ten,

▼ H4. This poster was part of Land Rover's campaign for the new 110, and emphasised the main selling points such as: coil springs; fifth gear; front disc brakes; improved steering and more comfortable interior.

▲ *H6. CWK 40Y is the second Land Rover 90 prototype. It has a modified Series III body and hardtop with the petrol filler in the normal 88in position, but with a wheelbase of 92⅞th in.*

In line with the expanding range for the 1990s, the 'old-style' model was given a name in its own right – the Land Rover Defender. Outwardly similar to the V8 and County models that had gone before it (in fact, the 'County' model designation is still used on some Defender versions), the Defender incorporated minor, visual improvements like new seat trim, special badging and colour-keyed decals.

Under the bonnet, however, is where the new Defender *really* differed from its predecessors, with the adoption of the new 2.5-litre direct-injection intercooled diesel engine from the Discovery models, producing 26 per cent more power than the *old* turbo-diesel unit. Maximum speed increased to 84mph (135kph) (from 75mph/120kph), while the Defender 90 accelerated from rest to 60mph (100kph) in just 15.7 seconds (down from the 'old' time of 22.5 seconds). Official fuel consumption figures also showed a dramatic improvement with the 90 model now achieving 28.3mpg on the urban cycle compared with the previous figure of 23.7mpg (11.9l/100km). Those who did not want a diesel engine could still opt for the legendary 3.5-litre all-alloy V8 petrol engine, as used so extensively by Land Rover over the years.

with similar styling touches and trim finishes and, of course, another completely redesigned chassis. The Ninety's wheelbase actually measured 92.9in (2,360mm), although this would hardly have sounded tempting as a model name for the newcomer! Just like its 'big brother' One Ten, the Ninety represented the latest in Land Rover luxury . . . without losing sight of the fact that it was still very much a hard-working vehicle.

MORE IMPROVEMENTS

Throughout the 1980s, the Land Rover came in for steady improvement, in both its long *and* short wheelbase forms. Mechanical changes included the eventual adoption of a turbocharged version of the 2.5-litre diesel engine, providing a welcome boost to power and, in particular, on-road performance, even though in reliability terms, the 'pre-Tdi' turbo diesel engine has been described as 'the worst engine Land Rover has ever produced'. However, an engine which gave 28 per cent more torque and 25 per cent more power than the non-turbo diesel was a step in the right direction. Thankfully, the ubiquitous Land Rover met with widespread commercial success once again, with steadily improving sales figures worldwide as the 1990s approached. But it was clear that this much-loved vehicle could not hold on to a major share of the

▲ *H7. The interior of a One Ten, from around 1984, which came complete with wind-down windows for the first time! Engine options now included the 3528cc V8, at first, and 2¼-litre petrol and diesel units, later giving way to 2.5-litre units. Introduced in March 1983, 110in models offered coil sprung suspension, five-speed gearbox and permanent four-wheel-drive à la Range Rover.*

world market without some assistance from new designs. More and more customers were now demanding sophistication as well as rugged, off-road appeal. The company needed something else along the lines of the Range Rover, but at a rather more affordable price. The answer was . . . the Discovery.

There was certainly plenty of life left in the 'old faithful' Land Rover though, and in 1990, in time for the 1991 model year, the company announced yet another series of improvements across the range.

From Spring 1994, the Defender range of utility permanent four-wheel-drive vehicles was fitted with Land Rover's new R380 manual gearbox and the latest 300 Tdi turbocharged diesel injection engine. An increase in power from 107 to 111bhp complemented an increase in torque from 188 to 195lbf/ft, particularly useful when

▲ *H8. By traditional standards, all Ninety, One Ten and Defender interiors have been comfortable, although still with restricted seat movement and legroom.*

towing. The 300 Tdi met, at that time, all known future emissions legislation.

Land Rover's new manual R380 gearbox was exceptionally strong, but had a light and precise action. Reverse gear now had full synchromesh and was moved to behind fifth from the previous position behind first. Gearchange quality and ease of use were further improved with a new clutch mechanism, which needed significantly less pressure to be fully depressed.

▲ H12. The 110 County station wagon was criticised by some for being too luxurious! However, the extra length allowed it to be a much more useful five-door design. Its list of equipment included tinted windows, side-stripes, halogen headlights, cloth seats, sunroof, and more besides. If you intended using your Land Rover for high mileage, every day motoring, this is one of the most user-friendly models available second-hand!

▲ H9. The Land Rover Ninety Pick-Up, also with Range Rover-style coil spring suspension, a special chassis, five-speed manual gearbox and a choice of 2.5-litre petrol or diesel engines.

▲ H10. Also available in the Ninety Series was the hardtop 'van'. . .

▲ H13. The 2.5-litre petrol and diesel engines were both developments of what had gone before. In 1986, the turbo diesel (with indirect injection) was introduced, providing 28 per cent more torque and 25 per cent more power but still with excellent economy. The engine was under-developed and unreliable.

▲ H14. The engine shown here is the 1990 200 Tdi (turbo direct injection) unit, easily the most reliable diesel engine that Land Rover had ever built up to that point, and a vast improvement on the old turbo diesel unit. Although dimensions such as bore and stroke are the same, the later engine is as desirable as the earlier one is unreliable.

▲ H11. . . . and the rather neat looking County station wagon, bringing the traditional Land Rover shape more up to date.

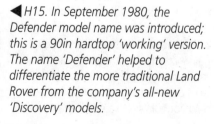

◀ H15. In September 1980, the Defender model name was introduced; this is a 90in hardtop 'working' version. The name 'Defender' helped to differentiate the more traditional Land Rover from the company's all-new 'Discovery' models.

▲ H16. Here an early 110 is put through its paces at Land Rover's own testing ground on the so-called 'Jungle Track'. An unadorned 90 Tdi gave immense ruggedness, much improved economy and quite a surprising turn of speed.

▲ H19. With bright body colour, rear-mounted spare and US-only 'soft-top', the North American Defender 90 is hardly recognisable as a Land Rover at first glance.

▲ H17. That improved Tdi diesel engine meant that for the first time, the 110 Station Wagon had sufficient power in diesel form.

▲ H20. This otherwise unadorned 1992 Hard Top 90 Tdi, from the Land Rover Press Fleet, poses in the author's garden, showing off its black wheelarch 'eyebrows'.

▲ H18. When, in 1992, the Defender 90 was introduced to the United States, it was almost a case of 'coals to Newcastle', bearing in mind the Jeep-inspired origins of the original vehicle. This 1994 V8 illustrates the canvas tilt-covered version introduced in the USA.

◄ H21. For a completely basic truck/van, the 90 Tdi was nippy but was comprehensively trounced by the 300 Tdi-engined vehicle, introduced in 1994.

▼ H25. The High Capacity Pick-up has completely different rear body panels. It has more load space than 'ordinary' 110 Pick-ups, but paradoxically . . .

▼ H26. . . . load capacity is slightly diminished, although it took this trip to the author's local timber yard without batting an eye-lid (except for the 'eye-lid' vents beneath the windscreen) – ideal for a warm day late in May!

▲ H22. The 300 Tdi engine – with catalytic converter option – gave superb performance and fuel economy, as well as the 'cleanest' Land Rover diesel to date.

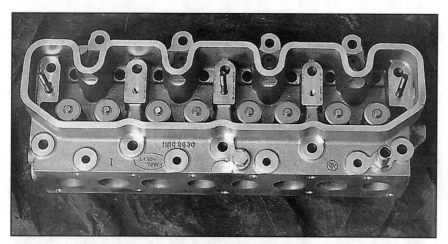

▼ H27. The author's wife, Shan, takes out the 2.5 tonne Ifor Williams trailer and pronounces the combination, 'The best tow ever!'.

▲ H23. The 300 Tdi's increased power came largely from cylinder head developments, although the structure of the engine and the siting of its ancillaries were also changed.

▼ H28. And here's the ultimate testament to the ruggedness of the One Ten. Liveridge British 4X4 refurbished this early '80s vehicle in 1998, and it immediately went back into service, in 'as-new' condition, with a Midlands' Forestry company, ready for another 15 to 20 years' service!

▲ H24. At the same time, the new R380 manual gearbox was fitted – still with permanent 4x4, of course, and the best Land Rover gearbox yet!

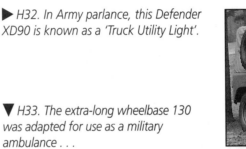

H32. In Army parlance, this Defender XD90 is known as a 'Truck Utility Light'.

H33. The extra-long wheelbase 130 was adapted for use as a military ambulance . . .

H29. Because the new Land Rover was more comfortable than its predecessors, the company knew it had to prove the new vehicle's toughness. This is the Land Rover 90 that successfully competed in the Camel Trophy, one of the most gruelling events through which an off-road vehicle can be put.

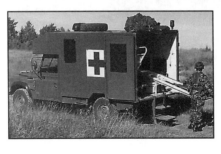

H30. In the Land Rover tradition, 90s are frequently used in amateur trials and events.

H34. . . . and is shown here undergoing trials in a British Army exercise.

H31. Another Land Rover tradition is the supply of vehicles for military purposes. This cut-away shows a Defender XD110 with hardtop and 24 volt electrics, as supplied to the Army.

H35. A vehicle that is tough enough for military action is tough enough for most civilian purposes, too, as this 110 equipped with winch assembly demonstrates.

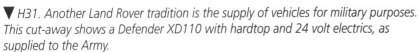

▲ H36. British International Helicopters at Penzance heliport make use of this adapted Defender as a fire fighting tender. (This is typical of the author's holiday snaps . . .)

▲ H39. . . . but this 'stretched' 110, known as the 130, with a 127-in wheelbase is a popular choice for those who need to carry a crew and who also need a large load capacity – the 130's gross vehicle weight is 3.5 tonnes.

▲ H37. Not all Defender adaptations are quite as predictable! This cumbersome looking Defender 'boat' was used as a course 'vehicle' at Cowes week.

▼ H38. Land Rover build this spectacular adaptation as 'The World's Longest Land Rover'. . .

▼ H40. All of which is why, in 1996, you could buy this new Defender 110 Country Station Wagon Tdi, and know that it would be a delight to use and take all the hard work you could throw at it.

▲ *H41. At its launch in 1989, the Land Rover Discovery was available only in three-door form (the five-door didn't arrive until the following year).*

DISCOVERY

As mentioned earlier, not everyone is prepared to accept what can be termed a 4x4 utility-type vehicle. The discerning buyer of the 1990s wants a little extra, particularly with so many potential customers looking at vehicles like the Mitsubishi Shogun, Isuzu Trooper and Toyota Land Cruiser for everyday transport, which means 99 per cent *on-road* driving. Land Rover saw the need for a British rival to such established Japanese models; their answer laying in the November 1989 launch of the Land Rover Discovery, a model which, almost overnight, took the market by storm.

The Discovery met with immediate acclaim from the motoring press, most road-testers rating it as the best vehicle in its class. The public were impressed too – as soon as supplies started to build up. A quite lengthy waiting list had been necessary right from day one, but Discovery took little time in becoming the best-selling 4x4 leisure vehicle in the UK – a clear indication that, once again, Land Rover had come up with a brand new vehicle that people *wanted* . . .

Initially available only in three-door form, Discovery was a distinctive looking vehicle. Although it was not *excitingly* different to look at its styling was

attractive and unlikely to get confused with any of its rivals. A choice of two engines was offered, the 3.5-litre V8 in carburettor form and the 2.5-litre direct-injection intercooled turbo-diesel unit.

Based on a wheelbase of 100 inches (2,540mm), Discovery was about the same size as most of its Japanese rivals. And, unlike the original Land Rover, it was aimed fairly and squarely at the leisure market, for those people who wanted 4x4 everyday transport

(whether for its usefulness or for its 'trendy' image that had developed throughout the '80s), with no loss in terms of standard equipment and comfort. The Discovery was certainly well equipped, with such luxuries as electric windows, central locking, electrically adjustable door mirrors, alloy wheels and seating for up to seven people; and its price was competitive at approximately £17,000, very similar to some of the top-of-the-range Japanese offerings.

The Discovery certainly was not 'all-show-and-no-go' however, for it boasted superb off-road capabilities (as would be expected from any new Land Rover). Permanent four-wheel-drive followed the Land Rover tradition, with high and low transfer settings for when the going got *really* tough! While the Discovery was pure Land Rover under the skin, the refinement and superb driving comfort of this newcomer was a new experience for anyone used to the Land Rover 90 and 110 models.

One of the few criticisms levelled at the Discovery was the restriction of being available only in three-door form. Such criticism was soon answered however, when the 1991 model year Discovery was announced. In came a new five-door version, plus a whole host of other improvements to the model in general.

▼ *H42. When a small company (such as Land Rover was) develops a new vehicle, the investment, relative to its size, is enormous. The Discovery development programme was known as the 'Jay' project and this was Land Rover's development team.*

▶ H43. The Discovery's interior was a revelation for Land Rover, it being designed by an 'outside' company of stylists. The Discovery is short of nothing in the way of creature comforts.

▼ H44. Discovery was launched with a choice of two engines, the petrol model being fitted with the carburettored V8 engine shown here. (Fuel injection did not arrive until the 1991 model year.) Also available was the new 200 Tdi direct-injection turbo diesel unit.

For 1991, the 3.5-litre V8 petrol engine came as standard with fuel injection, thus offering improved performance and top speed – up from 101.6mph (163kph) to 106.5mph (171kph), with the 0–60mph (0–100kph) acceleration time now taking just 10.8 seconds as opposed to 12.7 seconds. Impressive figures for a vehicle of its type.

There is no doubt that, with the right sort of product development throughout the '90s, Discovery has a good future ahead of it and should help to boost Land Rover's now-healthy sales figures still further, not just in Britain but throughout Europe too.

THE RANGE ROVER

There remains another major model in Land Rover's history yet to be covered, and as the flagship of the company for more than two decades, it is perhaps fitting that it is featured toward the end of this brief survey. This is particularly so

◀ H45. Although it was launched in 1970, the Range Rover story has a direct relevance to the 90, 110 and Defender series. YVB 153H is the earliest Range Rover still surviving today and this photograph illustrates the excellent amount of axle articulation available on these vehicles.

as it also represents the most expensive standard-model passenger vehicle ever to roll off the Land Rover production lines. That vehicle is the Range Rover.

In much the same way that Land Rover saw a need for a less agricultural vehicle when it developed Discovery, so the Range Rover was conceived in the late 1960s. The concept behind the Range Rover actually goes back much further, to the early 1950s in fact, when it was suggested that a more comfortable, bigger and more stylish alternative to the Land Rover could happily sell alongside its established, workhorse cousin. At that stage, the Road Rover (as it was then known) would be based on the chassis and components of the Rover P4 saloons and use only *rear*-wheel-drive. In effect, a purpose-built estate car with no cross-country abilities. Thankfully, such ideas were given up by the time the '60s dawned, the company then directing its efforts towards the development of the new Rover 2000 P6 saloons.

With the Rover 2000 not only launched but also proving highly successful by the mid-1960s however, it was time to consider the idea of an 'upmarket' Land Rover once again. It was now decided that this newcomer should employ *permanent* four-wheel-drive. It was to be a 'station wagon' based around a 100-inch wheelbase and, it was decided, would use the six-cylinder 3-litre engine from the *big* Rover saloons. Few people were happy with this engine though, for such an important new model. And so it was with great joy that those working on the project heard that Rover had secured the rights to an all-alloy GM-designed V8 engine, the unit that was to become the highly successful and much respected Rover V8 mentioned earlier. It was almost as though the whole project had been given new meaning, now that there could be used, a powerful, lightweight engine in keeping with the proposed upmarket image of the vehicle.

Exactly what that image would be still wasn't too clear to many. There would be no competitors by which to judge the new Rover, so the planners were left to follow what few guidelines had been set.

▲ *H46. Early Range Rovers were relatively basic and utilitarian, in the Land Rover tradition.*

The vehicle had to be bigger, faster and more civilised than a 'normal' Land Rover, but just as practical and still recognisably Rover. Such practicality dictated features like a high ground clearance, yet there was still uncertainty over how the *styling* should look. Two of the leading figures in the Range Rover development, Spen King and Gordon Bashford, set about building a mock-up of how they thought the newcomer should be shaped, rather than wait for the styling department to come up with ideas. The end result looked remarkably similar to how the finished Range Rover was to be at its launch in July 1970. It was always intended that the new model would be two-door only, to save on development costs and to ensure structural rigidity.

The Range Rover's development survived the company's merger with British Leyland in the late 1960s with ease, the new owners being particularly keen for the development to continue (much to the relief of all concerned!). And so it was that, just before the '60s came to an end, pilot production runs of the new Range Rover were under way, ready for the much publicised launch in the summer of 1970.

Introduced with a price tag of around £2,000, the Range Rover was considered remarkably good value at launch for a four-wheel-drive go-anywhere vehicle . . . but then it was never intended to be anything other than upmarket compared with the Land Rover. Despite rumours of an average fuel consumption of around 15mpg (19l/100km), stories of production troubles and claims of poor build quality and even early rusting on those panels made of conventional steel (most were aluminium), the public *loved* the Range Rover. It boasted near 100mph (160kph) performance and, with its exceptionally high driving position, allowed both driver and passengers a commanding view of the road ahead. It was a vehicle that fortunately (for Land Rover) portrayed the kind of image to which so many people aspired. In true Land Rover tradition, the Range Rover immediately built up a cult following, with long waiting lists soon appearing, particularly once exports began. The situation became so intense that a black market existed for Range Rovers for quite a while, as demand continued to outstrip supply by a massive margin.

The potential for the development of the Range Rover has always been immense, but throughout the 1970s it was almost ignored by the decision-makers at British Leyland/Leyland Cars. It soldiered on, its popularity still strong, but changes to it over the decade of the '70s were few and far between compared with its subsequent development.

◄H47. After 20 years of Range Rover production, the vehicle was becoming increasingly refined – though no less practical.

◄H48. In 1990, a Range Rover Vogue was the ultimate in luxury from Land Rover. Detail changes have been introduced throughout the Range Rover's life, this particular model being fitted with the viscous coupling transfer box. Simply select high or low ratio and let the vehicle do the rest!
The visually similar, Range Rover Vogue Turbo D relies on a 2.5-litre VM turbo-diesel engine for its power. Luxury and reasonable economy all in one!

◄H49. Goodies abound in this really upmarket Vogue SE! A few years ago, the idea of Land Rover producing a vehicle with an interior as plush as this would have been considered ludicrous.

Despite having been in production for nearly ten years, by the time the '80s arrived, Land Rover management was only then beginning to realise (or at least make use of) the potential that had been going to waste. Throughout the 1980s, the Range Rover went from strength to strength, being gradually moved further and further upmarket.

A four-door version was at last introduced, and soon began to outsell the two-door quite substantially and nowadays, something in the region of 90 per cent of new Range Rovers are bought in four-door form. The Range Rover's interior was greatly improved over the years, becoming positively luxurious in the top of the range versions. In fact, for the first time ever, *several* variants of the Range Rover were available as official models from Land Rover dealers, climaxing in the Vogue version – a particularly upmarket derivative that is still in production today, offering true luxury car appointments without losing any of the original's practicality and off-road abilities.

On the mechanical side, the Range Rover's development included the availability of automatic transmission, and at long last, a turbo-diesel engine option.

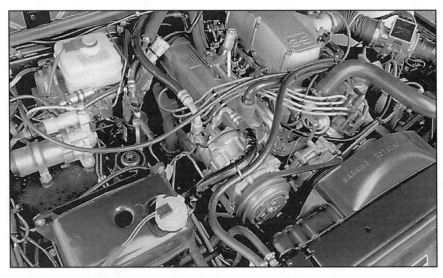

▲ *H50. In its 1990 form, the venerable Rover V8 was a 3.9-litre unit with electronic fuel injection. A far cry from the de-tuned V8 Land Rovers of a few years earlier!*

INSTANT 'CLASSIC'

Then, in September 1994, Land Rover introduced an all-new Range Rover, with more of everything. More room, more size, more power – and more cost. The old-style vehicle continued to be built for a few months and the 'old' vehicle instantly became dubbed the Range Rover 'Classic'.

The new Range Rover, by moving up-market, enables Land Rover to push

Discovery a little further up the cost and equipment ladder, leaving room for the most radical Land Rover to date . . .

▼ *H51. This aerial view of a Range Rover chassis illustrates the essential components that were used in developing the Land Rover 110, 90 and later Discovery.*

1. *Third differential unit*
2. *Coil springs with beam axles*
3. *Self levelling unit*
4. *Disc brakes all round*
5. *Tandem brake pipes*
6. *Brake servo*
7. *Transmission parking brake*
8. *Four-speed all synchro. gearbox*
9. *Radial ply tyres*
10. *Collapsible steering column*
11. *19-gallon fuel tank*
12. *Impact absorbing fascia*

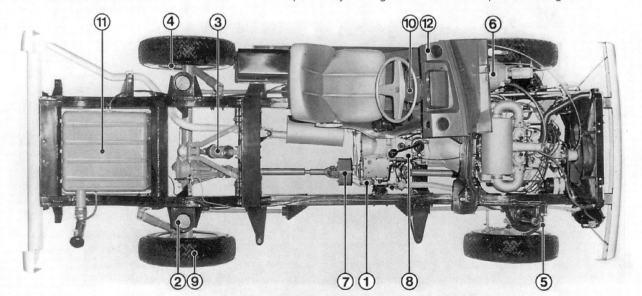

F FOR FREELANDER; F FOR FUN!

The very first 1948 Land Rover placed function way above form in its list of priorities. (But then, a train of thought, from the Ancient Greeks to Mini designer Alec Issigonis, holds that if something *is* right, it *will* look right!) And the modern Defender follows that honourable tradition. However, Land Rover exists to make money, not score debating points. The appeal of the Japanese, everyday urban 4x4 was undeniable and Freelander, launched at the 1998 Frankfurt Motor Show, was designed to match that appeal – with a number of traditional Land Rover virtues retained.

With the ride comfort and handling qualities that are expected from a saloon car, Freelander is nevertheless a robust, authentic off-roader. Its contemporary styling gives a distinctive and powerful presence in the city, but it provides a real ability to escape from the constraints of the urban environment: scope for serious off-road fun with genuine Land Rover credentials, unrivalled by non-specialist imitators.

Freelander was launched as a three-door soft-top and hardtop versions and a five-door station wagon, each with 120Ps petrol or 97Ps diesel power units – both award-winning car engines

▲ H53. Freelander was the first new Land Rover under BMW ownership. This is the Hardback model . . .

specifically adapted to meet the demands of on and off-road driving.

According to Land Rover, Freelander represents a contemporary application of the technical knowledge and vast experience that has made Land Rover's Defender, Discovery and Range Rover the most celebrated range of 4WD vehicles in the world. But, while the exterior and interior designs subtly reflect that illustrious heritage, Freelander broke significant new ground for the company and the four-wheel-drive market in general.

Freelander was the first Land Rover product to be based on a unitary body

▲ H52. A Land Rover without a separate chassis! Whoever heard of such a thing? But the unitary construction provides Freelander with extra stiffness as well as impeccable on-road behaviour. This is a five-door model and was launched for sale in January 1998.

▲ H54. . . and this the soft-top model, with the emphasis on fun!

with an integrated chassis – achieving a remarkably low weight with exceptional rigidity and strength. All-round independent suspension – another first time for Land Rover – enhanced driving comfort, while new materials, including the extensive use of plastics, combine strength with durability and impact resistance.

Freelander's 4x4 system was all-new too. Its 'intelligent' permanent 4WD system features a viscous coupling between front and rear differential units. In addition, certain models have three important features: anti-lock braking; electronic traction control – which reduces the risk of wheel slippage and automatically adapts to any driving situation, allowing the vehicle to keep going on surfaces which defeat its rivals – and another world first for Land Rover – hill descent control (HDC).

HDC was devised to minimise the hazards of descending slippery gradients. It adapts the ABS braking system automatically to cut descent speeds to a fixed, low maximum and cater for any twists or bumps in the way ahead. All the driver has to do is engage a switch on the gear lever – and it works surprisingly well!

Styling was also radical. A remote control 'drop glass' system on some models means that the rear door does not need to be opened to load the vehicle, while on the soft-top model, the hood folds upwards away from the loadspace area, and incorporates detachable rear side screens.

At the time of its launch, Land Rover admitted that it saw Freelander not only as an extension of its presence in a new market sector, but as a vehicle that will

actually attract new people to the concept of 4WD leisure motoring.

'To be frank, most of the current cars in this market have little to offer when they go off the conventional road' says Richard Elsy, Freelander Project Director. 'They are rarely durable enough to stand consistent recreational use, and are incapable of anything but the most elementary off-road work. In the end, people are bound to be disappointed by them.'

'Freelander is the answer – the only real answer. It can comfortably be used as a family or a fun car; but that genuine all-terrain presence is always there – not a dominating presence, but one which is inherent in the vehicle. The only skill that may be required is the flick of a switch! It's a serious product with a superb pedigree – but most of all, it's fun.'

DEVELOPMENT MILESTONES
90, 110, DEFENDER

March 1983
Announcement of new generation Land Rover One Ten with coil spring suspension and 110in wheelbase. Five-speed all-synchromesh gearbox on four-cylinder models. V8 version with Range Rover transmission also available.

January 1984
Introduction of 2495cc diesel four-cylinder engine, directly replacing 2286cc type.

June 1984
Introduction of new generation Land Rover Ninety with shortened version of One Ten chassis and coil spring suspension – but wheelbase actually 92.9in (2,360mm)! Available only with four-cylinder engines and with five-speed all-synchromesh gearbox.

May 1985
Launch of five-speed all-synchromesh Spanish built 'Santana' manual gearbox for V8-engine Land Rovers. At the same time, V8 engines made available for the first time on the Ninety model. This is the first time that a V8 has been offered in a SWB. Series III assembly ended a few weeks later.

September 1985
Introduction of 2495cc petrol four-cylinder engine, directly replacing 2286cc type.

October 1985
Completion of the 1,500,000th vehicle off the production lines at Solihull.

October 1986
Introduction of 85bhp turbocharged version of existing 2.5-litre diesel engine, optional for all Land Rovers.

1988
40th Anniversary of Land Rover. Over 1.6 million vehicles sold worldwide.

1990
New 200 Tdi 2.5-litre turbocharged direct injection diesel engine for Land Rover. Defender name first used.

1992
Land Rovers sold in America for the first time since 1974.

1993
45th anniversary of Land Rover.

1994
Defender receives all-new Land Rover R380 manual gearbox and more powerful 300 Tdi diesel engine.

1995
Freestyle choice option pack introduced.

1998
50th anniversary of the world's finest 4x4 by far.

DEFENDER ENGINE TYPES

The following list is a useful compilation of engine types used in 90, 110 and Defender models up to 1998. The biggest differences lie between the old 2.5-litre turbo diesel and the 200 Tdi, while the 300 Tdi shows even more changes over its predecessors. Don't be fooled by the identical engine capacities!

Type: 2¼-litre 4 cyl. OHV Petrol (74bhp)

Bore x Stroke:	90.49 x 88.9mm
Capacity:	2286cc
Model/s and years:	90: June '84–August '85
	110: March '83–August '85

Type: 2.5-litre 4 cyl. OHV Petrol (83bhp)

Bore x Stroke:	90.49 x 97mm
Capacity:	2494cc
Model/s and years:	90: August '85–July '94
	110: August '85–January '92

Type: 2¼-litre 4 cyl. Diesel (60bhp)

Bore x Stroke:	90.49 x 88.9mm
Capacity:	2286cc
Model/s and years:	90: Not fitted
	110: March '83–March '84

Type: 2.5-litre 4 cyl. Diesel (68bhp)

Bore x Stroke:	90.49 x 97mm
Capacity:	2494cc
Model/s and years:	90: June '84–July '94
110:	March '84–January '92

Type: 3.5-litre V8 OHV Petrol (114/134bhp)

Bore x Stroke:	88.9 x 71.1mm
Capacity:	3528cc
Model/s and years:	90: May '85–July '94
	110: March '83–July '94

Type: 2.5-litre 4 cyl. Turbo Diesel (85bhp)

Bore x Stroke:	90.49 x 97mm
Capacity:	2494cc
Model/s and years:	90 and 110: October '86–September '90

Type: 200 Tdi 4 cyl. intercooled TurboDiesel (107bhp)

Bore x Stroke:	90.49 x 97mm
Capacity:	2494cc
Model/s and years:	Defender range: September '90–March '94

Type: 300 Tdi 4 cyl. intercooled Turbo Diesel (111bhp)

Bore x Stroke:	90.49 x 97mm
Capacity:	2494cc
Model/s and years:	Defender: March '94–on.

BUYING A LAND ROVER 90, 110, DEFENDER

The bulk of this book was written with the assistance of Liveridge British 4X4, based not far from Land Rover themselves, near Birmingham. A major part of Liveridge's business is building what they call 'Refurb.' vehicles – older 90s and 110s completely restored from the chassis up to customer specifications, producing a virtually as-new vehicle at far less cost. I felt that we could do no better therefore, than to ask Chris Howard, proprietor of Liveridge, to talk us through what to look for when buying a 90, 110, Defender. After all, Liveridge have seen them all and know exactly what to look out for!

WHICH MODEL?

Chris always starts by asking prospective customers how many miles a year they think they will be doing in their Land Rover. This has a major bearing on which type of engine to go for. Petrol engine vehicles run more sweetly, are much quieter, are cheaper to maintain and cheaper to buy. On the other hand, they do use a lot more fuel than diesel engined vehicles – hence Chris's initial question. He reckons that if you do less than 6,000 to 7,000 miles (10,000km) a year, you would be better off buying a petrol engined vehicle. He then asks what the vehicle is most likely to be used for. V8 engine vehicles are incredibly thirsty but are second to none when it comes to pulling heavy loads. Of course, if you live in a part of the world where petrol/gasoline is cheap, this latter point won't bother you at all and you will probably want to go for a V8-engined vehicle in any case. The other downside to V8 engines is that they do cost more to maintain and to replace when they eventually wear out.

At the lowest end of the scale, if all you are looking for is a simple workhorse and you really don't care about performance, a normally aspirated (non-turbo) diesel could well be your best bet. If you don't mind the noise, the 60mph touring speed and all the usual drawbacks of a basic, commercial diesel engine, the vehicle will be inexpensive to purchase, inexpensive to run and relatively reliable.

Other pointers to bear in mind relate to carrying capacity (the weight capacity on all models is good but the load area on a short wheelbase vehicle is pathetic), the number of seats (up to 12 on a long wheelbase), ground clearance, vehicle height and available parking space (long wheelbase vehicles are bigger in every respect) and whether or not you actually need five doors. Long wheelbase five-door vehicles are, generally speaking, the dearest of all, while long wheelbase three-door hardtops are generally the cheapest. An idea which appeals greatly to the author is the Liveridge 'Special' – a three-door LWB hardtop which has been converted with rear side windows and rear seats providing, in many ways, the best of all worlds, especially with Series III doors fitted in place of 90/110 doors. But more of that anon!

Another point to bear in mind with regard to long wheelbase vehicles is that they are better for pulling heavy weights – they are more stable than short wheelbase vehicles and are slightly more comfortable, too. The extra fuel they consume by virtue of their extra weight is negligible, according to Chris. On the other hand, for those who intend carrying out off-road competition work, a 90 is much more nimble and manoeuvrable than a 110.

Chris Howard makes a crucial point: You cannot use the criteria that you would normally use when looking at a second-hand car when choosing a second-hand Land Rover. Chris has plenty of experience of seeing Land Rovers that have been abused cosmetically but extremely well maintained mechanically. And, on the other hand he has seen a number of cosmetically done-up vehicles with hugely expensive mechanical problems lurking in the undergrowth. You can't even use the usual rule of thumb regarding mileage. I once owned a beautiful Series I that had done very low mileage but with a completely 'shot' engine. It had been used by a farmer as a power supply for his milking parlour. Hardly any miles per week, but dozens of running hours! Chris has seen many 110s with less than 30,000 miles on the clock but they have spent life in a quarry, on an army firing range or pulling boats up slipways, which has rendered the vehicle all but scrap. So, bearing these and other points in mind, here are Chris Howard's golden rules when buying a 90/110/Defender:

GOLDEN RULES

ENGINE CONVERSIONS

Avoid at all costs! A non-Land Rover engine is bound to lead to lots of inherent problems, such as: clutches that don't last the course; wear on ancillary components that weren't designed to do the job; cooling problems; the 'noise, vibration and harshness' problems that manufacturers spend millions of pounds ironing out; parts that can't be identified when they need to be replaced, such as clutches; a need for special exhausts to be made up, and the extra cost of Japanese parts. In addition, insurance may be difficult to find or extremely expensive, at best. On the other hand, Land Rover engine conversions, such as fitting a Tdi engine to an earlier vehicle, can be fine provided that the work is done properly and with all correct components.

RE-REGISTERED VEHICLES

This is a tricky one, because there are hundreds of re-registered vehicles around. If the vehicle has a 'Q' number plate (in the UK) it is obviously a re-registered import. Insurance can be difficult to arrange or at best expensive with a Q plate, but many vehicles are wrongly registered by DVLA who go on the information supplied to them rather than carrying out their own checks. In other words, you cannot guarantee that the information on the registration document will be correct. Have a specialist such as Liveridge check a vehicle which does not have its original bill of sale with it so that you don't get caught out.

HYBRIDS

Avoid like the plague! So many Land Rover parts across the years are interchangeable, that many creative souls cut them and shut them and fit them together and make hybrid vehicles out of them. A Series III Land Rover rebuilt onto a Range Rover chassis can be a nightmare to work on or, indeed to insure. A 1970 Land Rover with a 90 chassis is not uncommon, and if you come across, say, a 90 with a pre-90 chassis plate and registration document, turn round and run! Stolen vehicles are sometimes given new identities using an old registration document from a scrapped, earlier vehicle, so don't take chances!

DIESEL CAMBELTS

Find out the last time the cambelt was changed on a diesel engine. If there is no actual invoice to prove that the cambelt has been changed within the specified time, allow for adding the cost of fitting a new one onto the purchase price of the vehicle. You must not, under any circumstances, run the vehicle beyond its specified cambelt change because if the cambelt breaks, the engine will be scrapped.

OWNERSHIP

To make sure, in the UK, that the vehicle really is owned by the person who says he/she owns it, that it isn't a stolen vehicle or a written-off vehicle and that it doesn't have outstanding finance, invest a few pounds in checking with HPI (Tel: 01722 422422) who will need to know the registration and VIN number so that they can check their records.

WHAT TO LOOK FOR

NUMBERS GAME

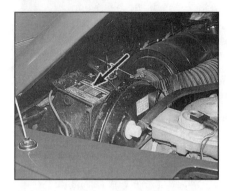

▲ B1. The first thing to look for is the chassis or VIN plate in the engine bay. If it's not there, don't touch the vehicle unless you can have a specialist firm check it over for you.

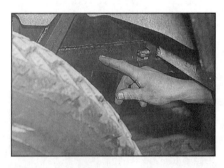

▲ B2. Double-check the chassis number, just behind the left-hand front wheel position, shown here. Of course, on older vehicles, the number can be made invisible by rust and a changed or repaired chassis won't show the number you are looking for.

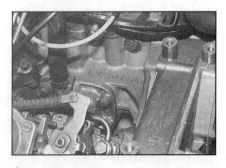

▲ B3. Also check the engine number against the VIN plate and/or registration document.

CHASSIS

▲ B4. While you're in the area of the chassis, check the rear crossmember. It's okay for an older vehicle to have had the rear crossmember replaced (provided it has been done properly) . . .

▲ B5. . . . but you must also check for general corrosion underneath the vehicle. A couple of important pointers here: look for areas of chassis that are too clean when compared with others. It could indicate that someone has been busy with body filler – and also look out for wavy areas which will provide the same clue. Don't rely on a British MoT certificate, especially if it is a few months out of date. Also note that the regulation MoT testing hammer is inadequate for the weight of a Land Rover chassis and that some test stations, incorrectly, don't seem to regard outriggers as structural chassis components. In other words, ignore what the MoT certificate says!

BODY AND BULKHEAD

With the bodywork on a Land Rover, what you see is what you get. But do note that you can't get rid of oxidation in aluminium, especially in the doors, which corrode like nobody's business! The problem is that they are made of aluminium and steel in close juxtaposition and that actually causes corrosion to take place. The front of the bulkhead can also rot and it has been known for this to happen so badly that the doors and hinges have flapped about!

ENGINES

Look out for oil leaks on diesel engine vehicles. Turbo diesels are prone to creating crankcase pressure which blows oil out of the seals. Look out for the left-hand chassis leg or the top of the engine covered in oil.

Untoward diesel engine noises are very difficult for the untrained ear to pick out – because of the general cacophony that goes on with a diesel engine! – but listen for tappet noise on a V8 engine, which will be very expensive to put right. Do bear in mind that oil pressure is congenitally low on V8 engines and doesn't really signify very much.

▲ B6. Looking at the condition of the engine oil might give you a few clues to maintenance on petrol engine vehicles, although on diesels, the engine oil is black even when it's relatively fresh.

TRANSMISSION

Select low ratio on the transfer box and ensure that it's okay. Check for noise or an inability to engage low ratio.

All gearboxes seem to leak a bit but check the oil level because if it has been allowed to fall, the gearbox could be damaged. Backlash can be expensive to put right, especially if it is between the output shaft on the box and the input shaft on the transfer box. On the other hand backlash can be confused with warn UJs, or rear suspension knuckle or bushes.

Check the clutch for overall condition or slipping and don't fall for the vendor's trick of saying that it needs adjusting. It can't be adjusted!

Differentials are tricky to assess and it's difficult to ascertain freeplay by moving the propshafts – and it can't be done at all with the handbrake on because this locks the transmission. Listen for droning from the differentials especially on the over-run.

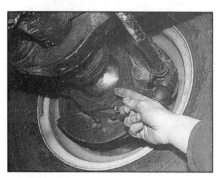

▲ B7. Check the condition of the swivel housings. They are chrome plated and should be clean and free from pitting. If badly pitted, they will be useless and costly to replace. Some leakage from the housing seal it to be expected, but signs of excessive oil loss could mean worn swivel pins. Some movement in the swivel pins is acceptable but, if excessive, the bushes or bearings will need to be replaced. See the relevant section of this manual.

STEERING

Steering is checked for wear at the joints in all the usual ways but note that a power steering box is very expensive to replace. As well as checking for wear, you must check for leaks – a leaking box or pump invariably needs replacement.

CONSUMABLES

There are a number of items which you could regard as consumables because they will invariably wear and need replacing in due course, but if too many of them are worn at once when you are purchasing a vehicle you will have to bear in mind the extra cost. You should therefore check the condition of the shock absorbers, tyres, exhaust, universal joints, bushes and springs and if any are in need of replacement, use them as a bargaining point.

▲ B8. Leaking shock absorbers (inside the springs) invariably need replacement and broken springs will be indicated by a vehicle which is down at one corner.

INTERIOR

▲ B9. The interior is another case of 'what you see is what you get' and everything can be replaced – albeit at a cost. An important tip is to check around each seat belt anchorage point, especially behind the seats where the inertia reel mountings can be found. If there is any corrosion, welding will be needed. Also, seat belts tend to get caught, become frayed and will need replacing in order to pass the MoT. And they're quite expensive!

COOLING SYSTEM

Check the condition of the radiator which can be quite expensive to replace, especially on turbo diesel and Tdi models with a built-in oil cooler. On the Tdi, there is also an intercooler which should be checked.

TAX TRAPS

When a UK resident buys a Land Rover, they will be faced with the thorny question of VAT. At the time of writing, VAT is levied at the standard rate on commercial vehicles. In general terms, a hardtop Land Rover with no rear windows, or a pick-up, is a commercial vehicle and attracts VAT. If you are a registered trader, there is no problem if the vehicle is to be used for commercial use and you can claim the VAT back again. If the vehicle has side windows and seats, it is classed as a car and the only VAT payable will be on the dealer's profit, just as with any other car. However, 12-seat LWB Land Rovers are also classed as commercial vehicles and attract VAT! Bear the Tax Trap in mind when buying from a trader, but note that privately sold vehicles are not liable for VAT.

TOP TIPS FROM LIVERIDGE

Bearing in mind what we said at the start of the section about not being able to apply the usual criteria when looking at a second-hand car, here are Chris Howard's top tips for identifying a well-worked Land Rover:

1. Check the towing drop-plate. If bent, the vehicle has been pulling loads that are grossly too heavy for it.
2. Check the rear load area. Abused vehicles will show signs of heavy weights being thrown into the back with all the damage that you would expect.
3. Check the bonnet and wing tops. They will be dented if the vehicle has been walked on – a sure sign of abuse.
4. Check to see if the windscreen wiper covers have been knocked off. This often happens on abused vehicles.
5. Check the steering wheel. If it has been worn completely smooth, the mileometer could be telling you lies!

CLASSIC CAR INSURANCE

If you own a 'classic' Land Rover 90 or 110, you can save money and ensure that you aren't caught in the 'old-car-not-worth-much' insurance trap.

Classic car insurance is usually cheaper than private motor insurance. This is because classic vehicles are generally used less than the main family vehicle and with extra care, making them a good risk as the likelihood of a claim is lower.

Naturally, enough, most insurance companies will set some restrictions to qualify for this. Models considered to be 'classics', are usually supported by an owners' club. In addition, insurers specify that the car must be above a certain age, in most cases 15 years old, though other companies have different age limits. In addition, the car must not be the main vehicle or be used for more than a specified annual mileage. To an extent you can choose the mileage that suits you, but the lower this is the lower the premium.

Above all, there is a cardinal rule that must be remembered when insuring your 'classic' Land Rover 90 or 110. Make sure you can agree the value of your vehicle with your insurer. It's the only way to protect your investment, should the worst come to the worst.

One thing is for sure. If your vehicle is eligible, you really should consider an agreed value classic car insurance policy.

Chapter 2

Preparation and Essential Safety!

Professional motor mechanics are trained in safe working procedures, whereas the onus is on you, the home mechanic, to find them out for yourself and act upon them. However enthusiastic you may be about getting on with the job in hand, do take the time to ensure that your safety is not put at risk. A moment's lack of attention can result in an accident, as can failure to observe certain elementary precautions.

There will always be new ways of having accidents, and the following points do not pretend to be a comprehensive list of all dangers; they are intended rather, to make you aware of the risks and to encourage a safety-conscious approach to all the work you carry out on your vehicle.

Be sure to consult the suppliers of any materials and equipment you may use and to obtain and read carefully the operating and health and safety instructions that they supply.

PREPARATIONS

ESSENTIAL DOs AND DON'Ts

DON'T rely on a single jack when working underneath the vehicle. Always use reliable additional means of support, such as axle stands, securely placed under a part of the vehicle that you know will not give way.

▲ S1. You will need to go out and buy yourself a set of basic safety gear. These Wurth disposable overalls, ear defenders, goggles, face mask, disposable gloves and hand cleaners are all typical top-quality German products.

DON'T attempt to loosen or tighten high-torque nuts (eg wheel hub nuts) while the vehicle is on a jack; it may be pulled off.

DON'T start the engine without first ascertaining that the transmission is in neutral (or 'Park' where applicable) and the parking brake is applied.

DON'T suddenly remove the filler cap from a hot cooling system – cover it with a cloth and release the pressure gradually first, or you may get scalded by escaping coolant.

DON'T attempt to drain oil, automatic transmission fluid, or coolant until you are sure it has cooled sufficiently to avoid scalding you.

DON'T grasp any part of the engine, exhaust or catalytic converter without first ascertaining that it is sufficiently cool to avoid burning you.

DON'T allow brake fluid or anti-freeze to contact vehicle paintwork.

DON'T siphon toxic liquids such as fuel, brake fluid or anti-freeze by mouth, or allow them to remain on your skin.

DON'T inhale brake lining dust – it may be injurious to health (see Asbestos below).

DON'T allow any spilt oil or grease to remain on the floor – wipe it up straight away, before someone slips on it.

DON'T use ill-fitting spanners or other tools which may slip and cause injury.

DON'T attempt to lift a heavy component which may be beyond your capability – get assistance.

DON'T rush to finish a job, or take unverified short cuts.

DON'T allow children or animals in or around an unattended vehicle.

DON'T park vehicles with catalytic converters over combustible materials such as dry grass, oily rags, etc, if the engine has recently been run. As catalytic converters reach extremely high temperatures, any such materials in close proximity may ignite.

DON'T run vehicles equipped with catalytic converters without the exhaust system heat shields fitted.

DO wear eye protection when using power tools such as electric drills, sanders, bench grinders, etc, and when working under the vehicle.

DO use a barrier cream on your hands prior to undertaking dirty jobs – it will protect your skin from infection as well as making the dirt easier to remove afterwards; but make sure your hands aren't left slippery. Note that long term contact with used engine oil can be a health hazard.

DO keep loose clothing (cuffs, tie, etc) and long hair well out of the way of moving mechanical parts.

DO remove rings, wristwatch, etc, before working on the vehicle – especially the electrical system.

DO ensure that any lifting tackle used has a safe working load rating adequate for the job, and is used precisely as recommended by the manufacturer.

DO keep your work area tidy – it is only too easy to fall over articles left lying around.

DO get someone to check periodically that all is well, when working alone on the vehicle.

DO carry out work in a logical sequence and check that everything is correctly assembled and tightened afterwards.

DO remember that your vehicle's safety affects that of yourself and others. If in doubt on any point, get specialist advice. IF, in spite of following these precautions, you are unfortunate enough to injure yourself, seek medical attention as soon as possible.

FIRE

Remember at all times that petrol (gasoline) is highly flammable. Never smoke, or have any kind of naked flame around, when working on the vehicle. But the risk does not end there – a spark caused by an electrical short-circuit, by two metal surfaces contacting each other, by a central heating boiler in the garage 'firing up', or even by static electricity built up in your body under certain conditions, can ignite petrol vapour, which, in a confined space is highly explosive.

Always disconnect the battery earth (ground) terminal before working on any part of the fuel system, and never risk spilling fuel on to a hot engine or exhaust.

It is recommended that a fire extinguisher of a type suitable for fuel

and electrical fires is kept handy in the garage or workplace at all times. Never try to extinguish a fuel or electrical fire with water.

FUMES

Certain fumes are highly toxic and can quickly cause unconsciousness and even death if inhaled to any extent. Petrol (gasoline) vapour comes into this category, as do the vapours from certain solvents such as trichloroethylene and those from many adhesives. Any draining or pouring of such volatile fluids should be done in a well ventilated area.

When using cleaning fluids and solvents, read the instructions carefully. Never use any materials from unmarked containers – they may give off poisonous vapours.

Never run the engine of a motor vehicle in an enclosed space such as a garage. Exhaust fumes contain carbon monoxide which is extremely poisonous; if you need to run the engine, always do so in the open air or at least have the rear of the vehicle outside the workplace.

If you are fortunate enough to have the use of an inspection pit, never drain or pour petrol, and never run the engine, while the vehicle is standing over it; the fumes being heavier than air, will concentrate in the pit with possibly lethal results.

THE BATTERY

Never cause a spark, or allow a naked light, near the vehicle battery. It will normally be giving off a certain amount of hydrogen gas, which is highly explosive.

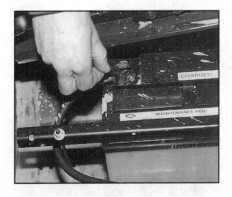

▲ *S2. Always disconnect the battery earth (ground) terminal before working on the fuel or electrical systems.*

If possible, loosen the filler plugs or cover when charging the battery from an external source. Do not charge at an excessive rate or the battery may burst.

Take care when topping up and when carrying the battery. The acid electrolyte, even when diluted, is very corrosive and should not be allowed to contact the eyes or skin.

If you ever need to prepare electrolyte yourself, always add the acid slowly to the water, and never the other way round. Protect against splashes by wearing rubber gloves and goggles.

MAINS ELECTRICITY

When using an electric power tool, inspection light, etc, which works from the mains, always ensure that the appliance is correctly connected to its plug and that, where necessary, it is properly earthed (grounded). Do not use such appliances in damp conditions and, again, beware of creating a spark or applying excessive heat in the vicinity of fuel or fuel vapour.

Also, before using any mains powered electrical equipment, take one more simple precaution – use an RCD (Residual Current Device) circuit breaker. Then, if there is a short, the RCD circuit breaker minimises the risk of electrocution by instantly cutting the power supply. Buy from any electrical store or DIY centre. RCDs fit simply into your electrical socket before plugging in your electrical equipment.

IGNITION HT VOLTAGE

A severe electric shock can result from touching certain parts of the ignition system, such as the HT leads, when the engine is running or being cranked, particularly if components are damp or the insulation is defective. Where an electronic system is fitted, the HT voltage is much higher and could prove fatal. Consult your handbook or main dealer if in any doubt. Risk of injury while working on running engines, eg adjusting the timing, can arise if the operator touches a high voltage lead and pulls his hand away on to a projection or revolving part.

WELDING AND BODYWORK REPAIRS

It is so useful to be able to weld when carrying out restoration work, and yet there is a good deal that could go dangerously wrong for the uninformed – in fact more than could be covered here. **For safety's sake** you are strongly recommended to seek tuition, in whatever branch of welding you wish to use, from your local evening institute or adult education classes. In addition, all of the information and instructional material produced by the suppliers of materials and equipment you will be using must be studied carefully. You may have to ask your stockist for some of this printed material if it is not made available at the time of purchase.

In addition, it is strongly recommended that *The Car Bodywork Repair Manual*, published by Haynes, is purchased and studied before carrying out any welding or bodywork repairs. Consisting of 292 pages, around 1,000 illustrations and written by Lindsay Porter, the author of this book, *The Car Bodywork Repair Manual* picks the brains of specialists from a variety of fields and covers arc, MIG and 'gas' welding, panel beating and accident repair, rust repair and treatment, paint spraying, glass-fibre work, filler, lead loading, interiors and much more besides. Alongside a number of projects, the book describes in detail how to carry out each of the techniques involved in car bodywork repair with safety notes where necessary. As such, it is the ideal complement to this book.

COMPRESSED GAS CYLINDERS

There are serious hazards associated with the storage and handling of gas cylinders and fittings, and standard precautions should be strictly observed in dealing with them. Ensure that cylinders are stored in safe conditions, properly maintained and always handled with special care and make constant efforts to eliminate the possibilities of leakage, fire and explosion.

The cylinder gases that are commonly used are oxygen, acetylene and liquid petroleum gas (LPG). Safety requirements for all three gases include:

Cylinders must be stored in a fire resistant, dry and well ventilated space, away from any source of heat or ignition and protected from ice, snow or direct sunlight. Valves of cylinders in store must always be kept uppermost and closed, even when the cylinder is empty. Cylinders should be handled with care and only by personnel who are reliable, adequately informed and fully aware of all associated hazards. Damaged or leaking cylinders should be immediately taken outside into the open air, and the supplier and fire authorities should be notified immediately. No one should approach a gas cylinder store with a naked light or cigarette. Care should be taken to avoid striking or dropping cylinders, or knocking them together. Cylinders should never be used as rollers. One cylinder should never be filled from another. Every care must be taken to avoid accidental damage to cylinder valves. Valves must be operated without haste, never fully opened hard back against the back stop (so that other users know the valve is open) and never wrenched shut but turned securely enough to stop the gas. Before removing or loosening any outlet connections, caps or plugs, a check should be made that the valves are closed. When changing cylinders, close all valves and appliance taps, and extinguish naked flames, including pilot jets, before disconnecting them. When reconnecting ensure that all connections and washers are clean and in good condition and do not overtighten them. Immediately a cylinder becomes empty, close its valve.

Safety requirements for acetylene: cylinders must always be stored and used in the upright position. If a cylinder becomes heated accidentally or becomes hot because of excessive backfiring, immediately shut the valve, detach the regulator, take the cylinder out of doors well away from the building, immerse it in or continually spray it with water, open the valve and allow the gas to escape until the cylinder is empty. If necessary, notify the emergency fire service without delay.

Safety requirements for oxygen include: no oil or grease should be used on valves or fittings. Cylinders with convex bases should be used in a stand or held securely to a wall.

Safety requirements for LPG include: The store must be kept free of combustible material, corrosive material and cylinders of oxygen.

Cylinders should only ever be carried upright, securely strapped down, preferably in an open vehicle or with windows open. Carry the suppliers' safety data with you. In the event of an accident, notify the police and fire services and hand the safety data to them.

DANGEROUS LIQUIDS AND GASES

Because of flammable gas given off by batteries when on charge, care should be taken to avoid sparking. Always switch off the power supply before charger leads are connected or disconnected. Battery terminals should be shielded, since a battery contains energy and a spark can be caused by any conductor which touches its terminals or exposed connecting straps.

When internal combustion engines are operated inside buildings the exhaust fumes must be properly discharged to the open air. Petroleum spirit or mixture must be contained in metal cans which should be kept in a store. In any area where battery charging or the testing of fuel injection systems is carried out there must be good ventilation, and no sources of ignition. Inspection pits often present serious hazards. They should be of adequate length to allow safe access and exit while a car is in position. If there is an inspection pit, petrol may enter it. Since petrol vapour is heavier than air it will remain there and be a hazard if there is any source of ignition. All sources of ignition must therefore be excluded. Special care should be taken when any type of lifting equipment is used.

WORK WITH PLASTICS

Work with plastic materials brings additional hazards into workshops. Many of the materials used (polymers, resins, adhesives and materials acting as catalysts and accelerators) readily produce very dangerous situations in the form of poisonous fumes, skin irritants, risk of fire and explosions. Do not allow resin or two-pack adhesive hardener, or that supplied with filler or two-pack stopper to come into contact with skin or eyes. Read carefully the safety notes supplied on the tin, tube or packaging.

GENERAL SAFETY NOTES
● Take care not to inhale any dust, especially brake dust, which may contain asbestos.

● Wipe up oil or grease spillages straight away. Use oil granules (cat litter will do the same job!) to soak up major spills.

● Use quality tools – an ill-fitting spanner could cause damage to the component, your car and, of course, to yourself!

● When fitting heavy items, remember the rule; bend your legs and keep your back straight. Know your limitations – if something is too heavy, call in a helper.

● Time is a vital element in any workshop. Make sure you've got enough to finish a job; rushed work is rarely done right.

● Children are naturally inquisitive. Don't allow them to wander unsupervised round or in your car, especially if it is jacked up.

FINISHING
When you've finished, clean up the workshop and clean and replace all your tools. You'll reap rewards in time saved next time out and in tools that last much longer and work much better.

PETROL SAFETY
Petrol is a highly flammable, volatile liquid and should be treated with great respect. Its vapour is extremely dangerous and will ignite at the slightest provocation and an empty fuel tank is thus more dangerous than a full one. Have a fuel tank internally steam cleaned if it is to be stored off the vehicle. When not actually in your fuel tank, petrol

should be kept in metal cans (or approved 'plastic' cans) and stored where there is no danger of naked flames or sparks. Cans should have a ventilation hole to prevent the build-up of vapour. If you work in a pit, extra care is required, as petrol vapour is heavier than air and will tend to build-up in the bottom of the pit.

ENGINE OILS
There is some danger from contaminates that are contained in all used oil – and diesel engine oil is worst of all! Indeed, prolonged skin exposure can lead to serious skin disorders and even cancer. Always use barrier cream on your hands and wear plastic or rubber gloves when draining the oil.

OIL DISPOSAL
Never pour your used oil down a drain or onto the ground. Environmentally, it is very unfriendly and will render you liable to action from your local council. In most EC countries, including the UK, local authorities must provide a safe means of oil disposal. If you're unsure where to take your used oil, contact your local Environmental Health Department for advice. To save transporting oil five litres at a time, use a large drum (say 25 gal) as interim storage. When it is full, take it for safe disposal.

WORKSHOP SAFETY – SUMMARY
1. Always have a fire extinguisher at arm's length whenever welding or when working on the fuel system – under the car, or under the bonnet.
2. NEVER use a naked flame near the petrol tank.
3. Keep your inspection lamp FAR AWAY from any source of dripping petrol (gasoline), for example while removing the fuel pump.
4. NEVER use petrol (gasoline) to clean parts. Use paraffin (kerosene) or white (mineral) spirits.
5. NO SMOKING!

If you do have a fire, DON'T PANIC. Use the extinguisher effectively by directing it at the base of the fire.

PAINT SPRAYING
NEVER use two-pack, isocyanate-based paints in the home environment or workshop. Ask your supplier if you are not sure which is which. If you have use of a professional booth, wear an air-fed mask. Wear a charcoal face mask when spraying other paints and maintain ventilation to the spray area. Concentrated fumes are dangerous!

Spray fumes, thinners and paint are highly flammable. Keep away from naked flames or sparks.

Paint spraying safety is too large a subject for this book. See *The Car Bodywork Repair Manual* for further information.

FLUOROELASTOMERS – MOST IMPORTANT! PLEASE READ THIS SECTION!
Many synthetic rubber-like materials used in motor cars contain a substance called fluorine. These substances are known as fluoroelastomers and are commonly used for oil seals, wiring and cabling, bearing surfaces, gaskets, diaphragms, hoses and O-rings. If they are subjected to temperatures greater than 315 degrees C, they will decompose and can be potentially hazardous. Fluoroelastomer materials will show physical signs of decomposition under such conditions in the form of charring of black sticky masses. Some decomposition may occur at temperatures above 200 degrees C, and it is obvious that when a car has been in a fire or has been dismantled with the assistance of a cutting torch or blow torch, the fluoroelastomers can decompose in the manner indicated above.

In the presence of any water or humidity, including atmospheric moisture, the by-products caused by the fluoroelastomers being heated can be extremely dangerous. According to the Health and Safety Executive, 'Skin contact with this liquid or decomposition residues can cause painful and penetrating burns. Permanent irreversible skin and tissue damage can occur. Damage can also be caused to eyes or by the inhalation of fumes created as fluoroelastomers are burned or heated.

If you are in the vicinity of a vehicle fire or a place where a vehicle is being cut up with cutting equipment, the Health and Safety Executive recommend the following action:

1. Assume unless you know otherwise that seals, gaskets and 'O' rings, hoses, wiring and cabling, bearing surfaces and diaphragms are fluoroelastomers.
2. Inform firefighters of the presence of fluoroelastomers and toxic and corrosive fumes hazards when they arrive.
3. All personnel not wearing breathing apparatus must leave the immediate area of a fire.

AFTER FIRES OR EXPOSURE TO HIGH TEMPERATURES:

1. Do not touch blackened or charred seals or equipment.
2. Allow all burnt or decomposed fluoroelastomer materials to cool down before inspection, investigations, tear-down or removal.
3. Preferably, don't handle parts containing decomposed fluoroelastomers, but if you must, wear goggles and PVC (polyvinyl chloride) or neoprene protective gloves whilst doing so. Never handle such parts unless they are completely cool.
4. Contaminated parts, residues, materials and clothing, including protective clothing and gloves, should be disposed of by an approved contractor to landfill or by incineration according to national or local regulations. Original seals, gaskets and 'O' rings, along with contaminated material, must not be burned locally.

SYMPTOMS AND CLINICAL FINDING OF EXPOSURE:

A. Skin/eye contact:
Symptoms may be apparent immediately, soon after contact or there may be considerable delay after exposure. Do not assume that there has been no damage from a lack of immediate symptoms; delays of minutes in treatment can have severe consequences:

1. Dull throbbing ache.
2. Severe and persistent pain.
3. Black discoloration under nails (skin contact).
4. Severe, persistent and penetrating burns.
5. Skin swelling and redness.
6. Blistering.
7. Sometimes pain without visible change.

B. Inhalation (breathing):
– immediate
1. Coughing.
2. Choking.
3. Chills lasting one to two hours after exposure.
4. Irritation.

C. Inhalation (breathing) – delays of one to two days or more:
1. Fever.
2. Cough.
3. Chest tightness.
4. Pulmonary oedema (congestion).
5. Bronchial pneumonia.

First aid:
A. Skin contact:
1. Remove contaminated clothing immediately.
2. Irrigate affected skin with copious amounts of cold water or lime water (saturated calcium hydroxide solution) for 15 to 60 minutes. Obtain medical assistance urgently.

B. Inhalation:
Remove to fresh air and obtain medical supportive treatment immediately. Treat for pulmonary oedema.

C. Eye contact:
Wash/irrigate eyes immediately with water followed by normal saline for 30 to 60 minutes. Obtain immediate medical attention.

RAISING YOUR LAND ROVER – SAFELY!

NEVER work beneath a vehicle held solely on a jack, not even a trolley jack. Quite a number of deaths have been caused by a car slipping off a jack while someone has been working beneath.

On the other hand, the safest way is by raising a car on a proprietary brand of ramps. Sometimes, however, there is no alternative but to use a jack and axle stands because of the nature of the work being carried out.

● Do not jack-up the vehicle with anyone on board, or when a trailer is connected (it could pull the vehicle off the jack).

● Before raising the vehicle with a jack, engage the differential lock (note that the warning lamp will only illuminate if the ignition switch is in the 'on' position).

● Pull the handbrake on, engage first gear (main gearbox) and low gear in the transfer box.

● Unlike most vehicles, the Land Rover's handbrake works on the transmission and NOT on the rear wheels. It is important therefore to follow the procedures outlined here in order to be totally safe, for if one front and one rear wheel were to be raised at the same time, it is possible for there to be no braking effect at all.

● WHEELS ON THE GROUND SHOULD BE CHOCKED AT ALL TIMES WHEN THE VEHICLE IS RAISED.

USING RAMPS

▲ RLR1. Make absolutely certain that the ramps are parallel to the wheels of the car and that the wheels are exactly central on each ramp. Always have an assistant watch both sides of the car as you drive up. Drive up to the end 'stops' on the ramps but never over them! Apply the handbrake firmly, put the car in first or reverse gear and follow the instructions above.

▲ RLR2. Chock both wheels remaining on the ground, both in front and behind so that the car can't move in either direction. These are pukka Land Rover chocks as supplied with new vehicles.

Wrap a strip of carpet into a loop around the first 'rung' of the ramps and drive over the doubled-up piece of carpet on the approach to the ramps. This prevents the ramps from skidding away, as they are inclined to do, as the vehicle is driven on to them.

USING A TROLLEY JACK

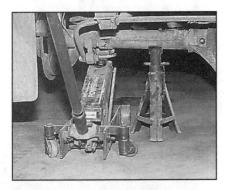

▲ RLR3. On many occasions, you will need to raise your Land Rover with a trolley jack – invest in one if you don't already own one. A SWL (safe working load) of 2 tonnes is required and a higher SWL adds a greater margin of safety. Ensure that the floor is sufficiently clear and smooth for the trolley jack wheels to roll as the Land Rover is raised and lowered, otherwise it could slip off the jack. Before raising the vehicle, ENSURE THAT THE HANDBRAKE IS OFF AND THE GEARBOX IS IN NEUTRAL. This is so that the vehicle can move as the jack is raised. Reapply brake and gear after the raising is complete. Always remember to release them before lowering again.

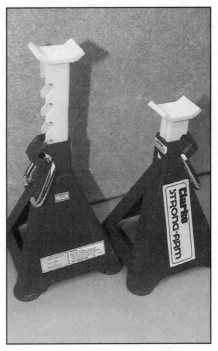

▲ RLR4. Axle stands also need to be man enough for the job. These inexpensive Clarke stands have an SWL of 3 tonnes.

At the front, position the jack so that the head engages the front axle casing below the coil spring. It should be positioned between the bracket to which the suspension members are mounted and the flange at the end of the axle casing.

At the rear, position the jack so that the head engages the rear axle casing below the coil spring, as close to the shock absorber mounting bracket as possible.

TYPES OF LIFTING JACK

The standard jack supplied with the vehicle is a screw type pillar jack. It fits in holes in the bodywork but, apart from the hard work involved in raising such a 'tall' vehicle, it is also far from stable. For emergency wheel changing you could carry a hydraulic bottle jack but use a trolley jack in all workshop situations.

Because Land Rover wheels are so much bigger and heavier than their car counterparts, they're more difficult to deal with. Use something like a spade to provide extra leverage and make the laws of physics take some of the strain!

MORE SAFETY NOTES

Whenever you're working beneath a car, have someone primed to keep an eye on you! If someone pops out to see how you are getting on every quarter of an hour or so, it could be enough to save your life!

Be especially careful when applying force to a spanner or when pulling hard on anything, when the car is supported off the ground. It is all too easy to move the car so far that it topples off the axle stand or stands. And remember that if a Land Rover falls on you, YOU COULD EASILY BE KILLED!

Do remember that, in general, a car will be more stable when only one wheel is removed and one axle stand used than if two wheels are removed in conjunction with two axle stands. You are strongly advised not to work on the car with all four wheels off the ground, on four axle stands. The car would then be very unstable and dangerous to work beneath.

Before lowering the Land Rover to the ground, remember to remove the chocks, release the handbrake and place the transmissions in neutral.

TOOLS AND EQUIPMENT

▲ HTE1. The Clarke power washer can be used a great deal in the early stages of cleaning body panels, chassis and mechanical components prior to stripping down.

▲ HTE2. An electric drill is an absolute 'must' and will be used a thousand and one times. Clarke include cordless drills-cum-power screwdrivers in their vast line-up. Cordless tools are safer and far simpler to use, while the power screwdriver feature can save a great deal of time when it comes to removing screws, nuts and bolts.

▲ HTE3. You'll need a good range of hand tools, as well. A suitable range is that made by Sykes-Pickavant, including the Speedline trade mark. Socket spanners have the superb 'surface drive' feature whereby force is applied to the flats of nuts rather than their corners, making it virtually impossible to round them off.

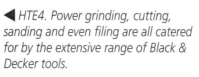
◄ HTE4. Power grinding, cutting, sanding and even filing are all catered for by the extensive range of Black & Decker tools.

▲ HTE5. A basic set of air tools will be invaluable if you have a compressor. This low-cost Clarke set includes spray and paraffin guns, a tyre inflator, blow gun and short air hose.

▲ HTE6. The Clarke 'Ranger' is a very popular 'first time buyer' compressor, just capable of completing a full respray, and fine for smaller jobs including for other purposes such as tyre inflating etc. For further details on compressors see Chapter 3, The Respray.

▲ HTE7. If you have any more than a tiny amount of welding to do, it is not worth considering anything but a MIG. Clarke now claim to be the UK's largest supplier of MIGs suitable for home and garage use and the cost of buying a small MIG unit is considerably less than equipping yourself with a typical gas welding set-up.

▲ HTE8. Clarke are also suppliers of a whole range of workshop equipment including bench and hand tools, compressors in all shapes and sizes and the arc welder shown here – adequate for Land Rover chassis welding.

▲ HTE9. For getting an engine out, you'll need heavy-duty gear. This Clarke hoist packs away into a really small floor area.

▲ HTE10. And for working on an engine, you just can't beat the use of a purpose-made engine stand, from the same company.

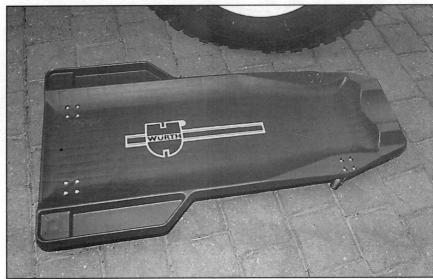

▲ HTE12. Taking parts off the vehicle will be a hundred times easier with a good quality car crawler, such as this plastic moulded crawler from Wurth.

◀ HTE11. Then, as the parts come out of the engine, or off the car, a parts washer will make the job easier and far more thorough.

◀ HTE13. If you've ever seen ancient cars running around in the Canary Islands or other 'dry' parts of the world, you'll appreciate that where there's little humidity, there's little rust. This Clarke de-humidifier can be used to keep your stored vehicle in a low humidity environment. A plastic sheet or canvas 'tent' is placed over the car and the de-humidifier is positioned in a gap at one end. It can be turned on for an hour or so every day or set at the machine's 'humidity stat.' to the required level and left on. You will be amazed at the amount of moisture the de-humidifier will extract from the air surrounding your car and deposit in its collection tray. Alternatively, an adequately draught-proofed garage will be beneficial.

◀ HTE14. Chubb produced what they claimed to be the first non-ozone damaging extinguisher for vehicles and workshops. This handsome beast can be mounted inside the vehicle and there is a larger workshop version. Not just recommended, but essential!

Chapter 3

Bodywork Restoration

More than almost any other vehicle on the road, each chassis-based Land Rover is just a giant kit of parts! It was deliberately made to be a vehicle that can be unbolted and bolted together at will and although the outer panels are difficult to repair by virtue of the fact that they are of aluminium, they couldn't be simpler to remove.

At least, that's the theory! In practice, the body panels on any older Land Rover will be held in place with nuts and bolts that are well rusted in and so the first step in bodywork repair is to soak with releasing fluid all the threads that you know you are going to have to undo. If you really want the releasing fluid to have a beneficial effect, carry this out several days before you intend to start work and then do the same thing again the day before. Even so, you'll have to face up to the fact that some fixings will undoubtedly have to be drilled out. Equip yourself with a centre punch and a set of new, sharp drills. Take care not to slip sideways when drilling one of the obstinate fixings because the drill will cause severe damage in the soft aluminium panelling. Panels themselves are unlikely to be corroded unless they are of steel – see later parts of this chapter – but they are quite likely to be damaged.

Almost all Land Rovers seem to have been treated roughly at some stage in their lives. However, you can take heart from the fact that all 90, 110 and Defender panels are available, 'off the shelf' in most cases.

The fact that the Land Rover was originally designed with ease of construction high on the list of priorities is now much to the advantage of any owner or potential restorer. If the vehicle was fairly quick and easy to build in the first place, the same may well be true when it comes to restoring one many years later.

Allied to this simple construction is the Land Rover's resistance to rust. With the exception of a few panels, such as the dashboard panel, door frames and tailboard frame, which are made of steel, the outer body of the Land Rover is made from a special light aluminium alloy.

The type of alloy used, originally known as Birmabright, was originally developed for aircraft use and is much stronger than pure aluminium. It also melts at a much lower temperature and will neither rust nor corrode under normal circumstances. Birmabright is work-hardening, becoming hard and brittle when hammered, though it is easily annealed. Exposed to the atmosphere, a hard oxide skin will form on the surface.

Aluminium alloy panels and wings can be beaten out after accidental damage in much the same way as sheet steel. As mentioned above though, this will lead to a hardening of the material, cured by applying heat to the metal followed by slow air-cooling (a process known as annealing). As the melting point of Birmabright is low however, it must be heated slowly and carefully; a rough but useful temperature control is to apply oil to the *cleaned* surface to be annealed; play the welding torch on the underside of the cleaned surface and watch for the oil to clear, which it should do quite quickly, leaving the surface clean and unmarked. Then allow to cool naturally in the air, when the area being worked on should again be soft and workable. Do *not* cool quickly with water or oil!

Another method is to clean the surface to be annealed and then rub it with a piece of soap. Apply heat *beneath* the area, as described above, and watch for the soap stain to clear, then allow it to cool naturally.

When applying heat for annealing, always hold the torch some distance away from the metal and move it about to avoid any localised melting.

RIVETING PANELS

Three types of rivet are used on the body:

1) Aluminium pop or 'blind' rivets are used only on box sections or where it is difficult or impossible to use any other type because of limited working space; these rivets are 'snapped-up' from one side only. The setting is controlled by the breaking of a headed steel mandrel which passes through the tubular rivet; the mandrel break occurs only when the thicknesses being riveted have been pulled together tightly and the rivet head on the blind side fully formed. The mandrels are either of the break stem or break head type, the latter being used in positions where the mandrel head is free to fall away after the rivet head is set. Where it is required to retain the broken off portion of the mandrel within the headed-up part of the rivet, as for example in box sections (where a loose mandrel head would rattle) or for sealing the rivet with filler or stopper, the break stem type is used. Either a mechanical or pneumatic hand tool can be used for fixing pop rivets.
2) Bifurcated or 'split' rivets are used for securing rubber and canvas together or to metal. The rivet is passed through the materials to be joined, a boss cap is placed over the tongues of the rivet, and these tongues then spread with a suitable drift.
3) Various sizes and lengths of round head rivets are used, and for these a suitably indented dolly is needed for the rivet head, while the tail of the rivet is peened over with a hammer, operated manually, electrically, or by compressed air.

GAS WELDING

Thanks to the growth in the home restoration market of the last few years, suppliers of gas welding gear are now selling some excellent equipment, obtainable from national companies. The type supplied by BOC uses mini oxy-acetylene bottles hired for a period of a few years at a time and refilled at quite low cost as and when necessary. Gas welding remains the most versatile technique of all, but has a few drawbacks in that a higher level of skill is required (why not enrol in one of the many welding classes run by local authorities?) and, if using acetylene, the gas bottles are less safe to store and use. (Also, check local by-laws regarding gas bottle storage.) Moreover, novice gas welded panels are almost certain to buckle and distort and will take a lot more work to be made to fit properly and to allow a smooth and ripple-free paint finish.

The early Land Rover workshop manuals state that Birmabright can be gas welded without major problems, though in practice, the welding of aluminium and aluminium alloy is extremely difficult for all but the most experienced welder. The principle difficulty is that, unlike steel, which goes through red and yellow to white heat when it is melted, aluminium displays no perceptible colour change before suddenly melting and 'flushing' away from the weld area before the welding rod can be added. Don't practise on your Land Rover's bodywork but buy a scrap panel from a breaker and experiment on that.

If you really want to have a go, the following guidelines should be adhered to: a small jet must be used, one or two sizes smaller than would be used for welding sheet steel of comparable thickness. For example, use a No. 2 nozzle for welding 18swg (.048in) sheet, and a No. 3 for 16swg (.064in) sheet. The flame should be smooth, quiet and neutral, though a slightly reducing flame may be used – in other words, there may be a *slight* excess of acetylene.

Use only 5 per cent magnesium/aluminium welding rod, Sifalumin No. 27 (use Sifbronze Special flux with this rod), or a thin strip cut from an old piece of aluminium alloy; do not use too wide or thick a strip though, as trouble may be experienced in making it melt before the material which is being welded!

Clean the surface of the panel being worked on to ensure it is free of all grease and paint, dry thoroughly and then clean the edges to be welded, plus an area at least half an inch (13mm) either side of the weld, with a stiff wire brush or wire wool. Cleanliness is essential! Also clean the welding rod or strip with wire wool.

An acid flux must be used when welding Birmabright, and you should follow the instructions *exactly* for whichever make of flux you decide upon (some flux is used in powder form, while others are mixed into a paste).

As we said earlier, one of the problems of welding aluminium and its alloys is that it does not go 'red hot' before melting, and so there is nothing about the appearance of the metal to show that it has reached welding temperature. With some experience, you will be able to gauge this point instinctively, but a useful guide initially is to sprinkle a little sawdust over the work; this will sparkle and char when the right temperature is approached.

As the flux you should use is highly acid, it is essential to wash it off thoroughly immediately after a weld is completed. The hottest possible water should be used, with wire wool or a stiff brush. Very hot, soapy water is ideal because of the alkaline nature of the soap, which will tend to 'kill' the acid.

Once again, we strongly recommend that you make a few welds on scrap aluminium alloy before an actual repair is undertaken if you are not already experienced in welding aluminium and its alloys.

The heat of welding will have softened the metal in the area of the repair, and it may be hardened again by peening with a light hammer. Many light blows are preferable to fewer heavy ones, but beware of the fact that hammering the metal will also tend to stretch it. Use a 'dolly' or anvil behind the metal to prevent denting and to make the hammering more effective – an old file used as a dolly will reduce the incidence of stretching to a minimum. Filing off surplus metal from the weld will also help to harden the work again.

WELDING TEARS AND PATCHING METAL

Although aluminium alloy will not rust, it is still prone to damage from general wear and tear, particularly if your Land Rover has been subjected to a great deal of off-road use during its life.

If one of the body panels is 'torn' and the tear extends to the edge of the panel, start the weld from the end *away* from the edge; also at this point, drill a small hole to prevent the crack spreading.

When welding a long tear or making a long welded joint, tack the edges to be welded at intervals of 2–4in (50–100mm) with 'spots'. This is done by melting the metal at the starting end and fusing into it a small amount of the filler rod, repeating the process at the suggested intervals. After this, weld continuously along the joint from right to left, increasing the speed of the weld as the material heats up. After the work has cooled, wash off all traces of flux as described earlier, and file off any build-up of excess metal.

When patching a hole in a panel for any reason, cut the patch to the correct shape for the hole to be filled, but of such size as to leave a gap of ½in (1mm) between it and the panel all round. Clean the patch and the panel, and then weld in the manner already covered. *Never* apply an 'overlay' patch as this will look awful! Once the patch is welded in place, a skim of body filler can be applied over the top and rubbed down smooth to give an even, level surface (this procedure is covered later in this section).

ELECTRIC WELDING

When your Land Rover was originally built, electric welding was used in some of its construction. As far as home restoration is concerned, electric arc welding equipment comes under two main headings, these being arc/rod welding and MIG (metal inert gas) welding equipment.

The first technique is ideal for welding a chassis but tends to be a bit too fierce for welding thin steel body panels. Panel welding *can* be achieved but only with an awful lot of care and even then the job can look rather messy. Special arc rod holders which operate in a pulse current delivery mode are available; carbon arc attachments can also be obtained quite cheaply to enable brazing work to be carried out, ideal for repairing and even replacing *unstressed* panels. The brazing attachment can also be used as a source of heat to help shift stubborn bolts and to bend exhaust pipes and so on. A further advantage of this equipment compared with other welding gear is that it is the most inexpensive while being quite versatile. On the other hand, brazed joints are not strong enough for major structural areas, a fact recognised by MoT test examiners in the UK who are instructed to fail any car that has been so repaired.

The type of welding that should probably be placed top of the list is MIG welding. Up until a few years ago, this welding option was only available as professional equipment well out of reach of the home restorer's pocket. Nowadays, cheaper models (though no less effective) have been developed for the amateur market. These machines are ideal for welding thin body panels, as well as chassis rails, and unlike gas welding, requires relatively little initial skill before good workmanship can be achieved. Usually only a few hours practise is required before you can start work with confidence on your Land Rover. The disadvantage with this type of equipment is that, on its own, it cannot generally be used as a source of heat for bending pipe and so on. It is worth pointing out that MIG welder models aimed at the non-professional tend to be supplied with disposable canisters of inert gas (argon, carbon dioxide or a mixture of the two), which tend to work out somewhat expensive. However, the good news is that mini professional gas cylinders may be hired and refilled from both BOC and Air Products which reduces the running costs significantly. (To use these,

relatively inexpensive gas cylinder valves also need to be purchased – well worth buying if you start welding regularly.)

SPOT WELDING

To complete the electric welding theme is the technique of spot welding, used quite extensively in the original manufacture of your Land Rover's body. Like the techniques described above, such equipment is now available for 'domestic' use. While spot welding is extremely useful in the initial manufacture of a vehicle, the Land Rover being no exception, its use in restoring old vehicles is more limited due to needing a full range of spot welding arms to reach into awkward corners (the length of which affects the welding performance) and which may cost nearly as much as the original tool. Panels to be welded also need to be really bright and shiny on both sides.

Aluminium and its alloys are very good conductors of heat and electricity, and it is therefore most important to maintain the right conditions for successful spot-welding.

SAFETY

At the start of many sections is a 'Safety' note. Naturally safety is the responsibility of each individual restorer or repairer and no responsibility for the effectiveness or otherwise of advice given here or for any omissions can be accepted by the authors or publisher. After all, the jobs you will be carrying out will be *your* responsibility so do take care to familiarise yourself with safety information available from the suppliers or manufacturers of the materials or equipment which you use. 'Safety Notes' are intended to supplement this information with useful tips, as is the additional information on workshop safety and workshop practise in the appendix – you are strongly advised to read the appendix before commencing any of the tasks detailed in this book.

Take note of information in the text on safety hazards. **NEVER drain petrol over a pit or anywhere where a spark could ignite the vapour, eg near a central heating boiler – outdoors is best. For obvious reasons, attempting to weld a fuel tank can be lethal and should be left to a specialist. Never use a flame near the fuel tank or lines. Drain fuel only into suitable containers. Do not use plastic containers which are attacked by petrol.**

The battery should be taken out prior to fuel tank removal, to prevent accidental shorting in the presence of fuel vapour. When storing the battery, take care to ensure that no object will fall unnoticed across the terminals and potentially cause a fire.

Paint stripper is damaging to the skin and eyes – read instructions before use and wear gloves, goggles and protective overalls. Ensure that the vehicle is firmly supported when lifted off the ground – a jack is NOT safe enough. Wear goggles when probing beneath the car and beware of rusty, jagged edges.

Never work beneath a car supported on a jack: use axle stands, ramps or a roll-over cage (see Suppliers Section) and, when using axle stands, or ramps, securely chock the wheels that remain on the ground.

FUEL TANK REMOVAL AND REPLACEMENT

FUEL TANK TYPES: There are two types of tank fitted to these vehicles: the end-mounted type, fitted to 90 models, and the side-mounted type fitted to the 110. Some 110s are fitted with twin-tanks – one of each type – with interconnecting pipework and two separate fillers.

SAFETY: Before carrying out any major body repairs, it makes good sense to drain and remove the fuel tank to a place of safety.

First, disconnect and remove the battery from the vehicle. Never drain a fuel tank indoors or where the highly flammable vapours can gather, such as over a pit. Store petrol drained from the tank in safe, closed, approved containers. If the empty tank is to be stored, have it steam cleaned to remove the petrol vapours. For very short term storage place a damp rag in any openings and keep the tank outdoors. Keep all sparks and flames away from the fuel system whilst working on it.

1. On all models there is a drain plug for the fuel tank or tanks well away from either of the tank positions! Look underneath the vehicle, towards the front, beneath the bulkhead and to the left of the vehicle's centre-line. You will find a bowl with a drain plug on the bottom of it.

▼ *FTR1. These are the components of the side-mounted fuel tank.* (Illustration © Lindsay Porter)

2. Some fuel tanks also have a drain plug on the bottom of the tank itself – check your vehicle to see which type you have. Buy a new drain plug sealing washer and fit it before refilling the tank.

3. Soak all of the mounting bolts with releasing fluid well before starting work.

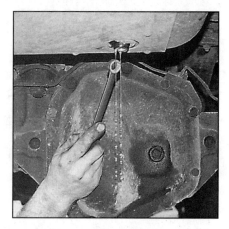

▲ *FTR2. SIDE-MOUNTED FUEL TANK. After disconnecting the battery negative terminal and draining the tank . . .*

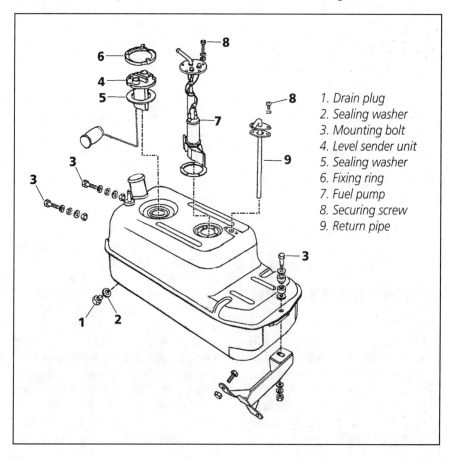

1. Drain plug
2. Sealing washer
3. Mounting bolt
4. Level sender unit
5. Sealing washer
6. Fixing ring
7. Fuel pump
8. Securing screw
9. Return pipe

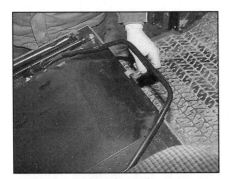

▲ FTR3. . . . take off the front seat cushion and the seat base cover, from over the tank. The level sender unit, pump and return pipe are all there.

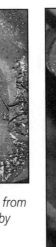

▲ FTR4. After removing the wiring from the sender unit, you can remove it by drifting the lugs (arrowed) anti-clockwise until the locking ring is free.

▲ FTR5. Disconnect the fuel hoses from the fuel tank, and wrap masking tape around their ends to stop dirt from getting in. BE SURE to close off the fuel 'flow' pipe (from the tank) to stop fuel running out of the pipe. Remove the pump by taking out the five screws.

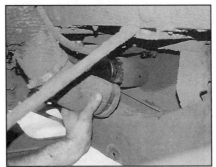

▲ FTR6. Take off the breather pipe from the filler pipe, where it connects to the tank and disconnect the filler pipe itself.

▲ FTR7. Place a trolley jack or stand beneath the tank (with a piece of wood over the head), to support it as it comes free, and remove the two front mounting nuts and bolts, followed by the rear nuts and bolts, in each case taking care not to lose washers or packing materials. Remove the three nuts and bolts holding the mounting bracket to the chassis and lower the tank.

If you want to remove the tank sender unit, tap the retaining ring anti-clockwise with a drift until the ring and then the sender unit can be removed. Always fit a new sealing ring when replacing the sender unit.

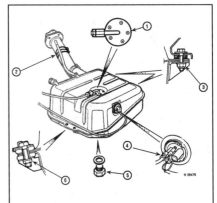

1. Fuel return pipe
2. Fuel filler hose
3. Tank rear mounting nuts
4. Fuel gauge sender unit
5. Tank drain plug
6. Tank front mounting nuts

▲ FTR8. END-MOUNTED FUEL TANK. The procedure for the end-mounted tank, shown here, is essentially the same as for the side-mounted tank, with the following extra points to bear in mind:

A. If an anti-roll bar, or a towing hitch drop plate with support bars is fitted, the anti-roll bar, or drop plate support bars will first have to be removed. On all models, you will gain better access if you remove the left-hand lashing eye from the chassis.
B. The fuel return hose connection on the top of the tank cannot be removed until the tank has been disconnected from its fixings and carefully lowered a small way on a trolley jack.
C. The sender unit is on the side of the tank, as shown.

FUEL TANK REPLACEMENT: Remember to refit the return hose to the tank on the end-mounted tank, before fully raising it into position – otherwise 'strong words' will ensue! With both types, fit all of the mountings but do not tighten any of them until all are in place. Similarly, fit the filler pipe, but do not tighten it until you have checked that there are no kinks, twists or other obstructions in the pipe.

BUMPER AND 'BUMPERETTE' AND REAR LIFTING BRACKET REPLACEMENT

▶ *FB1. The four bolts (1) holding the front bumper are easily reached at the top of the bumper, releasing the threaded plate (2) at the bottom. The optional 'bumperette' (3) is a straightforward bolt-on.*
(Illustration © Lindsay Porter)

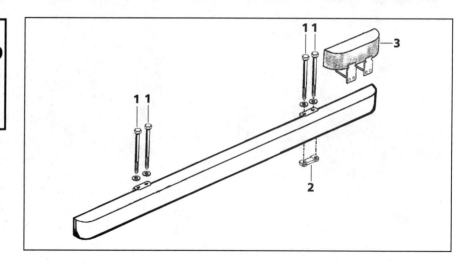

▲ *FB2. The bolts may need soaking in releasing fluid and you should be prepared for the weight of the bumper when lifting it away. This is a replacement PWB component, available in black or galvanised.*

▲ *FB3. Lifting handles, when fitted, are also straightforward bolt-on items.*

BONNET REMOVAL

If your Land Rover's bonnet is fitted with a spare wheel, unbolt and remove it, needless to say! If you're planning to strip the bonnet, remove the height control stop buffers and the catches.

▼ *BR1. Two types of bonnet prop have been fitted, as shown here. With the rigid-type of prop, nothing is fitted to the bonnet; with the scissors-type of prop (not suitable when a bonnet-mounted spare wheel is used), remove the split-pin and washer arrangement at the end of the prop rod and take out the pivot pin. 'Re-fit all washers and split pins from whence they came, for safe keeping', advises Liveridge's Chris Howard.*
(Illustration © Lindsay Porter)

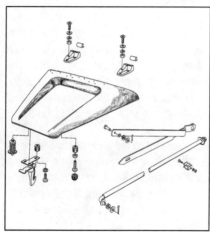

▲ *BR2. Lift the bonnet right back, unhook the bonnet and remove it. Retrieve the pivot bush from each hinge. It is advisable to cover the wings with a cloth to prevent scratches.*

As with most of the Land Rover's body panels, the bonnet is made of aluminium alloy and as such cannot rust. If it is severely dented, you can make it smooth once it has been removed, using the hammer and dolly mentioned earlier, remembering that it will become work-hardened and may need annealing during this process. Once the dents are virtually level again, a few skims of body filler will help to get an even finish prior to painting. Remember though, that if your Land Rover leads a hard life (with much off-road work, for instance), body filler may eventually crack. If possible, buy a replacement bonnet (you may be able to get hold of a second-hand one in better condition than yours).

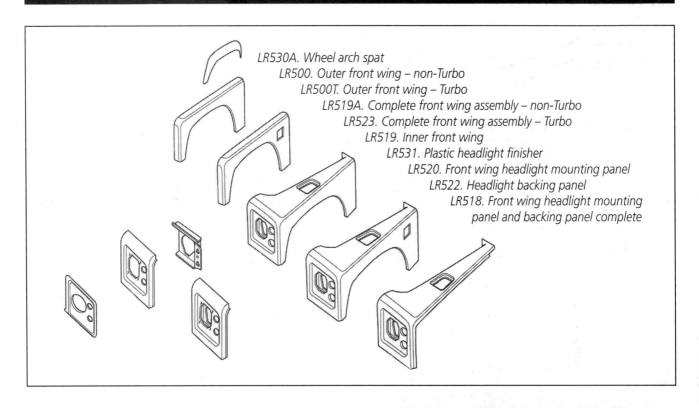

LR530A. Wheel arch spat
LR500. Outer front wing – non-Turbo
LR500T. Outer front wing – Turbo
LR519A. Complete front wing assembly – non-Turbo
LR523. Complete front wing assembly – Turbo
LR519. Inner front wing
LR531. Plastic headlight finisher
LR520. Front wing headlight mounting panel
LR522. Headlight backing panel
LR518. Front wing headlight mounting
panel and backing panel complete

FRONT WING REPLACEMENT

▲ FWR1. These are the front wing repair and replacement parts available from PWB. Note that Turbo models have an air intake aperture in the outer wing panel. Note also that you can buy each component of the front wing assembly – you don't have to replace it all if it isn't necessary! (Illustration courtesy PWB)

▲ FWR3. . . . which makes access to the mounting bolts . . .

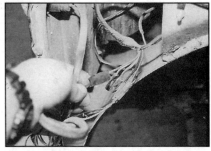

▲ FWR5. If you are replacing more than the outer panel, lights will have to be removed and wiring disconnected.

▲ FWR2. If you are only removing the outer wing and you don't wish to keep it, the quickest way is to cut through the aluminium . . .

▲FWR4. . . . so very much easier enabling you to work with a socket spanner. Cut edges of aluminium are not usually as razor-sharp as those of steel but even so, wear gloves – unlike this blasé mechanic!

▲ FWR6. The replacement outer wing panel is a straightforward bolt-on panel but be sure that you don't distort the wing when tightening these bolts into the A pillar. If necessary, use spacer washers so that the bolts can be correctly tightened. Also, check that panel gaps are acceptable.

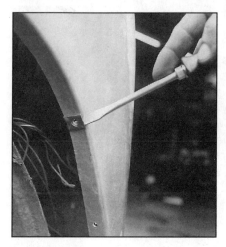

▲ FWR7. Before fitting the wheelarch spat, push on the threaded spring clips. If necessary, pre-drill the wing flange after marking the positions from the holes in the spat.

▲ FWR8. The spat can now be fitted onto the wing, using new fixing screws.

▲ FWR9. These are the separate inner wing panels, from PWB. Note that, as mentioned earlier, before removing this part of the wing, all of the wiring will have to be carefully removed and the headlight taken out, to avoid breakage.

▲ FWR10. And if you want to go the whole hog, here is a complete Turbo wing . . .

▲ FWR11. . . . and one of PWB's ABS plastic headlight finishers. It is simply held to the front wing with screws. Note that, on the more 'upmarket' models, wheelarch spats are painted in body colour.

FRONT GRILLE PANEL REMOVAL

▲ FGP1. The inner panel is fitted to the outer frame with a series of screws and washers around the perimeter of the grille, screwed into plastic inserts in the outer frame.

▲ FGP2. The outer frame itself is held with screws at the top, and hex-head bolts at the sides, screwed through the insides of the wings, into retaining nuts spring-clipped onto the grille panel itself, and with bolt-on bracing rods, as seen here.

SILL PANEL REPLACEMENT

FRONT AND REAR SIDE DOOR REMOVAL AND REPLACEMENT

▶ DR1. Start by disconnecting the check strap from the door. Front doors have a rod or flat plate check strap, held to the door with a clevis pin. Open out the split pin and remove it with pliers, making sure you 'save' the washer from above it. Pull out the clevis pin. Check straps on rear doors are held in place with lock nuts and plain washers. So that you don't lose the parts, re-assemble the clevis pin, washers and split pin (or the nut and washer) onto the door stay, or the stay bracket itself.

▶ DR2. If you're working by yourself, close the door so that it is held securely and take out the bolts holding the door hinge to the door pillar. There are captive nuts inside the door pillar. If you're carrying out a restoration, don't be tempted to disconnect the bolts from the door itself in the hope that you won't disturb the captive nuts in the door pillar because you will invariably have to carry out some restoration work to the bottom of the steel door pillars themselves. Be sure to retain the gaskets which fit between the hinges and the body. Remember to refit them when refitting the doors. Note, when refitting the doors, that there is a certain amount of adjustment available when the hinge fixing bolts are loose.

▲ SPR1. On all models, the sill panels are held on with screws and brackets underneath the vehicle. A mud poultice is likely to make the bolts seize solid and have to be cut away. Before cutting through the bracket, make sure that you see what comes with the replacement and what has to be retained.

▼ SPR2. These are PWB's replacement sill panels, the two lengths on the left corresponding to 90 and 110 vehicles, respectively.

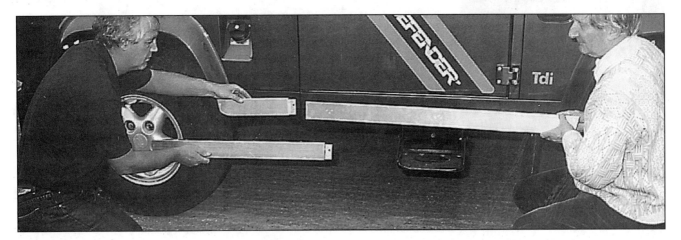

FRONT SIDE DOOR STRIPDOWN

All of the following was photographed at Liveridge who explain that 90 and 110 doors are the vehicles' Achilles' heel. They rust and rot so often that they offer purchasers of 'refurbished' vehicles the option of Series III doors, which last many years longer, have more robust lock mechanisms and are bolt-on replacements. Just a thought!

▲ *FSL1. This is the relatively rare, very early type of door with sliding glass in a separate door top, bolted to the main door panel beneath. It's very similar to the 'Series' door (see* Land Rover Series I, II and III Restoration Manual *by the same author) and is not covered here.*

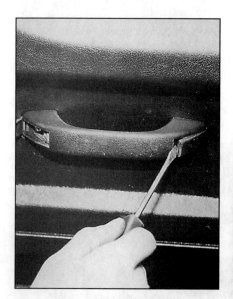

▲ *FSL2. DOOR TRIM PANEL. Open the two covers on the door pull, remove the two screws beneath and take off the door pull.*

▲ *FSL3. WINDOW WINDER HANDLE. The window winder handle has a trim cap in its centre which has to be levered out before the screw beneath can be removed. Pull off the handle and surround, making sure that you don't lose the washer from beneath the screw head.*

▲ *FSL4. DOOR LATCH HANDLE. Pull out the door latch handle and take out the screw from beneath. The trim panel can now be removed from around the pull handle.*

▲ *FSL5. Make sure the inner door lock button is up, then carefully pull off the surround trim.*

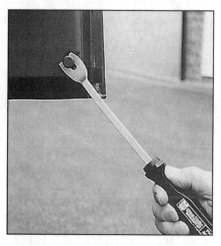

▲ *FSL6. If trim clips are fitted to the corners of the main door trim panel, remove them. The best way is with a tool such as this Wurth trim removal tool, but you can use a pair of screwdrivers and a great deal of care.*

▲ *FSL7. You can now free the trim panel by very carefully levering each clip from the door frame, in turn. With all the clips released, lift the trim panel up and away. If any of the retaining clips are broken, new ones can be purchased. On some doors, there may be retaining screws (whether original or not!) – remove them first. When refitting, make sure that all of the anti-vibration pads, placed between trim and door, are in position, and that all of the clips line up with their holes.*

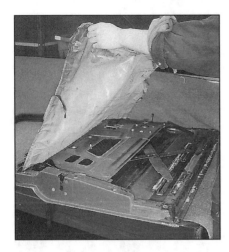

▲ FSL8. FRONT DOOR LEVERS AND LOCKS. After removing the door trim panel, the plastic sheet covering the door frame opening must be carefully peeled away and stored for re-use later. Try not to contaminate the sticky re-usable adhesive on the edges of the sheet.

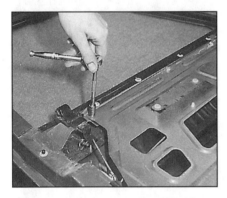

▲ FSL9. Undo the ring of bolts holding the door subframe in place . . .

▲ FLS10. . . . ease the glass over the base of the door frame, disconnect it from the rollers, at the bottom of the glass, and slide the glass out. With the subframe out, you can get at the door's innards.

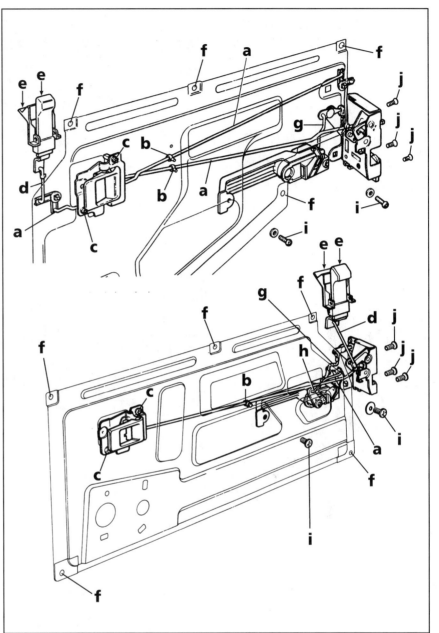

▲ FSL11. This Land Rover drawing shows a right-hand rear (top) and a right-hand front (bottom) door mechanisms. The letters in brackets in the remaining captions refer to this illustration. (Illustration courtesy Land Rover)

◄ FSL12. Locate the control rod/s (a) and disconnect the end/s from the latch mechanism. Disconnect the control rod/s from the plastic clip (b). Take out the two screws (c) holding the lever to the door, and remove the lever and control rod. Take off the spring clip (d) and remove the lock operating rod from the latch mechanism. Remove the two screws (e) holding the lock button to the door frame and remove it.

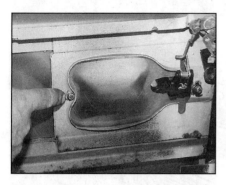

▲ FSL13. EXTERIOR DOOR HANDLE. You will now also have access to the exterior door handle. Disconnect the control rod (g) from the handle lever and the control rod (h) from the locking lever (front side doors only). Remove the two screws (i) and take off the handle . . .

▲ FSL14. . . . although, in the 'real world', Liveridge usually have to drill off the heads . . .

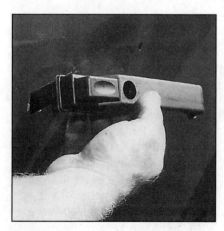

▲ FSL15. . . . and fit a new handle – not too expensive, fortunately.

▲ FSL16. The flimsy plastic components do break but are easily replaced.

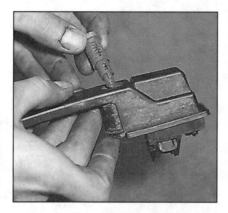

▲ FSL17. The lock barrel pulls out . . .

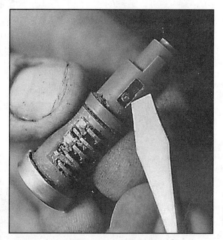

▲ FSL18. . . . but only after depressing the spring-loaded retainer pin – impossible to photograph in-situ.

DOOR LATCH. The latch assembly can be removed by taking off the three screws (j). It will also be necessary to take out the two screws holding the bottom end of the window glass runner to the door frame, so that the latch assembly can be manoeuvred free.

▲ FSL19. The outer glass seal is simply eased away from the frame. . .

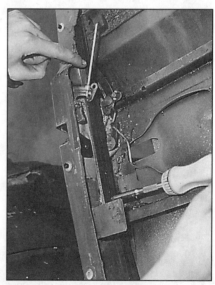

▲ FSL20. . . . while you'll have to chase around the insides of the glass runners with your screwdriver to hunt for the positions of the channel retaining screws.

SIDE DOOR RESKIN

▲ SDR1. Side doors for 90s, 110s and Defenders are notorious rotters! It has to be said that the basic design is faulty and if you rebuild the door as it was built at the factory, it will just rot out again. This door, shows typical signs of aluminium rot all along the base – when prodded with a screwdriver the aluminium just went right through. Fortunately, parts supplier, PWB, have come up with a process which can solve the problem.

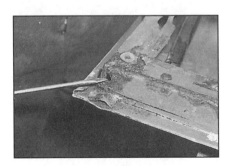

▲ SDR2. And this is the same door viewed from the other side. The steel frame has also started to corrode. Theoretically, aluminium should always corrode before steel when the two are in contact with one another, because aluminium becomes what is known as a sacrificial anode to steel when they are joined together. The aluminium gives up its life in an electrolytic process, one which is greatly encouraged by all the moisture that finds its way to the insides – and especially the bottom – of vehicle doors. Quite why Land Rover have continued to build doors with steel and aluminium in contact with one another is anyone's guess.

▲ SDR3. Before starting to remove the skin, the door must be stripped out as described in the previous section. A single pop rivet holds the door skin halfway along the window aperture. Drill it out.

▲ SDR4. You now have to work your way all around the door skin, levering up the folded over edge of the skin from the steel frame.

▲ SDR5. If there is any risk of causing damage to the steel frame, use a packing piece between lever and frame.

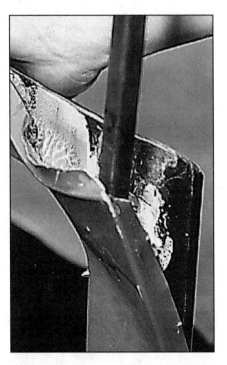

▲ SDR6. The door skin is frequently held to the steel frame with mastic (a half-hearted attempt by Land Rover to separate the two metals?) and the two often have to be strongly encouraged to come apart.

▲ SDR7. Lift the door skin off the frame . . .

▲SDR8. . . . and clean off any traces of rust from the surface of the frame. You will also have to cut out and repair any rusty sections of frame (most often found near the bottom of the door) and the door frame must be primered and painted.

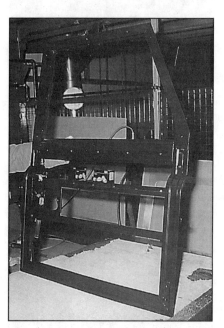

▲ SDR9. And here's one I made earlier! Actually, this is a brand new door frame as supplied by PWB. These frames are now plastic coated so that there is no chance of the steel and aluminium coming into contact with each other. Perhaps a similar effect could be achieved by using waterproof plastic tape, available from DIY centres for things like guttering repairs. PWB's ace door builder, Alan Agutter, shows how a replacement door skin is fitted.
Be sure to go all the way round the outside of the frame, tapping down with a hammer any raised areas of metal. If you don't, they will show through the soft aluminium skin after it has been fitted.

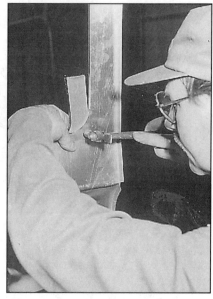

▲ SDR10. Likewise with the new skin itself. Alan goes all the way round with a hammer and dolly, taking out any tiny blemishes. It's worth spending time to get things right at this stage because you won't be able to get at it later.

▲ SDR11. Alan applies sealer from a roll all the way round the frame and on each crossbar. On the outer frame, he applies the sealer to each of the inner raised areas (the door skin will need to be tight against the metal of the outer raised area) and he puts a double thickness strip on the centre crossbar. He explains that a replacement door skin tends to bow outwards fractionally in the centre, come unstuck from the sealer and cause drumming. The double thickness overcomes this tendency.

▲ SDR12. Place the door skin on a work surface with something soft and protective such as cloth or corrugated paper between the aluminium and the work surface. Carefully lower the frame into place . . .

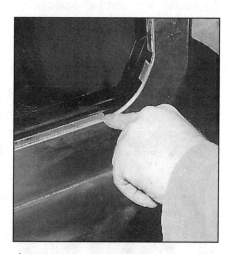

▲ SDR13. . . . and check that the lip is tight against the steel frame in the window aperture. When the lip is right, says Alan, all else will be.

▲ SDR14. You can now go all the way around the frame pressing it down on to the door skin.

▲ SDR15. You can now start hammering over the door skin flange on to the frame, but bear in mind the following important points:
i) Alan recommends that you start folding the flange over at the top of the curved area halfway up the door. This can be the trickiest part to do and it also starts you off by holding the skin in place at its centre.
ii) Use only a soft-faced mallet and make sure that the underside of the skin is not being hammered down on to a rough surface.
iii) Metal flanges should always be hammered over a little at a time, all the way along their length, before going back to the beginning and hammer over a little more. If you try hammering the flange over fully at one end, then work your way along, the metal will stretch and you will end up with wrinkled metal.

▶ SDR16. Make sure that the top of the door frame is supported with a piece of wood to take account of the fact that the door frame is angled inwards. You will have to use a drift – the broader the better – to hammer over the flange. A piece of hardwood would be better than steel.

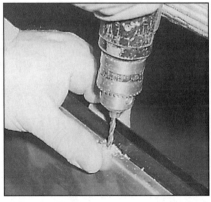

▲ SDR17. Don't forget to fit a new pop rivet to the centre of the lip in the window aperture.

▲ SDR18. Use a smooth file or medium abrasive paper to round off each of the sharp corners. If you are concerned about filing right through the aluminium, try rounding off the corner first with your hammer.

▲ SDR19. Drill right through the frame and through the new aluminium door skin to recreate the hinge holes.

▲ SDR20. If your door frame had rotted out, or if you want to purchase a completely re-built door such as this one, PWB can supply new, replacement doors with the plastic coated frame and ready primered aluminium skin.

▲ SDR21. Whichever route you choose, it then remains to refit the door components – once again taking great care not to damage the aluminium skin – before refitting the door to the vehicle.

REAR DOOR AND TAILGATE REMOVAL

▶ RDT1. When a heated rear windscreen and/or rear wiper is fitted, you will have to remove the door trim so that the wiring can be disconnected. The centre two hinge bolts (arrowed) are also behind the trim but, if no electrics are involved, you can get away with easing back the top part of the trim only.

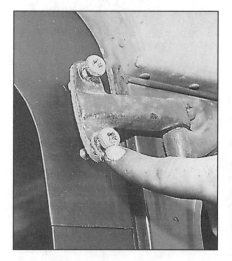

▲ RDT2. Unscrew the top bolts from the outside of the door.

▲ RDT3. The door stay will also have the be disconnected – pull out the split pin and remove the clevis pin, or take out the nut and bolt, if that is what has been used – and you could also unbolt the bottom hinge, the bolt ends seen here above and below the door stay.

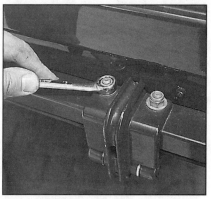

▲ RDT4. On the different types of pick-up model, tailgates are simply bolted to their hinges.

REAR DOOR – RESKIN

▲ RDR1. Except for the points shown below, the principles of reskinning a rear door are very similar to those of reskinning a side door. Once again, the alternative of buying a ready-built door presents itself, such as this one offered up by PWB's Tim Pickering (right) and John Ross. The door can be purchased with or without glass and the glass can be the type fitted with heating elements if required.

◀ RDR2. Alan Agutter demonstrates the four components that make up a rear door's door skin.

▲ RDR3. The main, lower skin panel is fitted first, following the principles described earlier, for the side door.

▲ RDR4. Next, the two side pieces are fitted, the overlap on the side piece running over the top of the lower skin. Finally, the top section is fitted with, once again, the overlap lying on top of the section beneath so that, in each case, water runs off, rather than into the panel.

The comments made earlier regarding electrolytic reaction between aluminium and steel apply just as much to the rear door as they do to the side doors of course – see the earlier section.

REAR DOOR GLASS

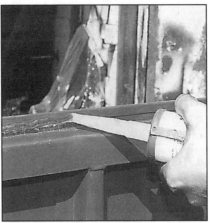

▲ RDG1. Fitting or replacing your own rear door glass is not at all difficult and removal – as all the best workshop manuals say – is the reverse of the fitting process shown here by Liveridge.

The whole of the aperture must be coated with a bead of sealant. Use the correct type of automotive glass sealant, available from your local paint factor or windscreen fitter – don't be tempted to use ordinary household silicon sealer.

▼ RDG2. Wear strong industrial gloves and fit the glass in place, pushing it against the door frame so that the sealant is continuous, with no gaps. If necessary, remove the glass, clean it up and start again.

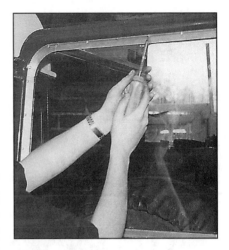

▲ RDG3. The glass is held in place with these aluminium retainers. Screw them into position on the frame using new screws, if necessary.

WINDSCREEN REMOVAL AND REPLACEMENT

The fixed windscreen glass is bonded in place. Its removal and replacement is a specialist job and is not covered here. See your local windscreen specialist.

REMOVING AND REPLACING A HARDTOP

▲ HT1. Although it is rather a large part of a Land Rover's bodywork, the rear hardtop is quite easily moved by two people – being made of aluminium, it's lighter than it looks and easier still if you want to split it into its constituent parts for any reason!

Before starting work, you will have to remove the rear door and the trim where relevant.

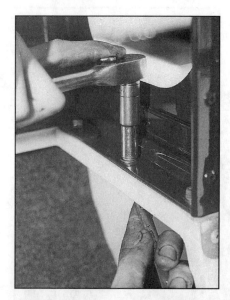

▲ HT2. The hardtop is held to the windscreen and lower bodywork with lines of nuts, bolts and washers. On models with four side doors, remove the bolts securing the hardtop to the door pillar.

▲ HT3. Look out for access slots for locking nuts, where relevant.

Then, with all the fixings removed, it's back to strong arm tactics and the hardtop can be lifted away. Note the positions of any rubber washers or seals as the hardtop is removed.

TRUCK CAB REMOVAL

The cab is held to the cab mounting rail at the rear body with more nuts, bolts and washers. (If you want to replace any of the individual components of the cab, they also bolt together.)

The cab can now be lifted away but note, when replacing it, that it is best to replace the sealing rubbers on the backrest panel capping and the front edge of the roof, because they go hard over time and will allow the elements in.

▼ CAB1. Remove the nuts, bolts and washers holding the cab to the windscreen and those fitting it to the rear panel.
(Illustration © Lindsay Porter)

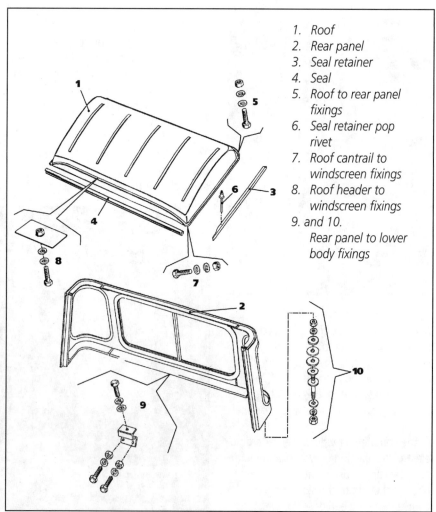

1. Roof
2. Rear panel
3. Seal retainer
4. Seal
5. Roof to rear panel fixings
6. Seal retainer pop rivet
7. Roof cantrail to windscreen fixings
8. Roof header to windscreen fixings
9. and 10. Rear panel to lower body fixings

FITTING GLASS TO A HARD TOP

There are two types of glass panel that you can fit to a hard top: a sliding glass arrangement, or a fixed glass panel. In addition there are glasses that fit to the rear panel and to the roof panel on some models.

Most body shops use a special tool for inserting the filler strip into the glazing rubber and you may find such a tool to be a worthwhile investment.

Liveridge also recommend working with the panel to be glazed in a horizontal position wherever possible and you should, at the very least, have at least one or preferably two people to help you fit the glass, otherwise there is a very strong risk of the whole thing dropping on to the floor before you have got it fitted into place!

▲ *FGH1. You will need a template to mark the sides of the hardtop so that exactly the right amount of material is cut out. There should be one supplied with the kit, but if not you will have to make your own. Take advice from the supplier on how much bigger than the glass the template needs to be – it all depends on the dimensions of the rubber moulding and you can't generalise. 'Moose', the Liveridge fitter, uses the standard template which they have made up for themselves and holds it in position while a helper first measures its position to make sure that it is correct, and then draws around it with a scriber or felt pen.*

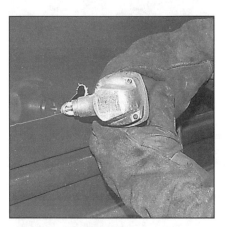

◀ *FGH2. After drilling a hole inboard of the cut line, 'Moose' uses the power-operated nibbler to cut tight up against the cut line. If you use a hand-operated tool or a jigsaw with a large anvil, be sure to mask off the paintwork so that the tool does not damage it. Always wear goggles when using a power tool.*

▼ *FGH3. The redundant panel can now be lifted away – note the heavy duty gloves.*

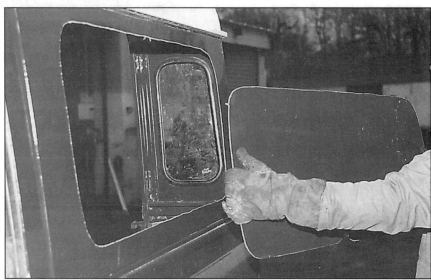

Start by cutting one end of the glazing rubber so that it's perfectly square – use a sharp craft knife dipped into soapy water to help the blade slice easily through the rubber.

Push the strip well into the aperture corners until it overlaps at the point where you first started, which earlier Land Rover manuals recommend as the bottom-centre although it would seem less likely to cause a leak if you were to start at the top-centre. Do note that the strip has a narrow groove and a broader groove and the narrow one is the side that pushes over the aluminium aperture in the hardtop.

Check again that the glazing strip is pushed well down all the way around and then cut it off to length *plus* 1in (25mm) – in other words, allow the sealing rubber to overlap by one inch. Now, pull the sealing rubber back off again for a little way in both directions from the overlap. Refit it, this time easing it back so that the one-inch overlap turns into a tight butt-joint.

Next, with the aid of friends and flat-bladed screwdrivers, ease the glass into the glazing rubber. Then start fitting the filler strip, after first squaring one end off with the craft knife. Commence fitting from the side opposite that from where you started the glazing rubber. This time, allow about a ¼in (5mm) overlap and cut the filler strip off square before pushing it home. If you can get hold of the special tool mentioned above, all well and good; if not, revert to the use of screwdrivers.

▲ *FGH4. This illustration goes back in time to show the end window being fitted – in exactly the same way. The sealing rubber is cut over-length (about ⅜in/10mm for the small windows and about 1in/25mm for the larger ones), pushed over the aperture and the ends butted up against each other. Don't make the join at the bottom; it's more likely to leak there!*

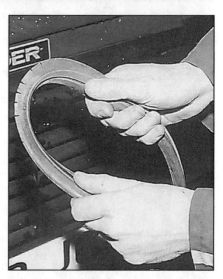

▲ *FGH6. The whole thing is kept in place with a further rubber strip which is inserted all the way around the outer slot in the rubber. Having the proper tool makes the job far easier, but you can carry this out with a couple of screwdrivers and a lot of patience. Note that the join is on the opposite side to that of the main rubber.*

▶ *FGH7. Don't try refitting old rubbers! Not only do they become brittle and crack but they also become hard, extremely difficult to work with and prone to letting in leaks. Renew the rubbers every time you remove the glass.*

▼ *FGH8. The finished job looks attractive and makes the vehicle much more user-friendly, especially when pulling out of angle junctions.*

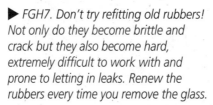

▲ *FGH5. The rear window glasses are easiest of all to fit because they taper towards the top and can be slid in from the bottom. The side windows will need to be fitted with at least one and preferably two assistants, an extra one working inside the vehicle. If the glass sticks in the rubber, wipe around it with a solution of washing-up liquid in water.*

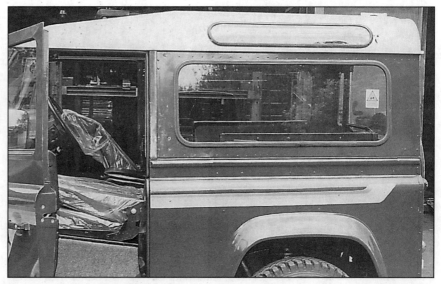

SUNROOF REMOVAL AND REPLACEMENT

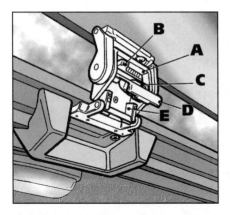

▲ *SRR1. After pulling the latch handle (A) down to the first open position, move the green button (B) to the right and open the panel as far as you can. The red button (C) should be moved in the direction of the arrow which allows you to open the hasp (D), which disconnects the latch handle and allows you to open the rear of the panel as far as possible. (Illustration © Lindsay Porter)*

▼ *SRR2. With the rear of the glass panel (B) raised, it can be pulled out of its hinges, disconnecting the pegs (A). (Illustration courtesy Land Rover)*

Back inside the vehicle, you can remove the two screws (C) and remove the trim (D). Still inside the vehicle, use a broad-bladed screwdriver to lever the inner finisher (E) away from the frame. It is held in place with 14 dowels. This exposes the frame retainer (F) which is held in place with screws (G). With the frame retainer unscrewed and removed, lift the external frame (H) from the outside of the vehicle, if necessary, first removing the seal (I). This is the seal which fits between the sunroof and the roof, it is adhesive backed and it has to be removed from the inner edge of the frame.

If you want to take the latch (K) from the glass sunroof panel, take out the two screws which pass through the glass (with a rubber grommet each side), and into the backing plate (L).

REFITTING. Make sure that the two centralising blocks (M) are securely in place and if not, fit with a suitable epoxy adhesive after cleaning the surfaces to be fixed together. Always use a new frame-to-roof seal (I), being sure to make the join on the clamp side, not the hinge side. Reassemble the remainder of the roof as the reverse of the fitting procedure but note that, when refitting the latch, you must make sure that the bar is properly located in its cradle (E) and that the latch hasp is closed over the bar while pushing the red button (C) in the direction of the arrow.

HOOD AND HOOD STICKS

One of the many charms of the 90, 110 and Defender range is the strong connection with the earliest Land Rovers. The hood and hood stick arrangement (sometimes known as the tilt cover) is a very similar carry-over from the earlier models. Hood arrangements vary from model to model but are essentially as shown.

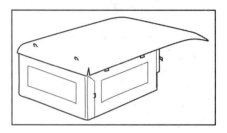

▲ *HA1. Note that there is one type of hood which is a full length affair, covering the cab . . . (Illustration courtesy PWB)*

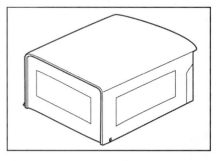

▲ *HA2. . . . while a different type fits the pick-up type body with a fully enclosed cab. (Illustration courtesy PWB)*

Before you attempt to fit a hood, make sure the cleats are in place on the rear side panels – they are sometimes missing, especially if panels have been replaced.

On all models, the hood sticks are held to the body and to each other with a series of clamps and clamp bolts. A combination of straps and draw strings is used to hold the hood taut and in shape.

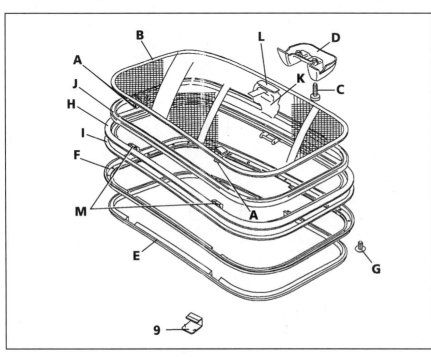

9

FRONT FLOOR REMOVAL

There are two separate sections of front floor. When the vehicle is new, removal is straightforward. But after the passage of time . . .

▶ *FFR1. The screws with Philips heads are self-tapping, and are screwed into plastic inserts. Removal should be no problem, provided that the screw heads are properly cleaned out first. Other (machine) screws fix into spring clips, while a third type has a nut and spring washer beneath, where it is exposed to the elements. Soak liberally with releasing fluid before starting work and be prepared, if necessary, to drill through the screw heads, if totally seized or rounded off. (Illustration © Lindsay Porter)*

Always refit (or replace) the seals around the perimeters of the floors before replacing them.

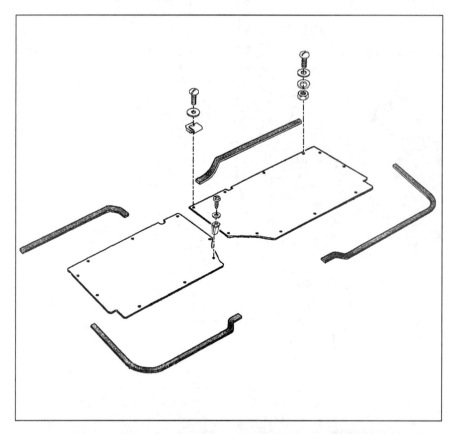

SIDE AND REAR BODY REPLACEMENT

Apart from the business of disconnecting wiring and fuel tank filler connections, where applicable, the business of fitting new side and rear body panels is one of drilling out rivets and spot welds and replacing with pop rivets. Be sure to remove the fuel tank or tanks before using power tools in the vicinity.

▲ *RSB1. Use a sharp, new drill and drill the heads off all of the pop rivets.*

▲ *RSB2. Treat all spot welds in the same way.*

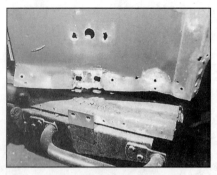

▲ *RSB3. It will still take quite a while to separate panels to be removed from their flanges. You will also have to remove the remnants of pop rivets and welds from flanges . . .*

▲ *RSB4. . . . and true up the surface of each flange with a hammer and a block of wood or other suitable dolly.*

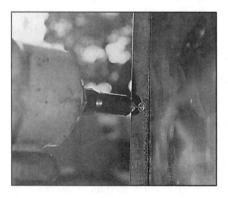

▲ RSB5. This is a PWB replacement rear panel for the 90 model – all versions are available – and was used by Liveridge . . .

▲ RSB6. . . . to repair this vehicle, after being carefully offered up into place, pop rivet positions drilled and new pop rivets fitted.

REAR BODY REMOVAL AND REPLACEMENT

▶ RBR1. These are the rear body components. On the left of this illustration can be seen the type of body fitted to 90s and non-Station Wagon 110s, while on the right can be seen the floor arrangements for 110 Station Wagons, with the lower front section for the forward facing rear seats. (Illustration © Lindsay Porter)

Either the entire section as a unit can be unbolted from the chassis, or each individual part can be disconnected, using a combination of screws, spot welds and rivets.

BULKHEAD FOOTWELL REPAIR

▲ BFR1. The first signs of corrosion in the footwell can be seen from inside the vehicle.

To carry out a thorough repair, you will have to remove the front wing and here you can see how corrosion has taken a hold.

▲ BFR2. If you can get one, you may wish to fit a complete repair panel to this area but, if one is not available for your 90 or 110, you may be able to adapt the Series IIA/III component as shown here.

▲ BFR3. Alternatively, you could fabricate your own repair patches, cutting away the corroded area of the old footwell one section at a time before welding in the new. (You should wear gloves, for safety's sake!)

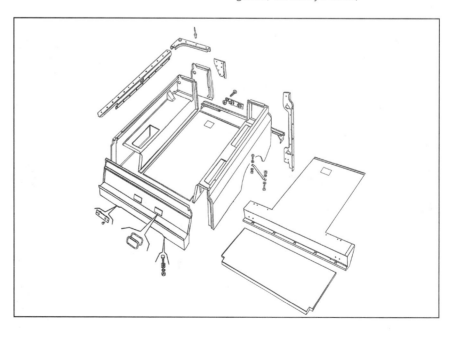

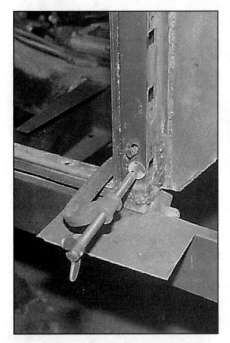

▲ BFR4. Small areas of corrosion to the base of the A-post are not uncommon on all traditional Land Rovers, right from the Series vehicles through to the Defender.

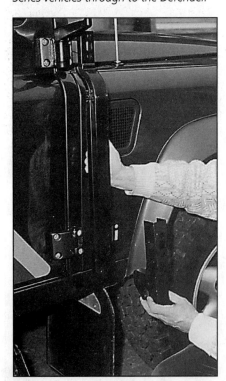

▲ BFR5. You could use a replacement A-post, such as the PWB component shown here, or even cut away as much of the repair part as you would need, leaving the upper part of your original A-post in place.

BULKHEAD REPLACEMENT

According to Chris Howard at Liveridge, there are several different ways of tackling this job. You might want to remove the bulkhead in connection with carrying out a chassis change, in which case you would want to do as much dismantling as possible. You might want to remove the bulkhead to renew it while leaving the rest of the vehicle in place, or you might want to remove it as part of a total vehicle 'refurb.', as Liveridge call it, in which case the process may be slightly different again. Follow whichever of the procedures shown here suits you best but start, in each case, by removing the battery and disconnecting the instruments, controls and warning lights so that the dash components can be removed.

The first job is to remove the following items, referring to the relevant section of this chapter: the bonnet, the front wings, windscreen frame, front floor plates and gearbox tunnel, the doors, and the hardtop. But note how Chris breaks the work down into the following routes: if you intend doing no more than carrying out a bulkhead replacement, take off the bodywork in as many large sections as possible. The front wings, the inner wings and the grille can be removed in one piece. See Body Removal and Chassis Change illustration BRC1. If a hardtop is fitted, you would also leave it in place but remove all the bolts from the top of the windscreen surround and loosen all the rest of the fittings holding the hardtop to the body. The hardtop can then remain in place after the bulkhead has been removed.

▼ BHR1. This is how the bare bulkhead looks. If you are carrying out a chassis change, you will want to leave all the lightweight items still bolted to the bulkhead, such as the wiring loom. On the other hand, you may or may not want to leave the heavyweight items in place. These include the steering column and box, the brake master cylinder and pedal box, the clutch pedal box, the heater matrix, and the wiper motor. If you leave them in position, Chris recommends that you use an engine hoist to lift off the bulkhead. (Illustration © Lindsay Porter)

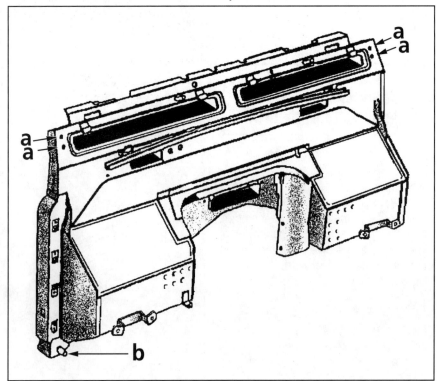

▲ *BHR2. The windscreen surround is removed from the top of the bulkhead by slackening the locknuts and fixing nuts holding the flip-over bolt to the forked bracket on the windscreen. It is also recommended that you take out the two Allen screws which hold the brackets to the bulkhead. See illustration BHR1, positions a.*

With the body panels out of the way, you can now disconnect all the wiring, unplug the bulkhead wiring loom, leaving it still in place fitted to the bulkhead – a quick and easy way of disconnecting and refitting the wiring, provided there have been no amateur add-ons later!

Disconnect the hydraulics. Chris recommends putting a clamp on the flexible hoses so that you lose as little fluid as possible and you are thus left with as little bleeding as possible.

▼ *BHR3. Disconnect the bulkhead/inner wing brackets from the chassis. Remove bolt (A) and you should, in theory, remove the bracket bolts (B). A tip from Liveridge is to undo the two bolts (C) instead. They are larger, easier to get at and come undone more easily.*

◀ *BHR4. Now the large bolt which passes through the bulkhead and the chassis outrigger (see also illustration BHR1, part b) needs to be undone . . .*

▼ *BHR5. . . . and the bolt drifted out from the rear. Note that the bolt is invariably ruined and you will need new ones every time.*

As you lift the bulkhead away, do so slowly and carefully and check that nothing is still attached.

CHASSIS INSPECTION

The chassis is at the heart of every traditional Land Rover. A bent wing can easily be replaced. A faulty gearbox is no problem (except for the cost!) and in general, the Land Rover is the ultimate in bolt-together vehicles.

In some way, the worst thing that can happen to a 90, 110 or Defender is for the chassis to rust, but in other ways it's not so bad. As the next section shows, all the major chassis repair sections are available and it's even possible to fit a completely new chassis. (In fact, it's more common than you might think!) The following section should give you a guide as to whether your vehicle is going to need

repairs to its chassis, how extensive they might be – and even, gulp! – if a new chassis is required.

Liveridge's 'Charlie Brown' takes us on a guided tour of all the well known 90 and 110 chassis rot-spots:

▲ *CI1. The front end of the chassis is notorious for rusting through.*

▲ CI2. The crossmember is one of the most convenient rot-spots, in as much as it can be unbolted and replaced with a new bolt-on member.

▲ CI3. Less conveniently, the front outriggers have inherited from their earlier 'Series' forefathers a tendency to rust away.

▲ CI4. At the rear of the vehicle, the chassis rusts well at this low point here . . .

▲ CI5. . . . at the outer ends of the rear crossmember . . .

◀ CI6. . . . and in the rear crossmember itself. The Land Rover tradition is carried forward in more ways than one!

CHASSIS REPAIRS

▼ CRP1. These are the chassis repair sections available from PWB. Note that there are differences between 90 and 110 chassis – the model-specific variations being shown here. (Illustration courtesy PWB)

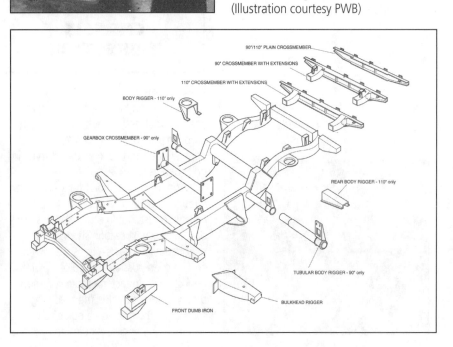

90"/110" PLAIN CROSSMEMBER

90" CROSSMEMBER WITH EXTENSIONS

110" CROSSMEMBER WITH EXTENSIONS

BODY RIGGER - 110" only

GEARBOX CROSSMEMBER - 90" only

REAR BODY RIGGER - 110" only

TUBULAR BODY RIGGER - 90" only

BULKHEAD RIGGER

FRONT DUMB IRON

▶ CRP2. The bulkhead outriggers are among the most corrosion prone parts of the chassis. If the bracing strut to the rear of the outrigger has also corroded, a new one, or a repair section will have to be fabricated and fitted. Using a hacksaw, you will need to cut through the joint carefully between the outrigger and the strut so that you remove the minimum amount of metal and create no distortion.

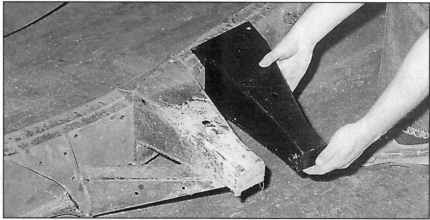

▲ CRP3. This is an outrigger to bulkhead bolt. It's invariably well rusted in but getting the nut off the bolt is only part of the problem! You may need to apply heat to the end of the outrigger in order to encourage the bolt to come free and you will almost certainly need to drift the bolt out. Use a large hammer!

▲ CRP5. The chassis side member must be cleaned up before attempting to fit a new outrigger. The angle grinder is now used with a grinding wheel or sanding pad to remove all traces of rust. Don't be surprised if, as in this case, a hole appears in the chassis. But there's no point welding over rusty areas – you'll simply be hiding the damage rather than repairing it, only to experience greater problems later. Cut out the rust and get rid of all the bad metal.

▲ CRP4. The old outrigger can be cut from the chassis with a hacksaw (plus patience); with a sharp chisel (plus strong gloves); or with oxy-acetylene (plus skill and experience); or with an angle grinder (plus a cutting disc, goggles and all glass covered to protect it from sparks).

▲ CRP6. The position of the outrigger can be determined by temporarily bolting it into place using a new bolt, as shown here.

▲ CRP7. Check, by measuring, that the outrigger is in exactly the correct place and then clamp it to the chassis before starting to weld. Note that this outrigger has flanges fitted to the side of it, similar to that shown in CRP1. If you can't buy an outrigger with flanges already fitted, weld them on before starting – it will make the work far easier to carry out and, for most welders, the job will be stronger.

The component should be tack-welded in place and its position checked before carrying out the final weld.

▶ CRP8. Other common rot-spots include the chassis front-end – PWB repair section shown here . . .

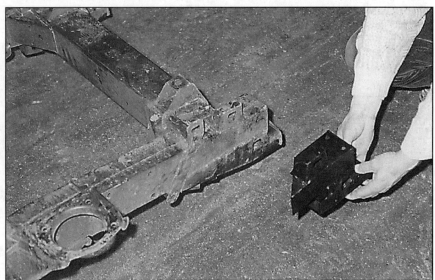

▲ CRP9. . . . and this type of outrigger, both of which are fitted in a similar way to that described for the front outrigger.

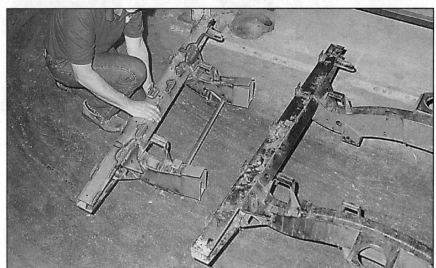

▲ CRP10. This crossmember is not welded but bolted into place, so replacement could not be simpler.

▶ *CRP11. On the other hand, this type of tubular outrigger could take a little more time. The inner, shanked end of the tube passes right through the chassis and you will have to grind the welds holding the tube into the chassis after first cutting the tube off flush with the chassis side member. When fitting the replacement part, it is essential that the mounting plates are all in precisely the correct position. Bolt the outrigger in position before welding it to the chassis.*

▲ *CRP12. You will see from illustration CRP1 that PWB, in common with other manufacturers, produce replacement rear crossmembers either as plain components (à la Land Rover parts) or with extension legs. As repair components, the plain crossmember is next to useless, unless you want to weld on your own extension legs. If the crossmember has rotted out, it is likely that the chassis ends will also have rotted and it is good to see this component complete with top brackets which also tend to rust out.*

▲ CRP13. The Liveridge mechanic uses a cutting wheel to cut through the old chassis. At this stage, the old top brackets are cut near to the chassis so that they can be trimmed back later, once the crossmember has been taken away. You could use any of the methods described earlier for outrigger repair for cutting through the chassis but be sure to support the crossmember on a jack or axle stands. This is because . . .

▲ CRP15. After cutting away the old top brackets so that the new ones slot nicely into place, Liveridge's Andy offers up the replacement crossmember. You will see the extensions on the chassis legs being pushed over the ends of the vehicle chassis as the crossmember is offered up.

▼ CRP14. . . . it is a very heavy component and could cause injury if allowed to drop in an uncontrolled manner.

▲ CRP16. Have the body fixing bolts ready – or at least a couple of them – so that the weight can be taken back into the vehicle quite quickly.

▲ CRP19. The weld can now be cleaned up before priming, painting and whatever rust prevention you want to carry out. Note the way the bracket on the bottom of the chassis has been carefully cut away from the old chassis rail before it is removed, bent out of the way, then welded back in position once the new component is in place.

▲ CRP17. If you are replacing the crossmember with the body off the chassis, you won't have anything with which to align the crossmember. However, it is essential that the new one fits exactly. Therefore, it is a good idea to make a simple angle-iron jig before cutting off the old crossmember so that you can be sure to replace the new one in exactly the same position.

◀ CRP18. With the crossmember repair section properly aligned, the opened ends of the repair section are welded up and are welded to the vehicle chassis. Note how all of the mud, paint and rust has been carefully cleaned away from the existing chassis so that the MIG welding used here gives a perfect weld.

▲ CRP20. The existing tow bracket is refitted to the vehicle so that the owner can tow again, safe in the knowledge that he won't be leaving the back end of his Land Rover behind him!

FITTING A TOW BRACKET

Fitting a tow bracket to a 90 or 110 is perfectly straightforward because the vehicle was built with fitting a tow bracket in mind.

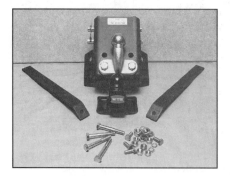

▲ *FTB1. You are strongly recommended to choose a top-quality tow bracket, such as this Witter unit. The Witter tow ball height is easily adjustable by removing the two pins and their retaining clips and sliding the tow ball mounting up or down the main mounting fitted to the crossmember. The two support brackets shown here connect from the main mounting bracket to the rear chassis rails. Note that, with a top-quality tow bracket durability is built in by supplying plated nuts, bolts and washers, a plated tow ball and pins, and heavily coated brackets and supports. The tow ball cover – essential for keeping grease off trouser legs – is supplied with the kit.*

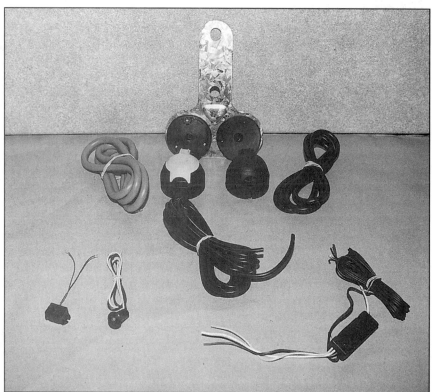

▼ *FTB2. The side arms (C) are fitted differently on 110 and 90 models. On 110s, the side arms are attached to the existing bolt of the towing eye and the towing eye fitted on the outside of the chassis. On 90s, the side arms are attached to the brackets which are welded on the chassis, along with the base of the main bracket (A) at point (E). The adjustable slider (A) can be moved up or down on the main bracket (A1) to give extra ground clearance when not towing, but both pins (P) must always be used.*

▲ *FTB3. Almost as important as the tow bracket itself is the wiring system. Witter recommend a company called Ryder Towing Equipment Ltd who pride themselves in not only supplying equipment but on supplying solutions to problems as well. Complete wiring kits are provided along with fitting instructions, and the unit shown here includes both 12N and 12S sockets, suitable for a caravan and its auxiliary components. Many Land Rover owners will only want to tow a simple trailer and the 12S socket would not be required.*

▼ *FTB4. It is a legal requirement that there is a visual or audible reminder that the trailer indicators are working. Ryder supply relays for many special purposes, such as a supplementary battery charging relay, or a fridge relay, both for caravans. Ryder offer an unrivalled range of tow-related electrical equipment plus free fault-finding advice. Good stuff!*

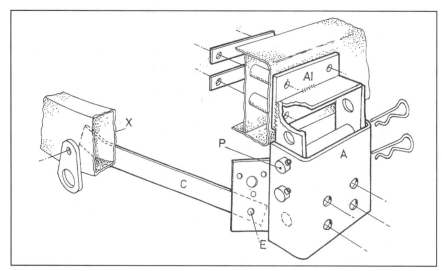

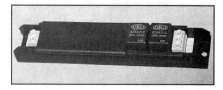

BODY REMOVAL AND CHASSIS CHANGE

Before starting work:

1. Remove the fuel tank or tanks – see the first section in this chapter.
2. Soak every mounting nut and bolt in releasing fluid several times over several days before attempting to remove them.
3. Have plenty of willing helpers available for lifting off – and even more especially for putting back on – the major body panels. Putting it on is more difficult than lifting off because you have to make sure that brackets are properly aligned, rubbers are in place, pipes and wires are not being trapped, and that involves one or two people scuttling around beneath the body as it is lowered on to the chassis.

Stripping a 90 or 110's body from its chassis and then transferring the mechanical components to a new chassis are, of course, very major operations but the good news is that they can be done and without the need for special skills, tools or abilities. You will need plenty of space to store the parts and to work on the vehicle – and plenty of patience!

Almost all of the dismantling and removal jobs required to fit a new chassis are covered elsewhere in this manual but here are a few more tips to help you on your way:

▲ BRC1. Start by removing as many ancillary components, such as doors, tailgate and bonnet, as possible. Then, if you follow Liveridge's recommendation, you will remove the front wings and front panel as a complete unit – after disconnecting all of the necessary wiring, of course.

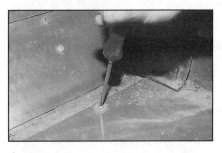

▲ BRC2. Minor body panels, such as floor and transmission tunnel can also be removed.

▼ BRC3. After taking off the hardtop (if fitted) the rear body can be removed, splitting it from the seat box. As with all the floor panels, gearbox tunnels and so on, there is an adhesive sealer between the two surfaces which will have to be levered apart.

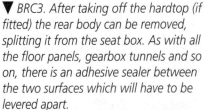

▲ BRC4. Body-to-chassis mounts vary between models although all are self-evident, after a little searching. This is a body-to-outrigger mounting on the High-Capacity Pick-up model.

▲ BRC5. In all cases, when undoing the (front) outrigger to bulkhead bolt, lock the head of the bolt with a spanner . . .

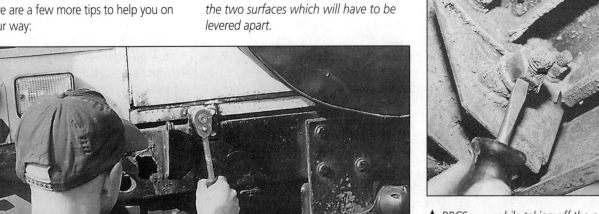

▲ BRC6. . . . while taking off the nut. Leave the nut flush with the end of the bolt to give yourself something to hammer against when drifting out the bolt.

▲ BRC7. Here is a complete chassis waiting to be fitted up to a 110. All chassis types are produced by PWB and are available through specialists such as Liveridge.

MINOR BODY REPAIRS

However well you look after your Land Rover, there will always be the risk of minor accident damage – or even worse! The smallest paint chips are best touched up with paint purchased from your local motor accessory shop. If your colour of paint is not available, some accessory shops offer a mixing scheme or you could look for a local paint factor in *Yellow Pages.* Take your vehicle along to the paint factor and have them match the colour and mix the smallest quantity of cellulose paint that they will supply you with.

Larger body blemishes will need the use of body filler – but aluminium bodywork demands the use of special filler since ordinary fillers won't adhere and will eventually break away. Always use filler with a reputable name, such as Pro-Panel GDF, made by Wurth, which is what we used to carry out this repair.

SAFETY: *Always* **wear plastic gloves when working with any make of filler, before it has set. Always wear a face mask when sanding filler and wear goggles when using a power sander.**

▲ BRC8. Next comes the long-winded business of transferring all of the mechanical components from the old chassis to the new. Budget for the replacement of all fixing nuts and bolts, as well as all suspension and steering rubbers unless yours are almost new.

▲ BRC9. And here is a built-up chassis with its bulkhead, dashboard and windscreen assembly lurking in the background on the right, ready to be fitted back up.

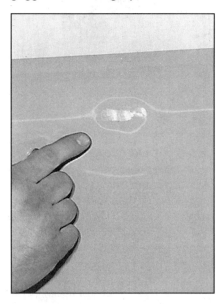

◄ BRC10. Don't forget to use new body-to-chassis mounting rubbers and to make sure that they are in the correct position as body panels are lowered into place.

▲ MBR1. The aluminium panels on a Land Rover dent quite easily and here we demonstrate how to carry out a small dent repair.

▲ MBR2. As we said earlier, we used a filler which is specially formulated to adhere to aluminium and galvanised body panels but if you are not able to get hold of this from a specialist motorist stores you can look up 'paint factors' in Yellow Pages and then ring around and find one that stocks it.

▲ MBR3. Wurth recommend that you remove the paint from the repair area and for a distance of 1in (25mm) all the way around the damaged area. The repair area should be left clean and dry and free of dust. If you can, get hold of some professional spirit cleaner in order to wipe the panel down and remove all contaminants that could cause paint problems. If not, wipe over the area with white spirit (mineral spirit) and then wash off with washing-up liquid in water – not car wash detergent. Take care not to power sand deeply into the aluminium!

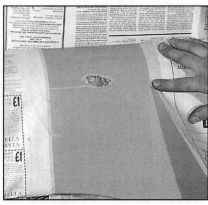

▲ MBR4. Mask off the area around the repair. You can, as we did, take off the masking tape and paper before spraying the finish coat, so that the overspray blends into the surrounding paint after it has been polished with cutting compound, available from any high street motor accessory store.

▲ MBR5. Use a piece of plastic on which to mix the filler and hardener, following the instructions on the can. Card 'picks-up' fibres into the filler and reduces its quality.

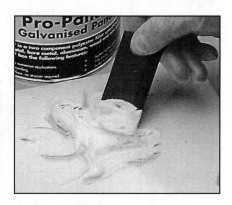

▲ MBR6. Mix the filler and hardener thoroughly until the colour is consistent and no traces of hardener can be discerned.

▲ MBR7, You can now spread the filler evenly over the repair.

▼ MBR8. If the dent is particularly deep, apply the paste in two or more layers, allowing the filler to harden before adding the next layer. The final layer should be just proud of the level required, but do not overfill as this wastes paste and will require more time to sand down.
(Illustration © Lindsay Porter)

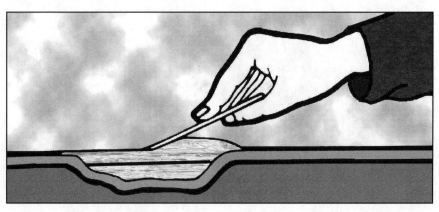

▲ MBR9. It is essential when sanding down that you wrap the sanding paper around a flat block. Sand diagonally in alternate directions until the filler is level with the surrounding panel but take care not to go deeply into the edges of the paint around the repair. There will invariably be small pin holes even if the right amount of filler was applied first time. Use a tiny amount of filler scraped very thin over the whole repair, filling in deep scratches and pin holes and then sanding off with a fine grade of sandpaper – preferably dry paper rather than wet-or-dry because you don't want to get water on to the bare filler – until all of the coarser scratches from the earlier sanding have been removed. (Illustration © Lindsay Porter)

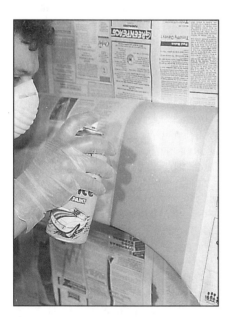

▲ MBR10. You can now use an aerosol primer to spray over the whole area of the repair but not right up to the edges of the masking tape . . .

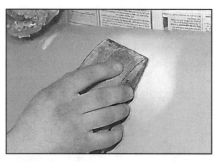

▲ MBR11. . . . and you can now use wet-or-dry paper to sand the primer paint since the filler is now protected from the water by the paint. Again, use a sanding block.

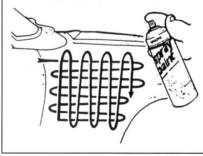

▲ MBR12. Before starting to spray, ensure that the nozzle is clear. Note that the can must be held with the index finger well back on the aerosol button. If you let your finger overhang the front of the button, a paint drip can form and throw itself on to the work area as a blob. This is most annoying and means that you will have to let the paint dry, sand it down and start again. One of the secrets of getting a decent coat of paint which doesn't run badly is to put a very light coat of spray paint on to the panel first, followed by several more coats, allowing time between each coat for the bulk of the solvent to evaporate. Alternate coats should go horizontally, followed by vertical coats as shown on the inset diagram.

You must always wear an efficient mask when spraying aerosol paint and only work in a well-ventilated area, well away from any source of ignition, since spray paint vapour, even that given off by an aerosol, is highly flammable. Ensure that you have doors and windows open to the outside when using aerosol paint but in cooler weather, close them when the vapour has dispersed, otherwise the surface of the paint will 'bloom', ie take on a milky appearance. In fact, you may find it difficult to obtain a satisfactory finish in cold and damp weather.

▲ MBR13. If carried out with great care and skill, this type of repair can be virtually invisible. After allowing about a week for the paint to dry, you will be able to polish it with a light cutting compound, blending the edges of the repair into the surrounding paintwork.

Do note that if your repairs don't work out first time and you have to apply more paint on top of the fresh paint that you have already used, allow a week to elapse otherwise there is a strong risk of pickling or other reactions taking place. Also note that a common cause of paint failure is the existence of silicone on the surface of the old paint before you start work. These come from most types of polish and are not all that easy to remove. Thoroughly wipe the panel down with white spirit before starting work and wash off with warm water and washing-up liquid to remove any further traces of the polish and the white spirit – but don't use the sponge or bucket that you normally use for washing the car otherwise you will simply introduce more silicones onto the surface!

69

PAINT YOUR WAGON!

The importance of getting the paintwork right on a restored Land Rover can't be over-stressed. You may have spent weeks of your life making your vehicle as sound as the day the makers conceived it, but unless the paintwork is right, the whole effect will be spoiled. It's a big mistake to believe that a vehicle designed as a workhorse won't benefit from being made to look its best. Re-painting a car is actually a major subject in itself, but provided you keep things simple, there will be enough information here to enable you to have a go at doing it yourself. If you feel you need to know more this author has written another book with Haynes called *The Car Bodywork Repair Manual* which is around the size of this book, but which does nothing but give information on how to fix car bodywork. So there's a very large amount of information in there on all aspects of paint spraying for the home sprayer.

But back to the specifics of the Land Rover: Your first decision must be to pick the type of paint you wish to use. The very best type of paint is not at all suitable for the home sprayer unless you possess well above average levels of equipment. It's known generally as 'two-pack' paint because the paint is mixed with a hardener before spraying, and it then sets rather like an adhesive. The finish from the gun is superb, the paint film is much harder than anything else on offer and it doesn't need polishing for many years, a wash and leather down restoring its shine. The snag is that the air-borne particles of paint are toxic, containing iso-cyanate; the family connection with the word 'cyanide' not being coincidental! Professionals use an air-fed mask when spraying with this type of paint, but the home sprayer would also have to be certain that the spray mist would not cause anyone else potential harm. This clearly is impossible in most domestic circumstances, such as where the garage is attached to the house or where children or other inquisitive souls could be in the vicinity.

The vehicles shown here are being resprayed at the Liveridge body shop, using two-pack paint in a professional booth, and that may be another option open to you; to go as far as you can in preparing the car then take it to a specialist (who will invariably criticise your preparation and want to do more – if he doesn't, ask yourself why!) and have the paint put on. This is actually quite a cost-effective thing to do because the most time-consuming part of the job is the preparation.

The only other type of paint that I could possibly recommend is cellulose enamel paint. Cellulose isn't and hasn't been used by any of the vehicle manufacturers for many years, but it is more suitable for DIY use. If a face mask of the correct type is used and the spray area kept ventilated, the fumes are not especially dangerous (but read carefully the Safety Section of this book) and the finish will be quite durable. It also has two advantages for the home restorer: any home paint job is almost certain to have bits of dust or kamikaze flies land in it and these can be most easily polished out from cellulose, and so can any runs that the unskilled sprayer might have incurred. Also, if cellulose is 'cut and polished' (rubbed down with extremely fine abrasive paper, then with polishing compound) it is possible to obtain the sort of 'mirror' finish that no other paint will give. The trouble is, it doesn't last, and you have to polish the shine back again, in the end polishing right through the paint over a period of years.

SAFETY:
Cellulose paint
The spray is volatile – keep away from all flames or sparks – and so are the fumes from paint and thinners, while thinner-dampened rags are also a fire hazard. The spray can cause you to lose consciousness if inhaled in a confined area. Always use a suitable face mask (see your supplier) and ventilate the work area. Protect hands with a barrier cream or wear protective gloves when handling paint. Keep well away from eyes.

Two-pack paint
Spray from this type of paint is toxic to the degree that it can be lethal! (The hardened paint on the car is not dangerous, of course!). Only use with an air-fed mask from a clean compressed air source (ie not from within the spray area) and never use this type of paint where the spray could affect others. It can also cause eye irritation and eye protection should be worn. Protective gloves should be worn when mixing and handling paint. Those who suffer from asthma or other respiratory illness should have nothing to do with this type of paint spraying! There is also a fire risk, with peroxide catalysts.

General
Don't eat, drink or smoke near the work area, clean hands after the work is complete, but never use thinners to wash paint from hands. Always wear an efficient particle mask when sanding down.

OBTAIN AND THOROUGHLY READ THE MANUFACTURERS' DATA AND SAFETY SHEETS BEFORE USE.

Starting work
For best results the old paint should be removed. (If spraying over old paint, you may have to apply a separate layer of a special isolating paint as different paints can show disastrous reactions if sprayed on top of one another. Check for this effect first by wiping over a small area of old paintwork with the new paint thinners. If wrinkling occurs, the two paint systems are incompatible and an isolator will be required. Check repaired and pre-primered areas too. Make sure that the areas where you don't want stripper to be applied are adequately masked over. Old newspaper is acceptable, but since newsprint 'leaching' out into new paintwork is not unheard of, strong brown wrapping paper is better. Ensure that you wear gloves (and wear safety glasses) in case of spills, etc. Stripper, as you might expect, is very corrosive and will damage eyes and skin if splashed on to them. Read the safety notes that come with the stripper before use. Let the old paint wrinkle up and then remove with a metal scraper, still wearing gloves and goggles! But take *great* care not to scratch or scrape the aluminium with the scraper blade.

It is far from unknown for Land Rovers to be painted, by brush or spray, in oil-based paints, more suitable for goods vehicles. Any attempt to spray two-pack or cellulose paint on top will involve a severe reaction taking place. There are two solutions if you don't wish to respray with the same type of inferior, slow-drying paint again. One is to strip off all of the old paint; another is to completely prepare the surface, then spray it with an isolator paint, which has a water base and thus will neither react with what is beneath nor the paint to be sprayed on top.

THE RESPRAY

▲ RS2. Going further up the scale, the Clarke 'Rebel' Air 50 is probably as large as the average DIY user will buy but it will cope easily with a full paint job or for powering most air tools. There are many other first class compressors in the huge Clarke range.

▲ RS1. The Clarke 'Ranger' is a very popular 'first time buyer' compressor, just capable of completing a full respray, and fine for other smaller jobs such as tyre inflating, etc.

▼ RS3. This is the compressor-operated Clarke random orbit sander which does an excellent job of quickly sanding filler, paintwork and primer without leaving scuff marks (by virtue of the 'random orbit' feature), saving hours of hand-work. Highly recommended! Before carrying out any preparatory work on your Land Rover, you should wipe down all the paintwork with wax-and-grease remover. This will get rid of grease and silicone deposits that will otherwise be integrated into the bodywork when you sand down – it won't just be sanded away!

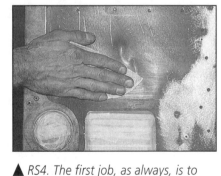

▲ RS4. The first job, as always, is to remove any bodywork blemishes. For those who are not skilled in panel beating, it is easy to make matters worse rather than better when hammering aluminium because it stretches so easily. Before starting to rub the surface down, wipe it over with a fresh cloth (not one that has been anywhere near polish) and spirit wipe, available from your local paint factor. If you let silicones settle on the surface to be painted, at any stage, your paint finish will be ruined and there will be nothing for it but to remove the affected areas and start again from scratch. Silicones will not stand out but will continually rise to the surface. You must therefore apply spirit wipe at every stage of the job. Mask off the surrounding components, rub down with medium-grade abrasive paper . . .

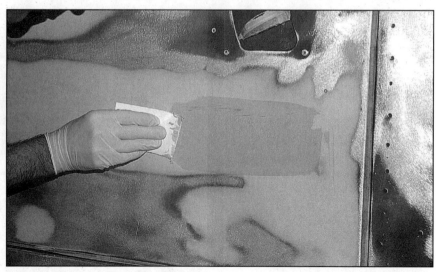

▲ RS7. You will invariably have to apply several layers of filler, so don't give yourself too much to sand off at any one time.

▲ RS5. . . . and mix filler, using the correct proportion of hardener with filler, mixing it until the colour is even and consistent. It is most important that you use the correct type of filler. Ordinary filler will not 'stick' to aluminium but cracks and drops out after a short time. Wurth Pro-Panel 'sticks' successfully to aluminium and galvanised steel. Note that you should always wear gloves and mix the filler on a hard surface, such as plastic or clean metal. Cardboard fibres will pick up in the filler and weaken it.

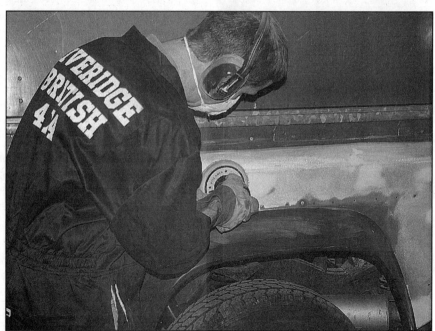

▲ RS8. For removing a good deal of filler, you can't beat the random orbit sander referred to earlier. Note that the Liveridge body man is wearing an efficient particle mask and ear defenders.

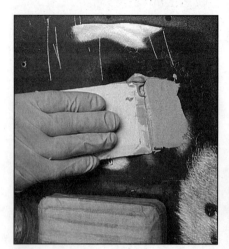

◀ RS9. When sanding a flat panel, you can't beat the use of a long-flat wooden sanding block to support the abrasive paper. Otherwise, you are bound to see ripples after the top coat has been put on, even though you won't see them while the panel is matt.

▲ RS6. Spread the filler on as required, but don't build it up too high.

▶ *RS10. The Liveridge bodyshop favour the use of a straight edge to check for ripples – excellent practice!*

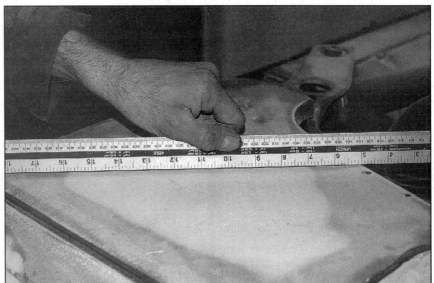

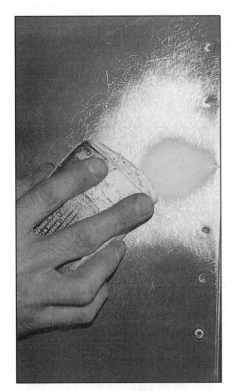

▲ *RS11. Inevitably, final 'blocking-down' has to be done by hand but once again, a sanding block supporting the paper is essential.*

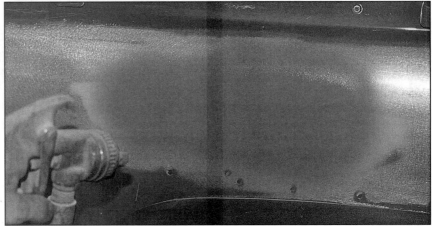

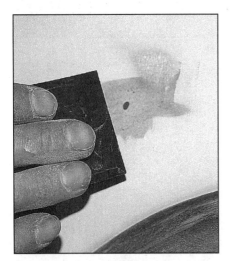

▲ *RS12. There are always minor blemishes in the surface of the filler after you have finished. Use purpose-made stopper, which is much finer than ordinary filler, to get rid of the tiny blemishes, then sand off with fine abrasive paper.*

▲ *RS13. Now here's another important point! Just as ordinary filler won't stick to aluminium, ordinary paint won't stick to it either. All areas of bare aluminium must be sprayed with special etch primer which 'keys' itself to the surface of the aluminium. If you rub through this etch primer when carrying out the final flatting before painting the vehicle, you will have to apply more or, sure as eggs is eggs, the paint will peal off the aluminium. If you wish to paint over the galvanised cappings, these will also have to be painted in etch primer first.*

▶ *RS14. If you're going for a top-quality job, you will now remove all of the old masking paper and remask all of the areas not to be painted. Then, you can get rid of all the dust that will be trapped in the old masking paper . . .*

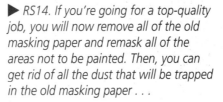

▲ RS15. . . .before fitting new. Large areas are best masked off by applying masking paper all the way around the perimeter and then filling in the 'gap' with brown paper available on the roll from your local paint factors. Beware: newspaper tends to leach and mark the surface beneath when it becomes wet with paint!

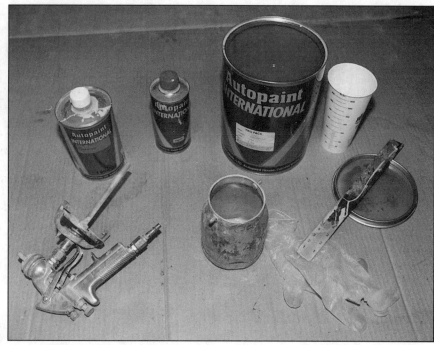

▲ RS18. Not all of the paint manufacturers want to provide vehicle paint for DIY use. In the UK, cellulose (and 2-pack, for professional use) are easily obtainable, along with all the peripherals, from Autopaints. See Appendix for contact numbers to find details of your local stockist.

▲ RS16. If you don't want to go to the trouble of fitting all new stuck-on decals, they could be masked off too.

▶ RS19. Use an air line to blow any dust from around the top of the paint tin before opening it. Clarke produce a trigger operated 'blow gun' if you prefer. The paint is poured into a clean container and mixed according to the manufacturer's specifications with the correct amount of spraying-quality thinners.

▲ RS17. The whole vehicle now has to be wiped over with a tak rag – a special cloth impregnated with a sticky substance, that picks up all small particles remaining on the surface to be painted. You must also wipe the entire surface down once again with spirit wipe to remove any of those pesky silicones which would otherwise ruin the surface of the finished job.

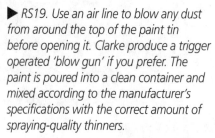

▲ RS20. If you are spraying at home, wet the floor to lay the dust before starting to spray. Take great care to avoid electrical connections and do not use electrical appliances anywhere near the wet floor.

▲ RS21. Starting at the rear, left-hand corner, the two-pack paint is being applied, working forwards towards the front of the vehicle. Work in vertical strips, covering each panel at a time.

▲ RS22. An accepted way of checking that your spray gun is being held the correct distance away is to use a hand span as a measure.

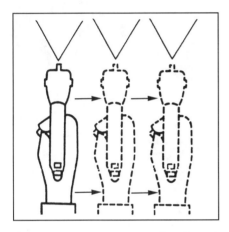

▲ RS23. Keep your wrists stiff and avoid swinging the gun in an arc from your elbow, to ensure even spraying. Always spray at a steady, even pace.

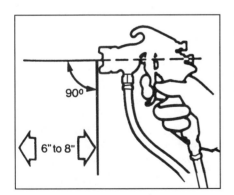

▲ RS24. Always hold the spray gun at right angles to the surface you are painting, keeping it between 6 and 8in (150mm to 180mm) away from the vehicle.

FITTING STRIPES AND DECALS

▲ FSD1. This refurbished Liveridge 110 is being fitted with its decals by Proprietor, Chris Howard. He says that, because a Land Rover's panels rarely line up precisely, as do those on a modern car, it is best to line up the decals and stripes by eye rather than attempting to follow the body contours, which vary from panel to panel. 'Moose', stands a little way away while Chris applies the first decal. Note that he has previously wetted the panel with a hand sprayer filled with water and a touch of washing-up liquid, and he has peeled the backing paper off the decal.

▲ FSD2. As the decal is fitted, Chris uses a squeegee to press it down to the panel, pushing out water and air bubbles as he goes.

▲ FSD3. Now 'Moose' takes a hand with fitting the stripes to the rear bodywork while Chris continues to line everything up by eye.

RUSTPROOFING

Only carry out rustproofing *after* all welding repairs, and *after* applying paint, or the silicones in the rustproofer may play havoc with your paint finish.

SAFETY: Wear gloves, a face mask and goggles when applying rustproofing materials. Keep such materials away from your eyes but if you do get any into your eyes, wash out with copious amounts of cold water and, if necessary, seek medical advice. All rustproofing materials are flammable and should be kept well away from all sources of ignition, especially when applying them. All such materials are volatile and in vaporised form are more likely to catch fire or explode. Do bear in mind that, if any welding has to be carried out on the car within a few months of rustproofing materials being injected into it, you must inform those who are carrying out the welding because of the fire risk. Cover all brake components with plastic bags so that none of the rustproofing material can get on to the brake friction materials, and keep away from the clutch bellhousing and from the exhaust manifold and exhaust system. Always carry out this work out of doors since the vapour can be dangerous in a confined space.

Some owners seem to think that because their Land Rover's bodywork is aluminium and the chassis is one of the toughest around, rusting can't be a problem, but that just isn't true. Land Rovers are designed to be around for decades rather than years, and to this end, the makers considered that 90, 100 and Defender models should be better protected against the rust bug than their Series I, II and III forebears. However, even the thick steel of the Solihull vehicle's chassis is capable of rusting away and, contrary to popular opinion, aluminium can corrode. When it does, it's even more difficult than steel to repair and where

aluminium is in contact with steel, it corrodes in double-quick time. Therefore, time and money spent on maintaining your Land Rover's bodywork will save you even more money in the long run than that spent on its mechanical components. Please remember that different models of Land Rover have 'access' holes (they weren't put there for that, of course) in different places, so it isn't possible to be specific about which chassis and bodies have to be drilled and which can use existing holes.

Do take note of the fact that in Britain, the Automobile Association has carried out research into rustproofing materials and has found that inadequately applied materials do more harm than good. A car's body panels are forever in the process of rusting unless there is a barrier in place to keep out the air and moisture which are necessary to help the rusting process along. However, if that barrier is inefficiently applied, the rusting process concentrates itself on the areas where the rustproofing is missing, which speeds up the corrosion and makes it even worse in the unprotected areas than it would otherwise have been. So, take great care that you apply the rustproofing materials as thoroughly as possible. It's not a question of quantity; more a question of quality of application – reaching every part of the car with a type of rustproofing fluid that 'creeps' into each of the seams, into any rust that may have already formed on the surface and using an applicator that applies the fluid in a mist rather than in streams or blobs which unfortunately is all that some of the hand applicators we have seen seem to do.

Also, you should note that the best time to apply rustproofing materials is in the summer when the warmer weather allows the materials to flow better inside the hidden areas of the car's bodywork and, just as importantly, the underside of the car and the insides of the box sections will be completely dried out. In spite of what anyone's advertising blurb says, you are better off applying rust preventative materials when the car is dry than when it is wet.

Before starting, make sure that all electric equipment, motors and electronic components, are covered up with plastic bags so that none of the rustproofing fluids can get into them. Never pressure-wash near them, either. Also, ensure that all drain channels are clear, so that any excess rustproofing fluid can drain out.

Then check once again that the drain channels are clear after you have finished carrying out the work, to ensure that the newly applied fluid has not caused them to be clogged up, otherwise water will get trapped in there, negating much of the good work you have carried out.

▲ *RP1. You will need to clean off the underside of the vehicle before commencing work. You can use a pressure attachment which uses your standard garden hose or a power washer – but you'll have to leave the car for about a week in warm dry weather so that it dries out properly underneath. Some garages have car washing equipment on the forecourt that enables you to wash underneath the vehicle. Get the mud and dirt from under the wheel arches and the chassis members, especially on their top edges where mud can sit and form a rust-inducing poultice. Scrape off any thick deposits of mud and remove any loose paint or underseal.*

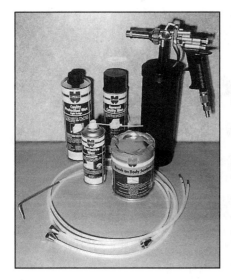

▲ RP2. Gather together all the materials and equipment you will need to carry out the work. All of the better rustproofing materials manufacturers, such as Wurth, make two types: one which is 'thinner' for applying to the insides of box sections and another one which is tougher and is for applying to the undersides of wheelarches and anywhere that is susceptible to blasting from debris thrown up by the wheels.

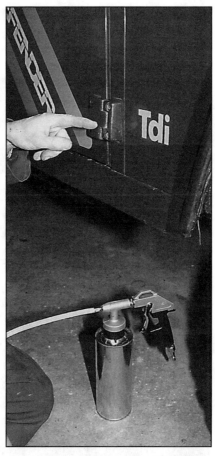

▲ RP3. Bear in mind the safety equipment you will need – referred to in Safety First! – opposite. You will also need lifting equipment and axle stands – see Chapter 2, Preparation and Essential Safety!, for information on raising and supporting a Land Rover above the ground and also for the correct procedures to follow when raising your vehicle with a trolley jack. You may need to park over newspaper for a couple of days after carrying out this treatment. Do remember that the vapour given off will be present for several days and you would be best parking out of doors for about a week after carrying out the work. The author has selected the top-quality German product from Wurth for use on his own vehicles. There is cavity wax for use with the Wurth application gun shown, brush-on surface protector and a number of complementary aerosol products. This application gun does a proper job of atomising the fluid and putting a thorough misting inside each enclosed box section. If you don't own a compressor, you will have to hire one in order to power the applicator but the results will be better than can be obtained with any hand-operated applicator.

◀ RP4. Water and dirt find their way down into the door hinge posts and then just sits there, rotting away the metal. The simplest way to protect against this is to drill the inside of the post and inject plenty of fluid.

90, 110 and Defender doors are mostly aluminium, but with a steel internal frame. Remove the trim panel and insert the nozzle to cover all the inside of the door, making sure you get plenty of 'creeping' fluid into the aluminium/steel joins, where electrolytic corrosion will occur. Naturally, the main problem is that moisture collects in the bottom of the doors and rots them out from the inside – use plenty of fluid here.

Some car manufacturers, such as Volkswagen, coat the engine bay and the engine with protective clear (or yellow) wax when new. (This wax should be washed off with a steam cleaner or with degreaser every two or three years and fresh wax applied.) It makes the engine bay look dingy but protects metal surfaces against corrosion, screws against seizure and helps to keep rubber supple. Provided that you keep the wax off manifolds and any other very hot areas and away from any electrical or brake components and out of the brake master cylinder – covering each item individually with taped-on plastic bags should do it – you could preserve the components in your engine bay in the same way. Check that the makers of whichever rustproofing fluid you select don't recommend against using their product for this purpose.

Think carefully before drilling holes to insert rustproofing fluid, especially in the chassis, where there are numerous holes already. If you do drill a hole in steel, make sure that you file off the rough burrs and then apply an anti-rusting agent, followed by a coating of paint followed by a layer of wax.

Always buy any blanking grommets you may want to use – a dozen or so are usually enough – before you drill any holes in the car's underbody. Grommets are often only available in a limited range of sizes and you will find it easier to match a drill bit to a given size of grommet than the other way around.

▶ *RP5. This part of your Land Rover is reached partly from beneath the car and partly from behind. Treat this area well because it is a major corrosion spot and its replacement is a major undertaking. There are plenty of access holes on the outside. Inject fluid from each end . . .*

▲ *RP6. . . . and from the centre, reaching both sides of internal divisions.*

▶ *RP7. Getting rustproofing fluid into the chassis is a must! There are plenty of access holes, but you'll have to play sleuth to ensure that the injector reaches every enclosed section. If any prove to be impenetrable, resort to the drill – it's essential to attain complete coverage. These front-end rails are favourite rot-spots.*

▲ *RP8. Look for (or drill) other holes in the main chassis rails and inject in both directions.*

▲ *RP9. The front crossmember can be another problem area unless you seek out holes like this one at the back.*

▶ RP10. Just as important as the chassis rails are the outriggers. They tend to trap dirt (and should be cleaned off regularly to help further to prevent corrosion) and must be treated inside and out, paying particular attention to chassis-body mountings.

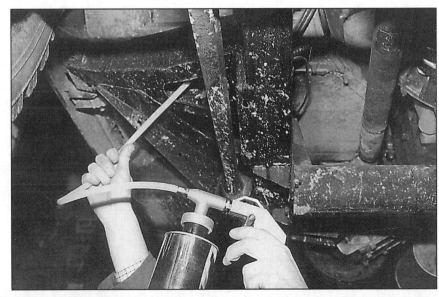

▼ RP11. Pay careful attention to the areas around the fuel tank – especially on top, where you can't see it – a great mud trap. Equally, the area under the battery tray (under the passenger's seat) can be subject to rust if the vent holes in the floor become blocked.

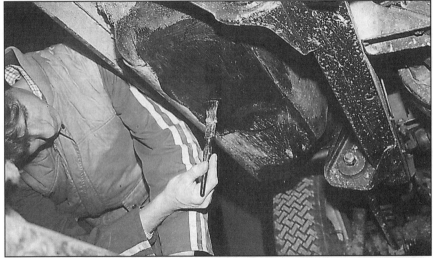

▲ RP12. Wurth Zinc Rich primers are a superb way of protecting bare metal before brushing on the body sealant – next best thing to galvanising, in fact!

◀ RP13. Don't forget to apply a little fluid to other rustable items under the vehicle, such as the brake and clutch lines, the jacking points and many other rust-prone parts.

Chapter 4

Engines and Transmission

Always clean the engine once it is out of the vehicle, and before starting work on it, so that you can see what you are dealing with. You will need lots of strong boxes to hold everything which comes off. Be methodical and make note of what nuts and bolts go where. Start with a nice clean engine and take all the auxiliaries off. Remove the flywheel and then the fuel pump, distributor pump drive, distributor, water pump, manifold and then the cylinder head as shown in a later section.

GENERAL SAFETY NOTES
– **ALWAYS disconnect the battery.**
– **DON'T try to lift off the cylinder head by yourself. Have an assistant to help you, especially with the earlier, cast-iron heads, and particularly if the engine is still in the vehicle.**
– **NEVER work or stand beneath an engine suspended on a hoist, or have an arm or hand in a position where it could be crushed. Even the sturdiest of hoists can give way or ropes or chains can slip. When attaching to the engine, try to use mechanical lifting fixings rather than tying ropes. Always have someone with you to lend a hand.**

– **With the engine out of the vehicle, ensure when working on it, that the block is securely chocked and that there's no danger of it falling over. Don't trust anything but the stoutest of benches. Preferably, use a purpose-built stand of the type shown here, or work on the floor.**

DIESEL ENGINES SAFETY NOTE:
Disconnecting fuel injection pipes can be dangerous! Even after the engine has not been run for some time, high pressure can persist in the injection system. The jet of spray that can be emitted when the pipes are first undone could cause eye damage, or could be fatal if the jet of fuel should penetrate the skin and enter the blood stream – which it is capable of doing! Follow the following precautions: 1. Wear goggles and industrial work gloves. 2. Wrap several layers of rag around the union as it is undone. 3. Disconnect the union slowly and carefully, releasing the pressure safely under the rag, until the pressure has dispersed from the pipework.

FOUR-CYLINDER ENGINE REMOVAL

▲ *ERM1. Start by disconnecting the battery leads, removing the battery, and taking off the bonnet or by tying it back to the windscreen.*

▲ *ERM2. Drain the engine and coolant.*

▲ ERM3. Then remove the air cleaner trunking and disconnect the following items: a) Front exhaust connections (it might be easier to remove the system as a single unit . . .

MODELS WITH AIR CONDITIONING:

Have the system discharged by a Land Rover dealer or air conditioning specialist. DO NOT attempt to do so yourself, for safety reasons. Disconnect the refrigerant pipes from the air conditioning compressor.

◄ ERM5. You can now remove the radiator. After fitting suitable lifting equipment, take up the slack sufficient to support the weight of the engine. Note that all Land Rover engines are relatively heavy and demand the use of suitable lifting gear. We use the Clarke hoist for our own vehicles.

▲ ERM4. . . . b) Heater hoses. c) Accelerator and cold-start linkage at the engine end. d) Distributor leads at ignition coil, on petrol engines. e) Engine earth connection. f) Engine mounting upper fixing. g) Fuel inlet and return pipes at the engine-end (be sure to plug the openings at the diesel engine's fuel injection pump, to prevent any dirt from entering). h) Oil pipes from the oil cooler to the filter adaptor on the block. i) Starter motor leads. j) Alternator leads. k) All other engine electrical leads at harness connectors. l) Release the disconnected cables from retaining clips at the dash panel. m) Release speedometer drive cable from cable clip. n) On petrol engines, and if necessary, disconnect the vacuum pipe from the distributor. o) Engine mounting upper fixing. p) The intercooler air trunking on 200 Tdi and 300 Tdi models. q) Transmission breather/wiring harness connector from the rear of the cylinder head. r) Drain the power steering fluid and disconnect the power steering pipes from the pump.

▲ ERM6. Remove the engine front mounting rubbers as follows: On both sides of the engine, disconnect the engine mountings from the engine block and the chassis. Lift the engine sufficiently to withdraw both engine mountings, complete. Then lower the engine to improve access to the top bellhousing bolts. You can now raise the engine to its original position to maintain alignment with the transmission. Remove all the fixings securing the flywheel housing to the transmission bell housing.

▲ *ERM7. Supporting the gearbox by using a suitable packing block or a jack, pull the engine forwards sufficiently to disengage the drive from the transmission, without putting any weight or strain on the transmission first-motion shaft or the clutch, through which it passes.*

FOUR-CYLINDER ENGINE STRIPDOWN AND REBUILD

The following section is an overview of how to strip and rebuild the engine of the 90, 110 and Defender. For specific details such as torque wrench settings and other relevant and important information, you will need to consult a good workshop manual relating to the type of engine you are working on.

2¼-LITRE AND 2.5-LITRE PETROL AND DIESEL ENGINES – OVERVIEW

All of the four-cylinder engines have many things in common – not surprising, since they all spring from the same source. Their cylinder blocks are of cast iron and their cylinder heads are of aluminium alloy (200 Tdi and 300 Tdi engines) or cast iron (all other types). Reboring the block is possible up to 0.040in (1.0mm) oversize above the 2¼-litre's and the 2.5-litre's standard bore size of 3.562in (90.47mm). Further reclamation is obtained by fitting cylinder liners and boring out to standard bore size. Liners may be rebored up to 0.010in (0.25mm) oversize.

The crankshaft is supported by five main bearings on all four-cylinder engines. Crankshaft thrust is taken by thrust washers on the centre bearing. All the crankshaft bearings are copper-lead lined, tin-plated steel shells. The camshaft is supported by four bearings and actuates roller-type cam followers, operating valve rockers through push-rods, and lead-tin plated bronze slides. Adjustment is made on the adjusting screws on valve rockers. These bearings are white-metal lined steel shells.

On 2¼-litre engines, the camshaft is chain driven and a chain tensioner is fitted. On all 2.5 litre engines, the camshaft is belt driven.

▲ *ERM8. Ensure that all cables, pipes and so on are clear; then hoist the engine from the vehicle.*

▶ *ERM9. When restoring a vehicle, this is a perfect opportunity to clean out the engine bay, tidy up the wiring and the hose runs and paint the area, if required.*

The engine is lubricated by a pressure fed oil system which incorporates a pump (one of two types) located in the crankcase sump and an external full flow oil filter.

REMOVING THE ANCILLARIES

▲ RTA1. With the engine still on the hoist take off the clutch assembly. Take very great care not to stand under the engine and you are strongly recommended to lower the engine down so that it is nearer the ground before carrying out this work.

▲ RTA3. Once the bolts and washer have been removed . . .

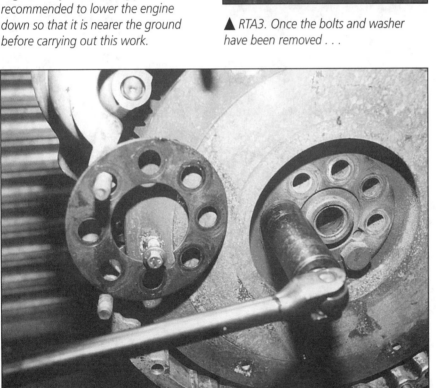

▲ RTA2. In order to remove the flywheel bolts, you will need to lock the flywheel to prevent it from turning. Liveridge's engine man, (and former professional speedway rider) John Hedderick, uses an old flywheel washer with a bolt re-inserted into the flywheel, but anything suitable will do.

▲ RTA4. . . . the flywheel can be eased away. John uses a pair of levers to free the flywheel from the crank . . .

▲ RTA5. . . . then, with a pair of bolts inserted into the flywheel to take the weight, he eases it carefully out of the housing. Take care; it's very heavy!

▲ RTA6. As you are stripping an engine down, you should make a note of all the faults you find on the way. This is a typical leaking rear oil seal.

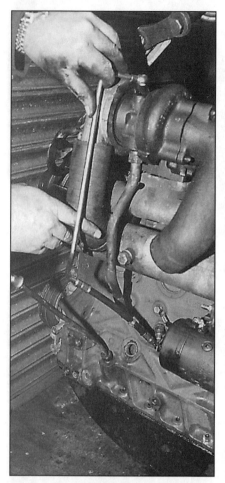

▲ RTA9. Next comes the starter motor – disconnect the wiring . . .

▲ RTA7. Any vulnerable exterior components, such as the external oil feed pipe can be removed at this stage . . .

▲ RTA10. . . . remove the securing bolts. . .

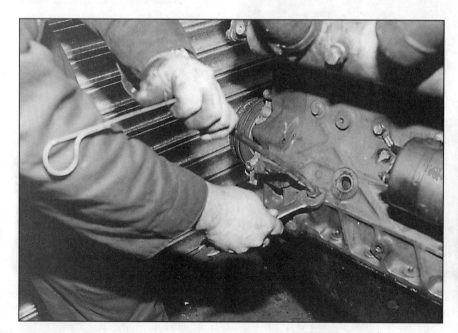

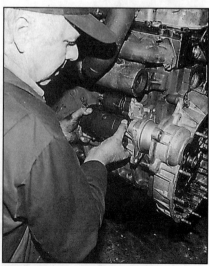

▲ RTA8. . . . as well as the dipstick tube, which screws into the block.

▲ RTA11. . . . and lift the starter motor out of the way.

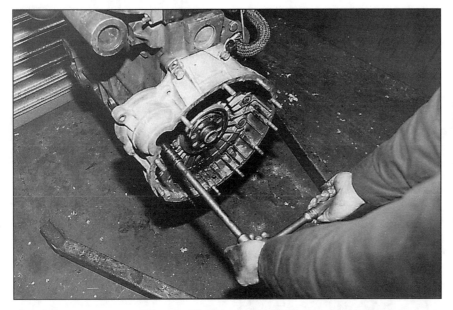

▲ RTA12. You can now take out all of the bolts holding the flywheel housing to the block . . .

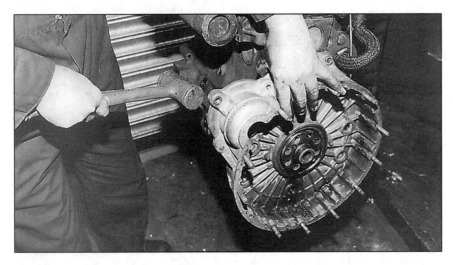

▲ RTA13. . . . tap it with a soft-faced mallet . . .

▲ RTA14. . . . and lift it away.

▲ RTA15. Supplied with the Clarke engine stand we used here, is a set of brackets which fit just about any engine. The brackets are arranged so that they suit the flywheel housing bolts on the end of the block and the bracket is firmly bolted in place.

▲ RTA16. The bracket is then inserted into the swivel head on the top of the engine stand and strip-down work proper can now commence.

FOUR-CYLINDER ENGINES – CYLINDER HEAD REMOVAL

The cylinder head can easily be removed with the engine in the vehicle. Disconnect the bonnet prop and tie the bonnet back against the windscreen with suitable padding between bonnet and screen surround. Disconnect the battery and drain the water from the engine and radiator. Remove the air cleaner complete with the hose and elbow that connects it to the carburettor or injection unit.

As you can see, this engine is out of the car but the procedure for carrying out the work is exactly the same as when it is still in the vehicle.

DIESEL ENGINES: Disconnect the pipes that lead to each injector.

ALL ENGINES: Disconnect all wiring and all hoses leading to the engine.

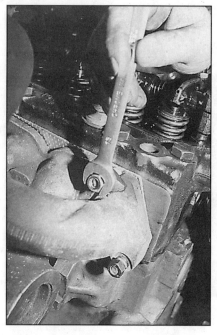

▲ CY4. On diesel engines, remove the fuel rail . . .

▲ CY1. First, the rocker cover nuts are removed and any clamps and fittings placed carefully in a plastic bag for safe keeping. It is then a simple matter to lift off the rocker cover.

▲ CY2. Remove the heat shield if it helps to gain access to the exhaust manifold. The manifolds bolt on to the side of the cylinder head, some of the retaining nuts being easily located while some will need the use of a socket on an extension probing between inlet and exhaust manifolds in order to remove some of the less accessible nuts and fittings. On some models, the manifolds and carburettor assembly can be lifted away complete.

▼ CY3. On turbo diesel engines, you can first remove the turbocharger or lift it away with the manifold.

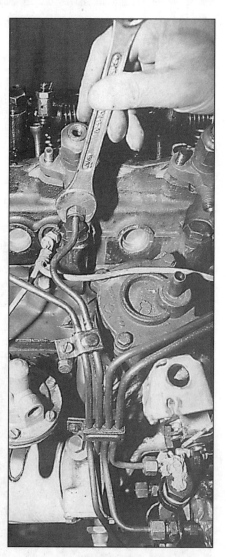

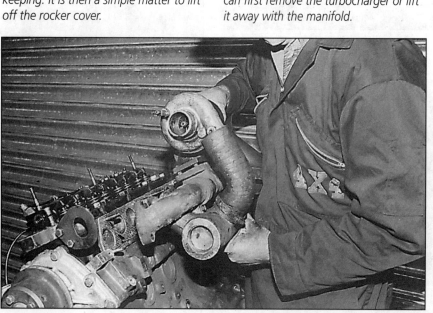

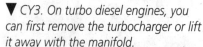

▲ CY5. . . . the pump-to-injector pipes . . .

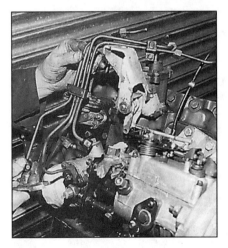

▲ CY6. . . . and lift them away.

▲ CY7. Unbolt and remove the injectors . . .

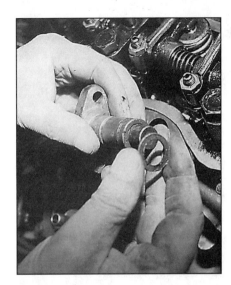

▲ CY8. . . . and the sealing washers, which should be renewed every time.

◀ CY9. Take out the small bolts holding the rocker assembly in place . . .

▼ CY10. . . . then the cylinder head bolts undoing the bolts gradually, a little at a time, in turn, taking off the pressure of the valve springs . . .

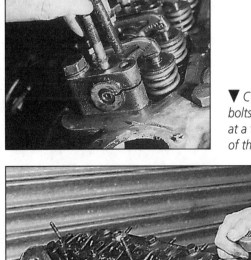

▲ CY11. . . . and lift off the rocker shaft assembly as a complete unit. Make a note of any ancillary components, such as the splash plate on petrol engines. Pull back each rocker arm on its shaft to check the shaft for wear.

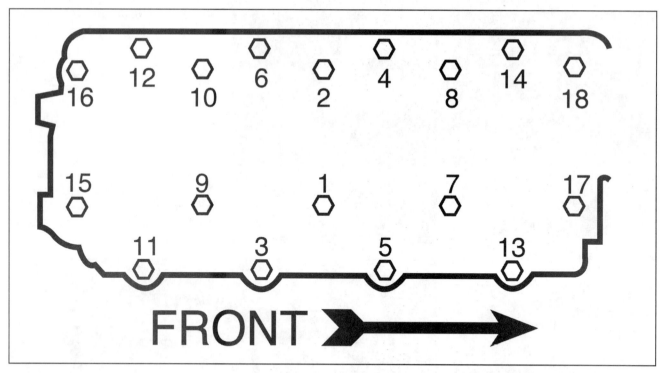

FRONT ➤

▲ CY12. However, you must undo the cylinder head studs in the opposite order to that shown here (in other words, highest number first) and follow this order (ie starting with 1) when tightening the head, as shown later. This is important with all engines, but it's extra critical on Tdi engines, because they are fitted with aluminium alloy cylinder heads.

▲ CY14. The external oil gallery pipe can now be removed – part remove the adjacent bracket to provide access to the special bolt.

▲ CY13. Before lifting off the cylinder head, take out the push rods and, so that you can put them back exactly where they came from, take a piece of card, push eight holes in it, write the numbers 1 to 8 alongside the holes and push the push rods into the holes ready for cleaning up and refitting later.

▶ CY15. With all the studs completely out, the head can now be carefully levered free, if it is stuck (but NOT by levering between head and block faces!) . . .

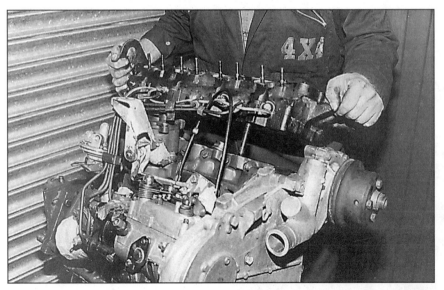

▲ CY16. . . . and lifted away.

▶ CY17. One of the turbo diesel's biggest failings is the pre-combustion chamber built into the head. (It's not there on Tdi engines because they are direct injection and don't have a pre-combustion chamber.) As on this turbo diesel engine, the pre-combustion chamber can come loose in the head . . .

▲ CY19. Take this opportunity to examine the bore in the cylinder block for wear and also for cracking between the cylinders and water jacket as well as for evidence of cylinder head gasket blow-by.

▲ CY18. . . . and here, John Hedderick found two of the pre-combustion chambers resting on the top face of the block when he had lifted the head away.
A useful tip is that, if you hear a tapping noise that sounds like a tappet but won't go away even after the tappets are adjusted, expect the worst on a pre-Tdi turbo diesel engine. Take the head off and investigate the problem straight away. If pre-combustion chambers come loose – and they do! – they can wear themselves free and tip into the combustion chamber, completely destroying the engine.

▲ CY20. Also look for evidence of cylinder head gasket blow-by on the cylinder head itself and again for signs of cracking, especially around the exhaust valve.

▲ CY21. You can now clean up the face/s of the block/s (taking very great care not to gouge the aluminium surface of aluminium alloy components) and also the piston crowns if they are very heavily encrusted with carbon, but before you do so, stuff rags into the push rod passages and also, preferably, into the oilways. Do try to leave the carbon around the outer edge of the piston crown – it helps as an oil seal. Let an old piston ring into the top of the block, push down to the level of the piston and clean the piston inside the piston ring.

▲ CY22. The cylinder head itself can now be overhauled as shown in the next section. Here is how to re-install the head. The new head gasket has been placed on to the block and a pair of old engine studs with their heads cut off have been screwed into two of the stud threads, to help with gasket and head alignment.

Before getting this far, you would be well advised to ensure that all the stud threads are entirely clean and that the studs themselves are not binding as they are being fitted. The best way of cleaning them out – unless you own a suitable tap set – would be to take an old stud, cut a slot about an inch along the length of the stud at the threaded end, and then screw the stud into the head. Any debris that has fallen into the threaded holes will be forced into the slot and, provided that the stud is unscrewed at regular intervals and the slot cleaned out with a hacksaw blade, the threaded hole will be completely cleared of debris.

▲ CY23. You can now lower the head back on to the block.

▲ CY24. If you have the foresight to put a screwdriver slot into the top of each 'dummy' stud, they can simply be screwed out with the head sitting in the correct position. You don't have to do it this way; it just makes life a little easier! You could just as well place the gasket and then the head on to the block, then insert a stud at a time, taking care to ensure that the first two pass cleanly through both head and gasket into the threaded block beneath without damaging the gasket.

▲ CY25. After placing the push rods back into position and ensuring that they bottom correctly in the spherical seats in the tappet slides, you can refit the rocker shaft assembly. On four-cylinder engines engage the tubular fixings referred to earlier and tighten the cylinder head and rocker shaft fixings in the order shown previously.

▲ CY26. The cylinder head bolts should be tightened until they just make contact with the head, and then, using a torque wrench, tightened down a little at a time, in the correct order, to the torque specified for your engine.

FOUR-CYLINDER ENGINES:
With the engine cold the tappet clearances can be set to 0.008in (0.20mm) on Tdi engines and 0.010in (0.25mm) for all other types. The tappet setting is most easily carried out in the following sequence with No. 1 tappet being at the front of the engine:

– Set No. 1 tappet clearance with No. 8 valve fully open.
– Set No. 2 tappet clearance with No. 7 valve fully open.
– Set No. 3 tappet clearance with No. 6 valve fully open; and so on. This is known in the 'trade' as the 'rule of nine'.

Some ancillaries are best replaced as a matter of course at this stage, such as the cold start sensor, the thermostat and the distributor cap on petrol engines.

FOUR-CYLINDER ENGINES, CYLINDER HEAD OVERHAUL

If yours is a turbo diesel, pre-Tdi engine, take careful note of the captions and photographs CY17 and CY18 in the previous section. You are

strongly advised to have the cylinder heads overhauled by a specialist with a written guarantee. According to Liveridge, the pre-injection chambers are notorious for coming loose and you will need to have the work carried out by someone who is capable of doing their utmost to ensure that they stay in place.

The valve gear on all four-cylinder engines is identical in principle although the components are not interchangeable between petrol and diesel engines, for instance.

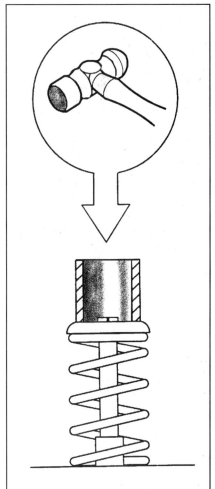

▲ CH01. Before using a valve spring compressor, 'crack' the joint between the valve collets and the caps. Going along each valve in turn, place a suitably sized socket over the head of the valve and give it a good blow with a hammer – they have a tendency to stick. (Illustration courtesy Sykes-Pickavant)

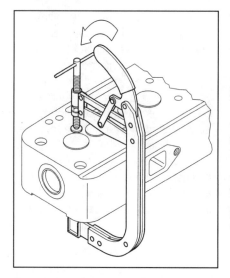

▲ CHO2. Using a suitably large valve spring compressor, fit the compressor to the valve assembly . . . (Illustration courtesy Sykes-Pickavant)

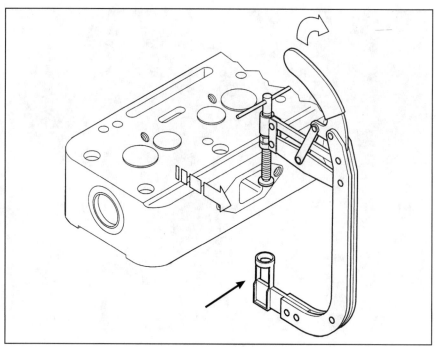

▼ CHO3. . . . and tighten the compressor screw (a) so that the valve spring cap (b) is tightened on the spring, allowing the collets (c) to be removed. You should wear goggles when carrying out this part of the work because of the risk of the compressor slipping and springs or collets flying about and causing severe damage.
(Illustration courtesy Sykes-Pickavant)

▲ CHO4. The compressor can now be removed slowly, either by releasing the pressure on the handle or unscrewing the screw, allowing the springs and valves to be removed. Note the way in which, typically, this Sykes-Pickavant compressor has a cut-away around the head (arrowed) which compresses the valve spring cap, so that the collets can be removed.
(Illustration courtesy Sykes-Pickavant)

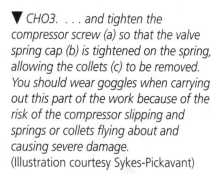

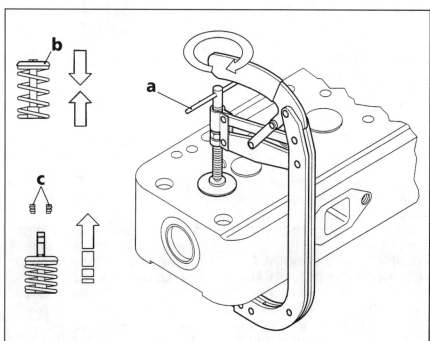

▲ CHO5. Badly worn valves will need replacing and severely burned valve seats will need recutting or inserts fitting by a specialist. Valves and seats made of modern materials are extremely difficult to lap in by hand in the traditional way. However, final bedding-in can be done with grinding paste which is lightly smeared around the valve seating area . . .

▲ CHO6. . . . before being lapped in with a valve lapping tool. Using this power drill-operated tool is much quicker and more efficient than the traditional method of twisting a stick with a suction tube on the end, like a bushman trying to start a fire by twirling a stick between his hands. When refitting the valve seals, you should note that new seals should be used each time. The inlet valves use seals with a plain exterior and a circular spring while the exhaust valves have the seals with a ridged exterior and no spring. The seal must locate in the groove in the valve guide.

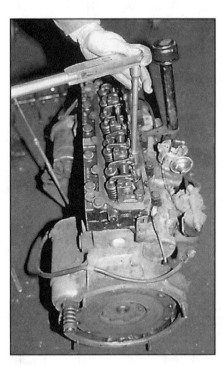

▲ CHO7. When refitting the cylinder head and valve gear, it is essential that the head is torqued down a little at a time, and finally to the correct torque, strictly in the order shown in illustration CY12 on page 88.

FOUR-CYLINDER ENGINE STRIPPING

▲ ES1. The main engine shown being stripped down in this section is a turbo diesel unit. Notes on other engine types – such as the petrol engine shown above – are added as the text goes along. Further information can be found in a good quality workshop manual. On diesel models, the fuel injection pump will have to be removed. Retiming the engine when the pump is refitted can be carried out statically at home, but dynamic timing should then be carried out by a specialist with the correct equipment.

▲ ES2. Using a specially large spanner and, if necessary, after locking the flywheel to the crank, start off by loosening the crankshaft pulley nut, making sure the engine is safe and well supported. A deep ¾in drive socket and a lump hammer will do it. You have got to shock the nut – it is no good pussy-footing around, because it won't come undone by gently pulling!

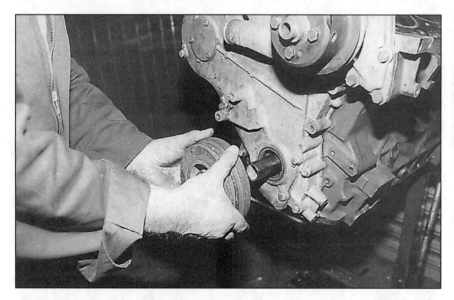

▲ ES3. The pulley slides off.

▲ ES4. The fan (where fitted) and water pump pulley need to come off, after undoing the four bolts shown.

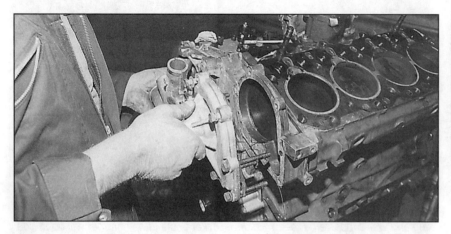

▲ ES5. Next, remove the water pump assembly, undoing the water pump retaining bolts.

▲ ES6. Remove the cover securing bolts and note their locations – several different lengths are used. (If you want to remove the camshaft sprocket, or the fuel injection pump sprocket, loosen it/them now, before the belt is removed.) Note carefully the different arrangement of the cover bolts for 300 Tdi engines.

200 AND 300 Tdi ENGINES. Check that the timing mark on the camshaft sprocket aligns with the web on the timing belt housing and that the Woodruff key in the crankshaft nose lines up with the arrow on the housing.

▲ ES7. Where applicable, make sure that the three bolts that hold the front of the sump into the timing cover are removed. (If the sump has been removed by now, this obviously won't apply.)

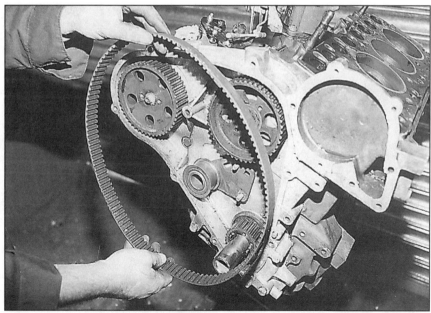

▲ ES10. . . . the timing belt can be removed.

▲ ES8. Land Rover continue to use just one Woodruff key even on diesel engines with a weighted damper on the crank pulley and those with a second pulley for power steering. As a result, if the crank pulley becomes the slightest bit loose, the Woodruff key and slot can become chewed up, destroying the crank. The author's suggestion is that you ask your machine shop if it would be possible to machine an extra slot for another Woodruff key, in line with the original one, further towards the front of the crank nose.

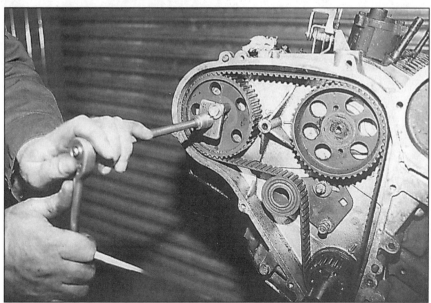

▲ ES11. The diesel pump timing pulley (where applicable) can be locked with the special tool shown here and the retaining bolt removed. If necessary, use some other means to lock the pulley.

▲ ES9. ENGINES WITH TIMING BELT. After slackening the belt adjuster . . .

▶ ES12. When removing the camshaft pulley retaining bolt, watch out for the rubber washer beneath.

▲ ES13. Pulleys can be difficult to move. If you don't have a purpose-made puller, a pair of long levers should do the trick. DON'T apply heat to the pulley, except that you could try pouring a kettle of boiling water over the pulley if all else fails.

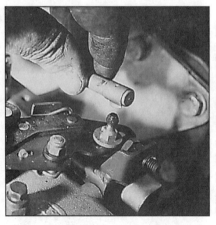

▲ ES15. The throttle lever is removed from the fuel injection pump by simply pulling it off its clip-on mounting.

▲ ES16. The mounting plate is unbolted and removed from the front cover plate . . .

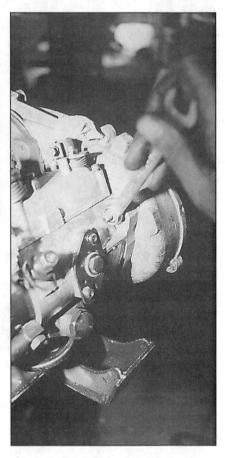

▲ ES17. . . . following which the pump can be unbolted from its mountings . . .

▼ ES18. . . . and lifted away. Note the way in which every aperture has been blanked off with clean rag so that no contaminants can get in – most important to prevent damage to the microscopically correct tolerances inside the pump.

▲ ES14. Remove each pulley from the vehicle.

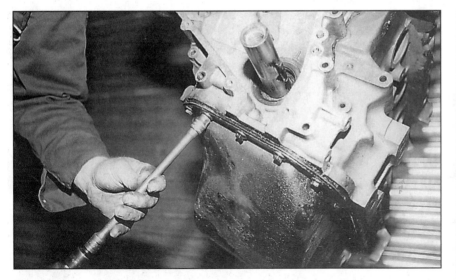

▲ ES19. On engines with a timing belt, the three sump bolts referred to in ES7 pass into the timing belt rear cover.

▲ ES20. The remaining bolts in the block are removed and the rear cover tapped free with a soft-faced mallet.

▲ ES22. The camshaft sprocket retaining bolt can be removed after knocking back the tab washer. The timing chain tensioner can now be unbolted and removed . . .

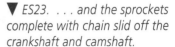

▼ ES23. . . . and the sprockets complete with chain slid off the crankshaft and camshaft.

▲ ES21. ENGINE WITH TIMING CHAIN. With the chain still in place, start by scribing a timing mark across the camshaft, camshaft sprocket and cylinder block.

▲ ES24. If (as is likely) the sprockets are difficult to move, use a pair of levers as described earlier.

▲ ES25. Behind the camshaft sprocket is the camshaft thrust plate which is removed after knocking back the two tab washers. Check the rear face of the thrust plate to make sure there is no excessive wear. Replace if necessary.

▶ ES26. Other components to inspect once removed include the timing chain itself. If a chain is capable of being bent like this one, it is well worn and must be replaced. You should also check the slipper plate and renew it unless the one you have taken off is almost new.

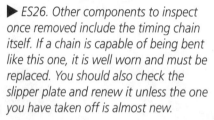

▼ ES27. ALL MODELS. On petrol engines, this is the mounting position for the distributor; here it is the diesel engine's vacuum pump.

▲ ES28. Unbolt and lift the drive away from the camshaft.

▲ ES29. You now have to remove the oil filter housing assembly . . .

▲ ES31. . . . and the two camshaft cover plates.

▲ ES30. . . . the fuel pump . . .

▲ ES32. Before you can get the camshaft out, you have to remove the distributor screw gear, which is found underneath the gasket at the oil filter mounting flange on the block. Push your way through the gasket with a screwdriver . . .

▲ ES33. . . . and take out the screw. Before removing the skew gear, you must make scriber marks between the skew gear flange and the cylinder block, and between the skew gear flange and the skew gear shaft inner face. This is to ensure that the skew gear is refitted exactly where it came from, and to ensure that the same teeth align with the camshaft drive.

▲ ES35. The drive gear screws up and out, in a clockwise direction.

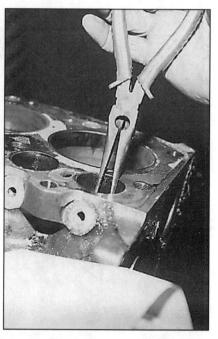

▲ ES37. After removing the screws, the cam followers can be carefully pulled out with long nosed pliers, or with a piece of hooked wire.

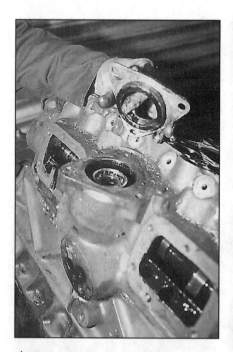

▲ ES34. Back at the top of the distributor/vacuum pump drive: on some engines, there is an extra sealing collar with an O-ring above the drive gear. It could have come out earlier; John just happened to take it out now.

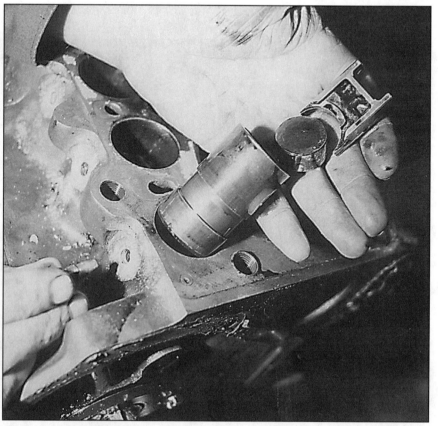

▲ ES36. A line of fixing screws holds the rather complex cam follower assemblies in place.

▲ ES38. You can start pulling the camshaft out from the front of the block with that same pair of long nosed pliers . . .

▲ ES39. . . . but you should be very careful when removing the camshaft! You must support it as it is removed, and turn it so that the cam lobes do not catch on the five, soft, thin-walled bushes in the block. If you just drag the camshaft out, you will probably damage the bushes which will cause a drop in oil pressure when you next come to run the engine.

▲ ES40. John turns the engine on the engine stand so that he can start work on the bottom end. No matter how carefully you have drained the block, more oil and water will have been trapped and will pour out on to the floor. Have a couple of containers, and large amounts of newspaper or sawdust ready.

▶ ES41. Also be ready for the oil pump driveshaft which can slide out through the vacuum pump/distributor drive opening as the engine is turned.

SAFETY: Used engine oil – and used diesel engine oil in particular – is known to be carcenegenic and you must wear impervious plastic or rubber gloves when carrying out this work. You are also strongly advised to use barrier cream on your hands – gloves are quite likely to split open in use.

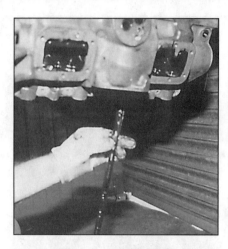

▶ ES42. Take out the ring of sump bolts and lift off the sump. Tdi ENGINE: After removing the sump, remove the ten bolts holding the ladder frame to the block. Tap the ladder frame with a soft-faced mallet to free it, then remove it. Now, on all but 300 Tdi engines, you can remove the oil pump which breaks very easily if you knock it sideways. Unlock the lock tabs – and take care! After unbolting the oil pump, it can be lifted away.

▼ ES43. The oil pump can actually be quite tricky to move, and John always uses the soft-faced mallet to tap the pump around and once it is turned . . .

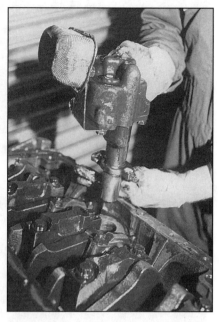

▲ ES44. . . . it becomes far easier to lift out. On non-Tdi engines, the oil pump drive shaft can now be removed, if necessary.

300 Tdi ENGINES. The oil pump is at the front of the crankshaft. With the timing belt housing removed, take out the screws and remove the oil pump cover plate. Mark the face of the outer rotor so that it can be replaced in the same position, then remove the rotors. To remove the timing chain or belt cover, you will first have to remove the fuel injection pump on diesel engines.

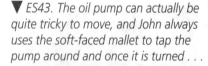

▲ ES45. A good tip from Liveridge is to put the crank pulley nut back onto the end of the crank so that the crankshaft can be turned easily and without trapping your fingers between the crank and the block.

▲ ES46. After unbolting each pair of big-end locknuts in turn . . .

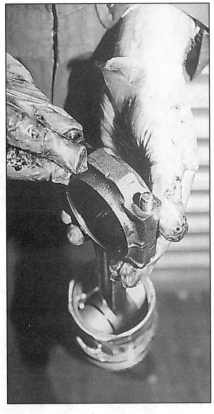

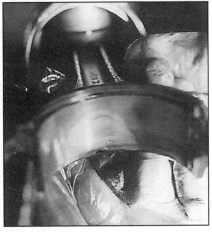

▲ ES48. Examine the bearings – this one has worn through the bearing surface to the copper backing plate beneath – and examine the crank journals for wear.

▲ ES49. Mark the conrods and caps so that you know which position they came from and immediately assemble each cap onto its matching conrod. It is essential that they go back together because they are manufactured in matching pairs.

▼ ES50. John now uses an extra-long bar to undo the main bearing cap bolts. They're done up to a very high torque, so take care not to pull the engine off its stand or workbench.

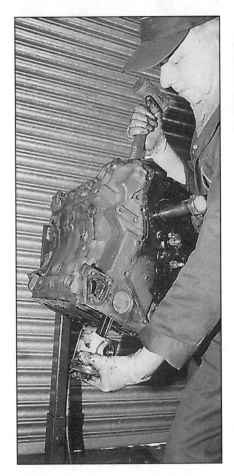

▲ ES47. . . . the caps can be levered away and the pistons and conrods tapped and pushed clear of the crank and out of the top face of the block using the handle of a hammer. Look out for broken piston rings and burned or damaged pistons.

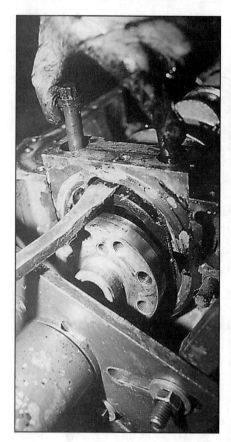

▲ ES51. The main bearing caps can be very difficult to remove. Here, John uses a lever because he knows that the main bearing shells will not be re-used. If necessary, you could make up a puller using the threaded hole in the top of the cap. Note that the bolts have splined heads rather than conventional hexagonal heads, for which you will need a special socket.

▲ ES52. John now lifts the crank – it's very heavy! – out of the block. Don't forget to retrieve and remove the crankshaft thrust bearings. There are two of them, one located each side of the centre main bearing cap.

▲ ES53. On turbo diesel and Tdi engines, there is an oil spray at the bottom of each bore which must also be removed. Take out the retaining bolts and check that the oil hole in the side of each bolt is clear, as well as the jet itself.

Before rebuilding an engine, and especially after the block has been machined, it is essential that it is thoroughly cleaned out. Remove any oil gallery plugs, wash the engine very thoroughly with degreaser and blow all of the galleys through with an air line (wear goggles!). Ideally, have an engine reconditioner, with a suitable cleaning bath, soak and clean the engine components for you.

▶ *ER1. On engines with a timing belt, the seal in the front cover pushes into a hole in the cover but does not fit up against a stop. It is therefore extra-important that this seal is driven in level and that it is fitted evenly and not sticking out on either side. Note that if any excess oil pressure builds up inside the engine, this seal can easily be popped out.*

▼ *ER2. This is the old oil seal being removed from the rear main bearing cap and the new ones must be fitted in the same way, except that the edge at the bottom of the 'L' – the bottom corner furthest away from the camera in this shot – must be chamfered with fine sandpaper to prevent any cork seal material being trapped. The seals should be dipped in fresh engine oil before being fitted to the cap which is then slid into place. If the seal does not seat properly, it will probably be because you have not cleaned out the groove before fitting it.*

ENGINE REBUILD

The engine rebuild proper starts with fitting the main bearing shells to the block. Before lowering the crank into place, flood the shells with plenty of fresh engine oil. Remember that when the engine starts up there will be nothing else there!

DIESEL ENGINES. Before fitting the crank, refit the oil jet tubes, having scrupulously cleaned them out. The jet tubes are 'handed' and can only be fitted in one position. Note that the retaining bolt is in fact a non-return valve and you must be certain, therefore, not to use an ordinary bolt!

Make sure that all of the oilways are free and, after the crankshaft and pistons have been fitted, check that the jet tubes do not catch on crankshaft or pistons.

Replace the crankshaft very gently, so that you don't disturb any of the shell bearings. Of course, before it has been fitted, the crankshaft will have been given a good clean – see the Clarke washer in Chapter 2 – and use an air line to blow out all of the airways, especially vital if the crank has been reground. This is where the Clarke compressor, also featured in Chapter 2, proves to be useful, but you must wear goggles! Make sure there is *no* swarf anywhere in the engine otherwise it will destroy the shell bearings straight away.

Remember to fit the new thrust washers to each side of the centre main cap. Fit the new caps to the main bearing shells and, with plenty of fresh oil on the shells, fit the caps and bolts into position. Make sure that the locating pegs are in position.

Fit all of the caps but without torquing them down tightly and check that the crank turns freely. If it doesn't, remove each cap, one at a time and find out which one is binding. The problem is most likely to be one of dirt between the cap and shell but it is possible that the wrong size of shells have been provided or that the crank has been ground to the wrong size.

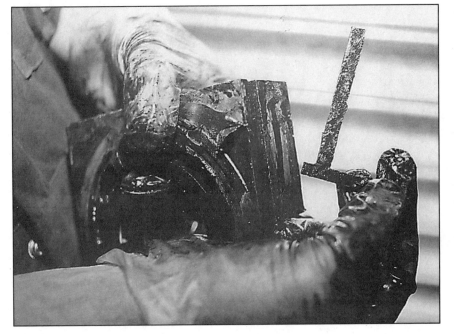

Land Rover recommend that the sump is not fitted for 12 hours after the rear main bearing is fitted so that the cork seal will have shrunk by as much as it needs to. The amount of cork seal standing proud of the crankcase sump face should be trimmed, but *not* flush with the face. Place a small washer over the protruding tip of the seal and cut the seal off level with the face of the washer. If you are not able to leave the sump off for the recommended 12 hours, Land Rover recommend that you trim the seal off leaving ⅛in (3.2mm) standing proud above the surface of the crankcase sump face.

When fitting the piston rings, be very careful to support the conrod in the vice in such a way that the piston cannot flop to one side. If it does so, you can easily break the skirt off the piston. The top two rings are identical but the bottom ring is a slotted oil control ring.

In an ideal world, everyone would fit piston rings using a piston ring spreader but another way is to carefully work each ring down the piston in a spiral motion, using a thin metal feeler gauge to slide it over the grooves. Note that if you break a piston ring you will probably have to buy a set, and they don't come cheap!

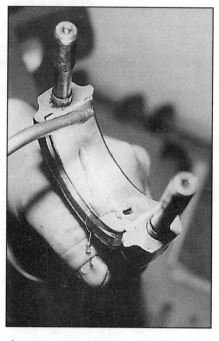

▲ ER5. As always, use lots of fresh engine oil on those bearings!

▲ ER4. After having first cleaned the journals, as for the main bearings, the conrod shell bearings are fitted with the nib and groove coinciding. Make sure that the conrod oilways are clear.

▲ ER3. A piston ring clamp compresses all of the rings but you will need to use plenty of oil to avoid a broken ring. Don't forget to stagger all the ring gaps so that the gaps are equidistant around the piston.

▲ ER6. Each conrod has a hole in the side of the rod – an oil feed hole which injects oil onto the bores. It should be checked to make sure that the oilway is clear before fitting the shell and it must be fitted facing the camshaft side of the engine.

Carefully insert the conrod into the bore and lower the piston into position. Once again, using lots of oil, carefully knock the piston through the piston ring compressor and into the bore with the shaft of a hammer, using the minimum of force. Make sure that the crank has been turned so that the conrod bolts won't damage it as the piston is tapped into place.

▶ ER7. The big-end caps are oiled, fitted and bolted into place and the crank turned each time to check for free running.

2.5-LITRE PETROL AND DIESEL ENGINES. Land Rover do not provide any information on fitting the skew gear to 2.5-litre petrol engines so it is safe to assume that the process is the same as for 2¼-litre petrol engines, shown above. For 2.5-litre diesel engines, Land Rover simply say that the skew gear has to be inserted into mesh with the camshaft gear and held in place with the retaining grub screw, as before. It does not appear that the skew gear on these engines has to be aligned as it is fitted.

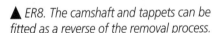

▲ ER8. The camshaft and tappets can be fitted as a reverse of the removal process.

▶ ER9. The skew gear has to be fitted in a specific position. It's quite a fiddle and it may take several attempts to get it right but it is necessary. The skew gear should be lubricated, inserted into mesh with the camshaft gear in the block, and as the skew gear is inserted it will turn anti-clockwise. When it finishes up, the main keyway should be 20° off the centre line of the skew gear assembly. On petrol engines, the keyway should be 20° above the centre line (a) but on diesel engines, it should be 20° below the centre line (b). As an added complication, the position may move slightly when the retaining grub screw is fitted, so you must check again with the grub screw in place. (Illustration © Lindsay Porter)

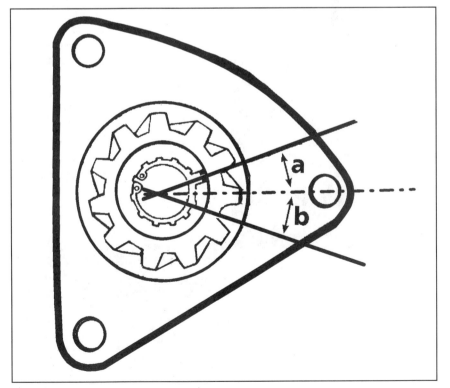

▲ ER10. Note that the grub screw on all of these engines screws into a location hole in the bush on the bottom of the skew gear assembly. You must make sure that this location hole lines up with the hole for the grub screw before fitting the screw.

▲ ER11. The drive chain sprockets can be fitted back in accordance with the markings made when they were removed. This is fine for petrol engines, but for diesel engines the story is more complicated! The timing chain is put on loosely, with sprockets aligned as they should be.

▲ ER12. In order to fit the timing tensioner, hook the aluminium sprocket in place first and then fix it in position with the three bolts. The slipper plate, to the right of the tensioner, will previously have been fitted, just touching the timing chain and preventing it from whipping about.

As mentioned earlier for the belt type of drive, the timing cover oil seal should be replaced as a matter of course.

You are strongly recommended – in fact it is essential – to replace the oil pump with a new unit when rebuilding the engine. Don't forget the oil pump drive, referred to earlier!

▼ ER13. These are the components of the non-adjustable oil relief valve. There should be no ridges and the spring should be clean and undistorted, otherwise replacements will be needed. Always fit a new copper washer.

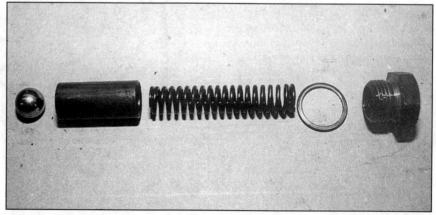

Before fitting the flywheel housing, you must fit a new main rear oil seal. Early engines also have an O-ring between the housing and the crankcase but later engines are fitted with a good bead of sealant in place of the O-ring. You are advised by Liveridge to use sealant also on the earlier engines, even with the O-ring.

▶ *ER14. Don't take chances with the core plugs! Chisel out the old ones, clean up their seats and fit new ones, drifting them in with a smear of sealer on each seat.*

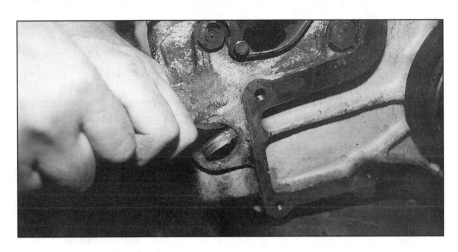

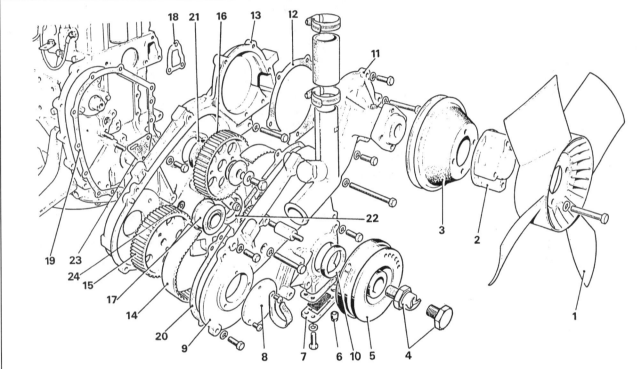

1. Fan blades	9. Front cover plate	18. Coolant gallery joint washer
2. Spacer	10. Front cover plate oil seal	19. Front cover to cylinder block
3. Fan pulley	11. Water pump	joint washer
4. Special bolt – later engines;	12. Water pump joint washer	20. Front cover plate joint washer
starter dog early engines	13. Cover	21. Camshaft front cover oil seal
5. Crankshaft pulley	14. Timing belt	22. Crankshaft cover oil seal
6. Wading plug	15. D.P.S. pump pulley	23. Triangular joint washer
7. Timing cover vent	16. Camshaft pulley	24. Fibre washer
8. Inspection cover	17. Jockey pulley (tensioner)	

▲ *ER15. Now to that business regarding diesel engine pulleys, and also the injector pump. After fitting the rear cover (13) yourself, you would be strongly advised to take the engine to a Land Rover dealer or a specialist, to have the pulleys correctly aligned and the injector pump assembled with the correct static timing. To do this work, a number of special tools will be required and it is essential that the static timing is carried out precisely and exactly because a diesel engine depends on it utterly for economy, power, and even the ability to run at all or run without causing self-destruction. You could then assemble the surrounding components yourself in the normal way.*

GENERAL FITTING NOTES

John Hedderick at Liveridge strongly recommends the use of sealant, such as the Wurth products we feature and suggested elsewhere in this manual, even where there are oil seals present. (Not in the area of the oil seals themselves, but as a second stage, around the oil seal area.) John also advises the use of sealant with every gasket and recommends that, especially on the diesel engine which is prone to vibration, every thread is held in place with Wurth threadlock. The oil seal in the front cover on engines with a timing belt (the one which is prone to blowing out under pressure) should be fitted, in John's opinion, with Wurth bearing lock to fix it firmly in place.

V8 ENGINES – OVERVIEW

There are two sizes of V8 engine; one for the UK (up to 1994) and one for the USA. All their cylinder blocks and cylinder heads are of aluminium alloy.

The single, central crankshaft is supported by five main bearings and is chain driven. The thrust is taken by the centre bearing. The bearings are lead-indium lined steel shells. The camshaft is supported by five bearings and actuates hydraulic cam followers. Adjustments cannot be made and the bearings are non-serviceable.

The engine is lubricated by a pressure fed oil system which incorporates a gear-driven pump located in the crankcase sump, and an external full flow cartridge oil filter.

OVERHAULING THE V8 ENGINE

The information here should be read in conjunction with the previous section, for four-cylinder engines, where the basic techniques, checks and safety matters are covered more thoroughly. There is not room in a book of this sort to cover every aspect of overhauling the V8 Rover engine, but the basic principles of rebuilding an engine are common to most engines. The major areas of interest, difference and difficulty are shown here, and you are recommended, as before, to use a good quality workshop manual in conjunction with these sections.

V8 ENGINE REMOVAL

1. Note safety notes referred to for the four-cylinder engines. Remove the battery terminals and drain all relevant fluids from the engine.
2. The V8 engine has to be taken out without the gearbox, and the front crossmember also has to be removed, from where it passes under the engine.
3. Next, the exhaust system has to be removed from the engine (it is actually usually easier to remove the whole system from the car than to try splitting the sections) and all the linkages to carburettor or injection unit, and all of the pipes and cables disconnected from the engine.
4. The radiator hoses have to be removed – take off the end of each one which is easiest to get at, leaving the other until later – and the radiator has to be removed from the vehicle.
5. After removing the semi-circular cover plate at the bottom of the bellhousing, the engine-to-bellhousing bolts can be taken out.
6. The engine's weight should now *just* be taken on an engine hoist, (but without putting any strain on the engine mountings), preferably connecting the hoist to the two 'factory' lifting positions on the engine. This type of hoist, produced by Clarke and available from many tool outlets, is ideal if you intend carrying out a lot of your own work, or you could hire one from a tool hire company.
7. Now, the engine mountings can all be disconnected. Undo the lower nut, leaving the mounting still connected to the engine.
8. Support the weight of the gearbox so that it cannot hang loose. You now have to take the weight of the engine on the hoist, so that it is free of its mountings, and slide it carefully forwards. The first motion shaft on the end of the gearbox must not take the weight of the engine (or of the clutch) as it is slid free.
9. Once the engine is free of the gearbox, it can be lifted high enough to be removed from the engine bay, and the vehicle can be rolled backwards, allowing you to lower the engine carefully to the ground, or, preferably, straight onto the engine stand, ready for working on. You can now remove all the following ancillaries from the engine, when fitted: starter motor; alternator and bracket; power steering pump; distributor and HT leads; clutch; fan blades, drive belt and pulley; air pulse rails from cylinder head; dipstick; engine mountings and brackets.

V8 ENGINES – CYLINDER HEAD REMOVAL

1. Start by removing the exhaust and inlet manifolds. Note that the exhaust manifold bolts are held with tab washers, which must first be bent back.
2. Once the various pipes and hoses have been removed from the inlet manifold (make a note of where they came from!) the inlet manifold can be removed with the carburettor.
3. After removing the 15 bolts holding the water pump in place, the pump and gasket can be removed. The bolts are of different lengths and their correct positions *must* be noted!
4. After taking off the rocker covers, the rocker shaft retaining bolts can be removed and taken off, complete with the baffle plate. Undo the shafts a little

Continued on page 114

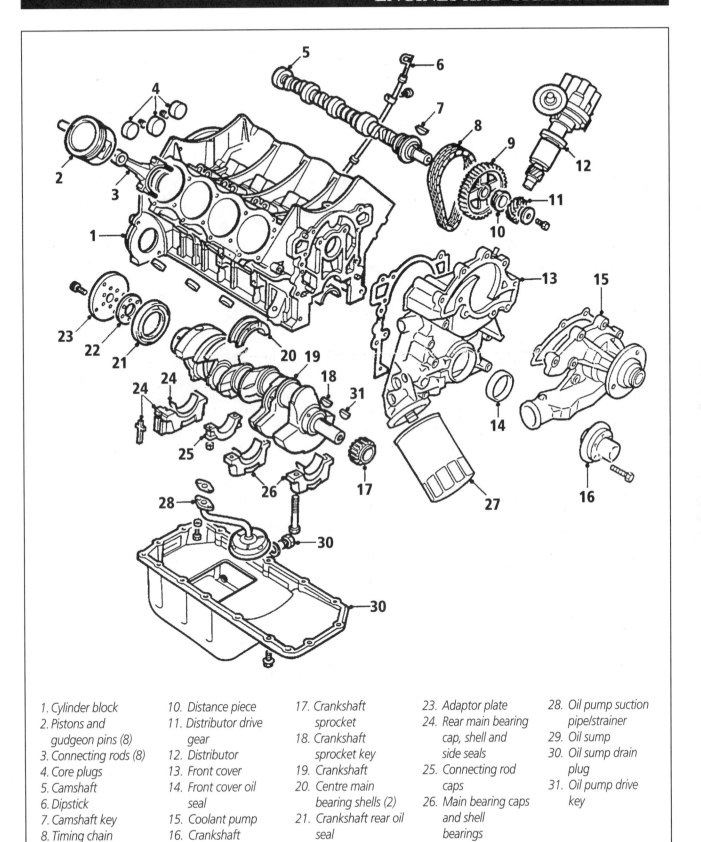

1. Cylinder block
2. Pistons and gudgeon pins (8)
3. Connecting rods (8)
4. Core plugs
5. Camshaft
6. Dipstick
7. Camshaft key
8. Timing chain
9. Camshaft sprocket
10. Distance piece
11. Distributor drive gear
12. Distributor
13. Front cover
14. Front cover oil seal
15. Coolant pump
16. Crankshaft damper/pulley
17. Crankshaft sprocket
18. Crankshaft sprocket key
19. Crankshaft
20. Centre main bearing shells (2)
21. Crankshaft rear oil seal
22. Spacer
23. Adaptor plate
24. Rear main bearing cap, shell and side seals
25. Connecting rod caps
26. Main bearing caps and shell bearings
27. Oil filter
28. Oil pump suction pipe/strainer
29. Oil sump
30. Oil sump drain plug
31. Oil pump drive key

▲ OVE1. These are the cylinder block, crankcase and timing gear components of the V8 engine . . . (Illustration courtesy Land Rover)

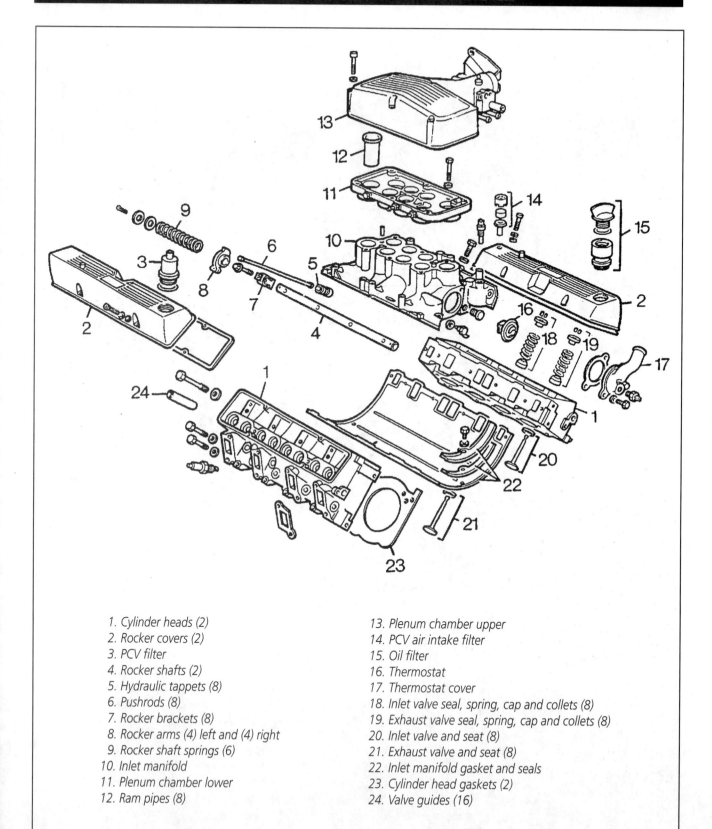

1. Cylinder heads (2)
2. Rocker covers (2)
3. PCV filter
4. Rocker shafts (2)
5. Hydraulic tappets (8)
6. Pushrods (8)
7. Rocker brackets (8)
8. Rocker arms (4) left and (4) right
9. Rocker shaft springs (6)
10. Inlet manifold
11. Plenum chamber lower
12. Ram pipes (8)

13. Plenum chamber upper
14. PCV air intake filter
15. Oil filter
16. Thermostat
17. Thermostat cover
18. Inlet valve seal, spring, cap and collets (8)
19. Exhaust valve seal, spring, cap and collets (8)
20. Inlet valve and seat (8)
21. Exhaust valve and seat (8)
22. Inlet manifold gasket and seals
23. Cylinder head gaskets (2)
24. Valve guides (16)

▲ OVE2. . . . and these are the cylinder head and inlet manifold components of the later injection engine.
(Illustration courtesy Land Rover)

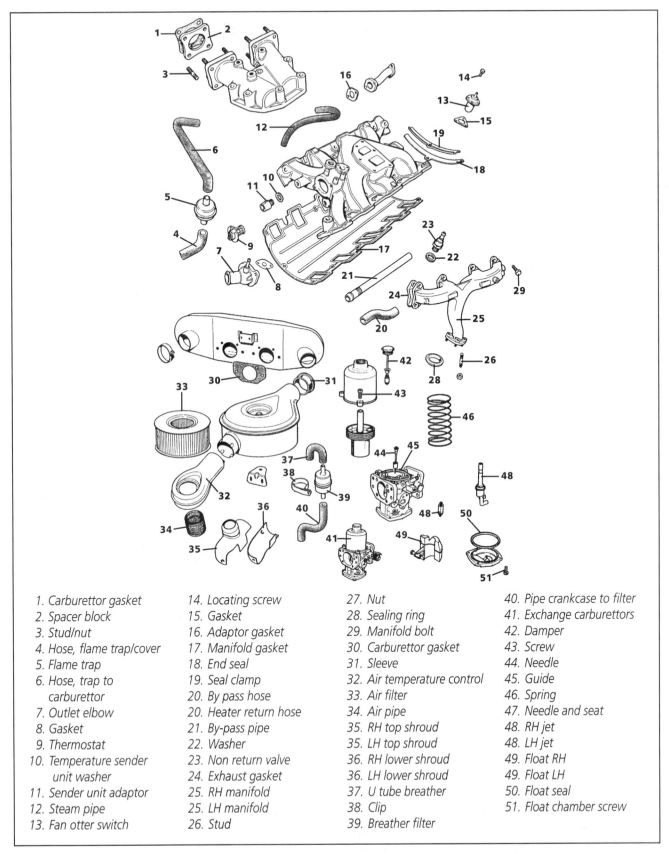

1. Carburettor gasket	14. Locating screw	27. Nut	40. Pipe crankcase to filter
2. Spacer block	15. Gasket	28. Sealing ring	41. Exchange carburettors
3. Stud/nut	16. Adaptor gasket	29. Manifold bolt	42. Damper
4. Hose, flame trap/cover	17. Manifold gasket	30. Carburettor gasket	43. Screw
5. Flame trap	18. End seal	31. Sleeve	44. Needle
6. Hose, trap to	19. Seal clamp	32. Air temperature control	45. Guide
carburettor	20. By pass hose	33. Air filter	46. Spring
7. Outlet elbow	20. Heater return hose	34. Air pipe	47. Needle and seat
8. Gasket	21. By-pass pipe	35. RH top shroud	48. RH jet
9. Thermostat	22. Washer	35. LH top shroud	48. LH jet
10. Temperature sender	23. Non return valve	36. RH lower shroud	49. Float RH
unit washer	24. Exhaust gasket	36. LH lower shroud	49. Float LH
11. Sender unit adaptor	25. RH manifold	37. U tube breather	50. Float seal
12. Steam pipe	25. LH manifold	38. Clip	51. Float chamber screw
13. Fan otter switch	26. Stud	39. Breather filter	

▲ OVE3. These are the manifolds and carburettor components of the far more common carburettor-fed V8 engine. Note that, as with any engine which has been in production over a long period of time, detailed differences will be found. (Illustration courtesy Land Rover)

Continued from page 110

at a time, each one in turn, so that they rise gradually under the pressure of the valve springs. The rocker shafts are removed next and you can then start to judge the condition of the engine, bearing in mind that oil sludging is 'Enemy No. One' of the V8 Rover engine.

5. The pushrods can be taken out (positions noted!) as well as the hydraulic tappets, although they can be left in until the head is off if they are reluctant to shift.
6. Hydraulic tappets must be replaced if their top surfaces show visible signs of excessive wear, or if the tappets were noisy in use. Check with your engine specialist if in doubt.
7. Evenly and gradually slacken the cylinder head bolts (*only* with the engine completely cold!) on each head, in the order shown.

V8 CYLINDER HEAD OVERHAUL

The principles of valve overhaul are the same as for four-cylinder engines. If the valve seats are worn or pitted, they can be renewed by your engine rebuild specialist, if necessary.

When refitting the valves, you must make sure that, with each valve pressed onto its seating in the head, the distance from the end of the stem to the face of the head is not more than 1.875in (47.63 mm). If it is, replace the valve, or take the head back to the reconditioners and have the seat recut to allow the distance to come within limits.

Early engines were not fitted with valve stem seals, but you are recommended to fit them to all engines, when rebuilding the head.

When refitting the head, the bolts *must* be retightened with a torque wrench, gradually, evenly, and in the order shown, otherwise the aluminium alloy head is likely to be distorted.

V8 ENGINE STRIPPING

1. Remove the flywheel, the crankshaft pulley and the sump, as described for four-cylinder engines.
2. Take off and drain the oil filter. (Note that, if you wish to remove the cover with the sump still in place, you will have to remove the front two sump bolts, as for the four-cylinder engine.) Remove the timing gear cover bolts and take off the timing gear cover . . .
3. . . . complete with oil pump and oil filter housing.
4. When removing the pushrods, store them so that they can be replaced from whence they came. Use the same system as for four-cylinder engines, but label the cards 'Left' and 'Right'. The hydraulic tappets must also be labelled for replacement in their correct locations, if they are to be re-used.
5. To remove the timing chain, take out the retaining bolt and take off the washer beneath, the distributor drive gear and the spacer from beneath. The wheels and timing chain can now be pulled off, complete.
6. Remove the camshaft, pistons, connecting rods and crank, as described for four-cylinder engines. However, note that the main bearing caps on 3.9-litre engines have an extra bolt on each side, passing horizontally through the block webbing and into each cap.

V8 ENGINE OVERHAUL AND RE-ASSEMBLY

1. TIMING COVER OIL SEAL. This is simply replaced after taking out the seven screws holding the oil seal shield in place. The new seal is fitted with the lip-side first and should be pushed in until about 1/16in (1.5mm) below the face of the timing cover.
2. CONNECTING RODS. When re-installing the connecting

rods, make sure that the dome-shaped boss on the rods faces towards the *front* of the engine on the *right-hand* bank of cylinders, and towards the *rear* of the engine on the *left-hand* bank of cylinders. To double-check: the domes on each pair of con-rods should face each other, and not away from each other.

3. CRANKSHAFT AND MAIN BEARINGS. a) The upper main bearings are located into the block – they are the ones with the oil drillings and oil grooves. b) the cross-shaped side seals are fitted to the grooves on each side of the main bearing caps. They must be fitted with the excess protruding and *not* cut off to length. c) Apply jointing compound to the rear half of the rear main bearing cap, where it butts up against the block. d) To fit the round seal on the rear flange of the crank, tension the rear main bearing cap by ¼ turn, then back off each bolt by one full turn. Make sure that the oil seal guide and the crank journal are totally clean, and well coated with fresh engine oil. Push the seal – lip-side towards the engine, *but without handling the lip* – onto the crank journal until it seats against the step in the recess. It *must* go on evenly! The cap can now be tightened to the recommended torque. *Do not* run the engine at more than 1,000rpm when it is first started up, or the seal will be damaged – and all the weary work will have to be done again!
4. TIMING GEARS. a) Make sure that the crankshaft key is tapped into the keyway on the crank nose so that it 'bottoms' all along its length. This is because there must be clearance along the top of the key, as this is where lubricating oil for the timing chain and gears is passed. Check that the overall dimension of shaft and key is not greater than 1.187in (30.15mm) at any point. b) Make sure that the distributor drive gear is fitted with the groove *towards* the engine.
5. CYLINDER HEAD. Note that there are three bolt sizes. *Long* – Nos 1, 3 and 5; *Medium* – 2, 4,

6, 7, 8, 9 and 10; *Short* – 11, 12, 13 and 14. The tightening torques for the 3.5-litre engine are: *Bolts* 1 to 10: 65–70lbf ft (88–95Nm); *Bolts* 11 to 14: 40–45lbf ft (54–61Nm). Re-check each, after tightening all.

6. INLET MANIFOLD.
a) Coat both sides of the new manifold gasket seals with silicone grease and place the seals in position with their ends engaged in the notches between block and cylinder head. b) Coat both sides of the main manifold gasket, around the water passage openings, with sealer such as Hylomar SQ32M. Place the gasket in position, but make sure that the word 'FRONT' on the gasket is facing away from the head and is at the front of the head. c) Fit the gasket clamps, but do *not* tighten the bolts, and fit the manifold onto the cylinder head. d) Clean and apply thread lock fluid to the manifold bolt threads and tighten them a little at a time, working on alternate sides and tightening from the centre, out to the ends. e) You can now tighten the gasket clamp bolts to the correct torque.

7. TIMING COVER and WATER PUMP. The bolts for both of these components should be cleaned and the threads coated with a suitable thread lubricant/sealant before fitting.

8. SUMP.
On earlier engines, which use a gasket, a suitable gasket jointing compound should be smeared over the joint on the bottom of the crankcase, between the timing cover and crankcase to a width of about ½in to ¾in (15 to 20 mm). On later engines, a 'liquid gasket' is used.

9. DISTRIBUTOR.
a) Bring piston No. 1 to TDC on the compression stroke (ie with both valves closed). b) Turn the distributor drive shaft until the rotor arm is about 30 degrees anti-clockwise from the No. 1 spark plug segment position in the distributor cap. c) Turn the oil pump/distributor drive shaft in the engine until the tongue is in the position shown. d) Fit the distributor and double-check that the rotor arm is

now *in line* with the No. 1 spark plug segment position in the cap. Reposition if necessary. e) CHECKS: The vacuum unit must be at 90 degrees to the camshaft line. If the distributor will not seat right down the drive is not engaged. Push down on the distributor while turning the engine, then recheck the position of the distributor. f) Fit the clamp and bolt *loosely*, turn the distributor until the points *just* start to open (use a test lamp), then lock the clamp plate. This should provide a close-enough timing position so the engine can be run and dynamically set with a strobe light.

10. ROCKER COVERS.
a) Remove the gaskets, clean off all traces of adhesive from the gaskets with a very small amount of thinners on a rag (work out of doors and away from any sources of sparks or ignition), dry the surface and brush ordinary impact adhesive onto both sides of the gasket. After about 15 minutes, when the adhesive is touch-dry, refit the gasket to the rocker cover. After another 30 minutes, the cover can be fitted to the engine. b) Make sure that the *long* bolts are used on the *outer* side of each cover and the *short* bolts on the *inner* side of each cover.

11. EXHAUST MANIFOLDS.
a) Use a suitable high-temperature mating face sealing compound (Land Rover recommend Foliac J 166 or Moly Paul). Clean the mating faces on both head and manifold before applying and follow the maker's instructions for use. b) Remember to refit the tab washers, using new if necessary.

RECLAIMING THREADS IN ALUMINIUM COMPONENTS

Threads can be stripped in aluminium alloy all too easily, and it's quite common to come across threads that have been stripped by previous owners but left

unrepaired. The Wurth Time-Sert thread insert system – available from motor factors – see your local *Yellow Pages* – is claimed to offer certain advantages over wire thread inserts. It is said to guarantee the application of a full torque load and its thin cross-section is said to make it more suitable where space or wall thickness are restricted. Here's how the system is used.

▲ RTA1. *Use a power drill – with a strong preference for a pillar drill, rather than hand-held – to drill out the old thread, using the size recommended for the thread size – see Wurth's product sheet.*

▲ RTA2. *Locate the spigot of the Wurth counterboring tool in the hole and cut to the depth of the shoulder on the tool.*

▲ RTA3. Use the prescribed size of thread tap to cut a new thread, remembering to use the correct cutting oil and back off the tap regularly, in the usual recommended fashion.

▲ RTA4. Clean out the swarf from the hole. Work out the length of Time-Sert insert required. Screw the Wurth inserting tool into the insert, then screw the insert into the hole.

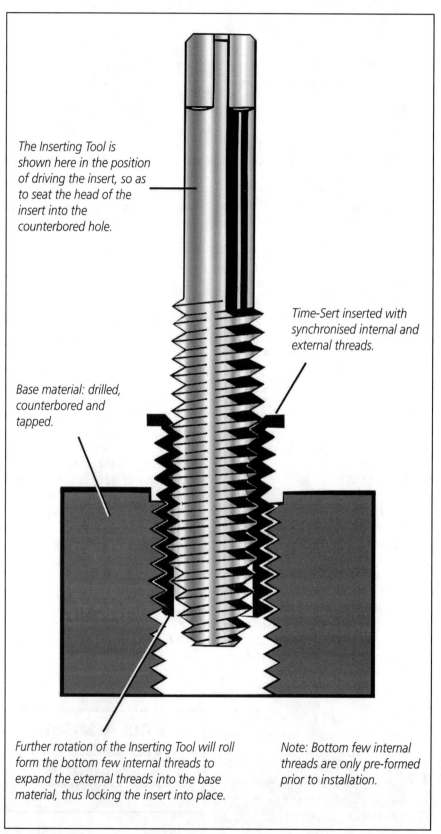

The Inserting Tool is shown here in the position of driving the insert, so as to seat the head of the insert into the counterbored hole.

Time-Sert inserted with synchronised internal and external threads.

Base material: drilled, counterbored and tapped.

Further rotation of the Inserting Tool will roll form the bottom few internal threads to expand the external threads into the base material, thus locking the insert into place.

Note: Bottom few internal threads are only pre-formed prior to installation.

▲ RTA5. The tool will turn with increased pressure, and then tighten up. This is because the bottom few threads of the insert are formed by the inserting tool as it is tightened.

▲ *RTA6. This ensures that the insert is seated and locked into position, allowing normal use of the original size fixing. (Illustrations RTA1 to RTA6, all courtesy Wurth UK Ltd)*

FLYWHEEL OVERHAUL

If the face of the flywheel has become badly scored by the clutch, you can have it refaced by an engineering company. On four-cylinder engines, Land Rover recommend that the maximum amount of metal which may be removed from the flywheel face is .030in (0.7mm). Check with the original specification for your particular model of Land Rover to ensure that the flywheel has not already been refaced in the past.

The starter ring can be replaced, as follows:

1. Either drill through the starter ring or hacksaw down as far as you can go, in both cases without touching the flywheel itself.
2. Use a sharp cold chisel and a heavy hammer and chisel through the flywheel as shown.

SAFETY: On rare occasions, flywheel rings have been known to shatter when split. Wear goggles and gloves and place a heavy cloth over the flywheel and starter ring with a small slit for the chisel to pass through.

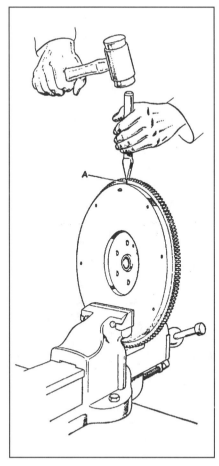

▲ *FL1. When the starter ring has become excessively worn, it is possible to remove it and replace with another one.*

3. Place the starter ring in a domestic oven at maximum temperature – but not more than 175ºC (350ºF) . which is the *maximum* temperature that Land Rover recommend the starter ring is heated to. Do not exceed this temperature.
4. While the ring is heating, (15 to 20 minutes should be enough once the oven is up to temperature), clean the inner face of the flywheel where the starter ring will sit so that it will be a good tight fit. Place the flywheel on a suitable flat surface.
5. When the starter ring is 'done to a turn', remove it from the oven using oven gloves and take great care not to be burnt or to cause any burns. There should now be a small clearance between the starter ring and the flywheel because of the expansion that will have taken place

in the starter ring. Naturally, the longer you take to find out, the more the ring will cool down and shrink back to its original size! Press the starter ring firmly against the flange of the flywheel until the ring contracts sufficiently to grip the flywheel. Keep a close eye on it and if necessary, tap the ring tightly down into the flange. Allow the whole thing to cool gradually; do *not* cool the starter ring down rapidly or you will cause internal stresses in the ring which may well result in it fracturing at some time in the future.

CLUTCH OVERHAUL

▲ *CL1. Clutch overhaul is covered thoroughly in your workshop manual but the key point is that you will need a mandrel in order to align the clutch plate so that the first motion shaft on the gearbox will enter the back of the engine when refitting gearbox to engine.*

Note that if the flywheel has been badly scored by a worn clutch in the past, it will be necessary to have it re-faced. You will have to remove the clutch pressure plate studs.

A tip from Liveridge is to lubricate the splines on the first motion shaft – clean them out thoroughly first – using copper grease so that the clutch moves freely on it.

You can follow the instructions in your manual to rebuild the clutch master and slave cylinders or, for the ultimate in longevity, you can fit new master and slave cylinders. Don't forget also to renew the flexible hose and also to replace the steel pipe with Automec's copper version, which will never corrode.

RE-FITTING THE ENGINE

NOTE: Engine removal and refit is broadly the same in principle for all types.

The following notes outline the principles in refitting an engine. Refer to the illustrations under 'Engine Removal'. Mark well the 'Safety Notes' under that section! Ensure that the top of the crossmember is totally clean, otherwise there is a chance of debris being trapped between the flywheel housing and bell housing – very expensive!

1. Engage a gear to prevent gear shaft rotation. Offer the engine to the gearbox – it may be necessary to rotate the engine sufficiently to align the gearbox primary pinion with the clutch plate splines. When aligned, push the engine fully to the rear and secure the bell housing to the flywheel housing, tightening the fixings evenly.
2. Lift the engine sufficiently to remove the packing or jack from beneath the gearbox and insert the engine front mounting rubbers. Then lower the engine and fit the upper and lower fixings to the engine mountings.
3. Remove the sling supporting the engine. Secure the speedometer drive cable in the cable clip adjacent to the fuel pump.
4. Connect the engine electrical leads at the snap connectors on the right-hand rear side of the engine compartment. Also connect the following:

A. The fuel inlet pipe to the fuel pump and secure the battery lead in the adjacent cable clip.
B. The alternator and starter motor leads at the dash panel.
C. The throttle cable.
D. The engine earth cable.
E. The distributor leads at the ignition coil.
F. The heater hoses in the engine compartment.
G. The front exhaust pipe to the exhaust manifold.
H. Diesel fuel pipe.
5. Once all this has been completed, the front floor, radiator, air cleaner and bonnet can be refitted.

THE COOLING SYSTEM

The radiator should give few problems, though corrosion and clogging up of the galleries can occur. Solder repairs are not successful long-term, because of the amount of vibration and flexing that takes place.

It is a commonly held belief that by removing a vehicle's thermostat, it will cool better – this is untrue, as a thermostat is there to control engine heat and, with the thermostat in position, the water is held in circulation round the engine for a longer time, giving the water more chance of picking up the heat. Take out the thermostat and the water will be going round the engine so quickly that it won't be able to transfer any heat, so the engine block may run hotter.

There are three rubber pads on the front chassis supports that hold the radiator; these are vital, for without them the radiator will fracture (due to distortion) and will simply need replacing all over again.

NEVER run a diesel engine without coolant, not even for a few seconds. You shouldn't run a petrol engine without coolant, for that matter, but a diesel engine is particularly susceptible to very rapid cylinder head damage!

After running any engine that has been refilled with water always re-check water level and keep an eye on the temperature. The engine will require topping up after the thermostat has opened.

EXHAUST SYSTEM

On all the four-cylinder engines, the front pipe bolts to the manifold with three studs which are threaded into the manifold itself. It is not unknown for the manifold to break at this point, necessitating renewal (or drilling and tapping). Use releasing fluid before removing. To avoid overstressing the manifold, do not connect the exhaust system to the manifold until it is in correct alignment, and do not tighten the connecting nuts until the rest of the system has been fully fitted into place.

On turbo diesel and Tdi engines the down pipe is connected to the turbocharger via a clamp as opposed to studs.

The manifolds on V8 engines can also fracture, and are not known for their 'free-flowing' nature! When manifolds need replacing, new Rover items can be very expensive, and it is not uncommon for owners to fit stainless steel tubular manifolds, which give better 'breathing' characteristics.

TRANSMISSION TYPES

The original Land Rover gearbox remained basically unchanged from 1948, for over 20 years. In late 1971 an entirely new main box was introduced together with the Series III model. Basic differences were that it had a larger diaphragm clutch and four-speed synchromesh, the earlier models only having synchromesh on the top two gears! In September 1980 the V8 option became available on the long wheelbase 109s and this was coupled to the permanent four-wheel drive Range Rover type of gearbox, the LT95, with a centre diff. This gearbox was used on the first V8 110s but was superseded by a gearbox with five speeds in 1985.

In 1983, the four-cylinder 110 was offered with the four-speed 'box, carried over from before but, on four-cylinder models, with the option of a new five-speed gearbox in an iron casing. The Land Rover 90 came on the scene in late 1984 and was also fitted with the four-speed transmission, but with the option of the five-speed gearbox. The new five-speed 'box had the model designation LT77, and was a unit originally fitted to Rover and Jaguar saloons, and the Triumph TR7! It had a totally new transfer box, the LT230R, with a mechanical diff-lock. This was replaced by an uprated version, the LT230T, introduced at the time of the first turbo diesel engines.

The V8 110 retained the four-speed one-piece Range Rover type of 'box, (the LT95) until 1985, and this had the servo operated diff-lock. In 1985, a very heavy duty Santana Spanish five-speed 'box known as the LT85, was introduced to the V8s and the transfer box was modified to Timken bearings as opposed to roller bearings, and this became known as LT230T.

With the advent of the 300 Tdi engine came yet another gearbox improvement, with the R380 gearbox unit.

The four-speed synchromesh gearbox has to be treated sensibly. The massive baulk ring system does not like being rushed! All these gearboxes have aluminium cases, including the transfer box, so are a little noisy when hot.

The five-speed boxes have proved to be very trouble free in use and a pleasure to drive, although they do need service tools to dismantle and rebuild when the time comes! One niggling fault, which is less of a problem for Land Rover owners than it is for TR7 owners, is that the synchromesh can be slow and prevent rapid gear changing. At one time, Rover dealers would recommend draining the gearbox oil and replacing it with automatic transmission fluid (ATF). It took a couple of thousand miles for the old oil to be 'washed' from the synchromesh components, but the ATF appeared to solve the problem. If your transmission unit suffers from this fault, it would be worth finding its serial number and taking it to your Land Rover dealer, to see if your gearbox is of the type that would benefit from this solution.

Unlike the transmission units in earlier Land Rovers, the gearboxes in the 110 and 90 models caught up with the power outputs of the various engines and are no longer the weak link in the transmission train.

SPECIFIC FAULTS IN THE GEARBOX

Problems in service can be put into three main pigeon holes: a) the 'keep an eye on it' type of problem; b) preventive action; c) major problems, which mean you have to get the tools out, but consult the workshop manual first! Before you start the series of tests, you must check the transmission oil levels, and get the engine and gearbox to working temperature.

1. Put the high/low lever into neutral and run through the gears. There should be no noise other than the gentle whirr of gears beating the oil.
2. Put the main box into neutral to press and release the clutch pedal. There should be no grumbling or heavy whirring noises, just the rotating shaft noise. If there is a noise when the clutch pedal is depressed it will probably come from the clutch release bearing, or if the noise is only there when the pedal is released it will probably be coming from the primary or lay shaft bearings. Some slap on tick over of the clutch release arm is acceptable as this is a design characteristic but excessive noise will indicate extensive wear in the clutch release arm.
3. If there is a squeal or grunt as the clutch is slipped for manoeuvring, it is probably caused by a dry primary shaft crankshaft bush in the flywheel. They are sealed-for-life graphite bushes and dry out or get damaged when you put a new gearbox in.
4. Whilst on the run, if you put your hand on the main gear lever and keep in 3rd gear, check that there is no rock in the gear lever between the drive and overrun condition. A worn or broken main shaft bush will allow the gears to move. Another cause is a loose rear main shaft nut, which will allow the main shaft to shunt.
5. Is the oil transferring from the main box to the transfer box? There is a possibility of a seal worn through or the bearing fretting in the bearing housing which separates the main box from the transfer box. This happens especially on the Series IIIs where the bearing housing is unpegged and the housing actually turns and wears the case. Another cause for this oil transfer is the breather plate on top of the gearbox or on the earlier ones, it is the filler cap which has a little hole to let the gearbox breathe. This can sometimes get blocked by mud on top of the 'box. This fault does not occur very often but was a common fault on Series III.
6. If when driving there is a heavy rushing noise in 1st, 2nd and 3rd, but all is quiet in top gear, the indication will be that the lay shaft bearings have failed. If there is a gritty noise take immediate action!
7. If you are unable to select 3rd and top, this is a common problem. There are little detent springs in the 3rd and 4th synchromesh, which break and fail to drop away but jam instead. Not applicable to later gearboxes.
8. If you have only got 4th gear accompanied by expensive clattering noises the chances are you have got a broken lay shaft.
9. If you can drive in 1st and 2nd gear but not in 3rd and 4th, the main shaft may have broken up at the front end, although this could also be a 3rd and 4th synchro problem.
10. If you can select all the gears with a great deal of noise but with no drive to the transfer box, the main shaft may have broken at the rear end. In addition, it is a common fault on 90s and 110s that the output shaft spline will strip allowing the output shaft to turn within the transfer box, giving the symptom of no drive.

11. Many gear selection problems can be caused by the gearbox remote. There are plastic bushes and pins that can wear out giving a sloppy feel to the gearstick and gears. There are two plungers within the remote that can give problems with reverse and 5th gear selection. The remote should be stripped, checked and properly inspected.

TRANSMISSION REMOVAL

The gearbox and transfer box are best separated before removal to cut down on weight and add to safety. You would need to remove the complete seat base to remove the gearbox from inside the vehicle. Liveridge remove all gearboxes and transfer boxes from underneath the vehicle and always split the two units.

The crossmember on 90s and 110s can be removed from the chassis as it is bolted on unlike the Series III where they are welded in civilian models.

The gearbox can now be removed from inside. The gearbox mountings should be removed completely from the chassis (obviously making sure the gearbox is supported on a hoist).
This aids removal and refitting back to the engine.

Remember that LT77 transmissions have transmission fluid in the gearbox and hypoid in the transfer box.

If the gearbox is to be removed from underneath then just the floor and centre turret need to be removed from the inside.

In both cases the gearstick should be removed.

On late Tdis the handbrake cable is easier to remove from the operating handle rather than the transfer box end.

The clutch slave cylinder should not be left hanging attached to the flexible hose as remaining hydraulic pressure can push the piston out.

If the transmission is to be removed from underneath, a suitable gearbox stand should be used.

The gearbox tunnels should always be removed when removing the transmission.

SEPARATING THE LT230R TRANSFER BOX FROM MAIN GEARBOX

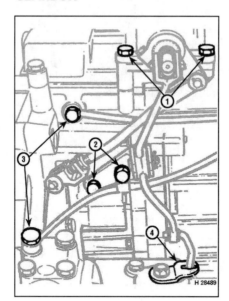

▲ TRB1. The following notes all relate to this drawing and all assume that the two units have been removed from the vehicle in one piece. It is possible to remove the transfer box with the main gearbox still in place in the vehicle, however.

a) Remove the four bolts (1) holding the transfer gearchange housing to the main gearchange housing.
b) Take out the two bolts (2) holding the pivot to the casing.
c) Remove the breather pipe connectors (3) from the casing.
d) Disconnect the diff. lock lever from the casing (4), removing the locknut, nut and split-pin or spring washer, as applicable. The transfer box will now slide from the main gearbox casing.

SEPARATING THE LT230T TRANSFER BOX FROM MAIN GEARBOX

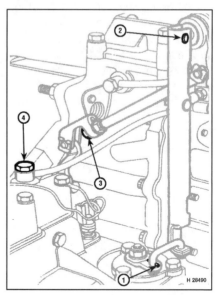

▲ TRB2. The following notes all relate to this drawing (early LT230T transfer boxes). . .

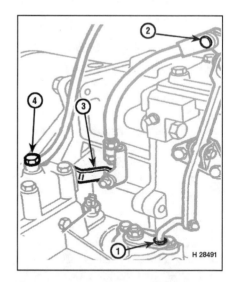

▲ TRB3. . . . or this drawing (later LT230T transfer boxes) and assume that the two units have been removed from the vehicle in one piece. It is possible to remove the transfer box with the main gearbox still in place in the vehicle, however.

a) Disconnect the diff. lock lever from the casing (1), removing the locknut, nut and split-pin or spring washer, as applicable.

b) Disconnect the selector shaft operating arm by removing the clevis pin (2). On later models, you will also have to disconnect the lower end of the selector shaft arm from the clamp on the gear selector lever (3).

c) Remove the breather pipe union and disconnect the breather pipes (4).

d) The bolts holding the two units together can now be removed and the transfer box will now slide from the main gearbox casing. Note that on early models, it will be necessary to raise the transfer gear selector lever to gain access to the main gearbox to transfer box retaining nut.

REFITTING THE TRANSFER BOX TO MAIN GEARBOX – BOTH TYPES

Before refitting the transfer box to the main gearbox, make sure that the Low Range is selected in the transfer box.

Clean the mating surfaces of the two gearboxes, make sure that the upper locating dowel is in place on the main gearbox casing, and fit the two units together, using the correct fixings in their original locations. Use a new lock nut or split-pin, where applicable, on the nut holding the diff. lock connecting rod to the lever on the transfer box. On LT230R models, note that the longest bolt fits at the rear, right-hand side of the housing.

Note that, on later LT230T models, the transfer gear selector rod has to be fitted into the clamp as the two units are brought together.

REFITTING TRANSMISSION TO VEHICLE

Refitting the transmission is the reverse of removal, with the following additional points:

a) The clutch will need to be perfectly aligned before starting work.

b) Some recommend that sealing compound should be applied to the mating surfaces of the flywheel housing and bellhousing (after checking that they are completely clean) immediately before re-assembly, although it is not used at the factory.

c) Put a large spanner and tommy bar on the crankshaft pulley nut and have a helper turn the engine (with spark plugs/glow plugs removed) as the two units are brought together, helping to align the splines on the first motion shaft and in the clutch. **ALWAYS ENSURE THAT THE BATTERY IS DISCONNECTED BEFORE TURNING AN ENGINE OVER. (A PETROL ENGINE WILL FIRE UP IF THE IGNITION IS ON.)**

d) Use a combination of lifting hoist and a trolley jack to change the angle, to line up the two units while they are slid together. Draw them together with bellhousing bolts (or even special long bolts, used just for the job of pulling the units together before being removed) but *do not* attempt to force the units together. If they absolutely refuse to get together, try re-aligning the clutch before trying again. Care should be taken not to damage the clutch diaphragm with the input shaft of the gearbox.

PROPELLER SHAFT REMOVAL AND REPLACEMENT

Both propeller shafts are removed and refitted in a similar way. Great care should be taken that universal joint (UJ) end caps are aligned correctly. If they are cocked over it will scrape the end cap. It should be checked, at all times, that the centre of the UJ will slide freely between both end caps. NEVER BE TEMPTED TO HAMMER CAPS DOWN. There are several different types of UJ that vary from year to year and it should be ensured that the correct size is fitted.

Sometimes if a UJ has been left for a period of time the end caps will break causing damage to the flange of the propshaft. If any damage at all is present the propshaft should be scrapped.

Many Land Rovers which are brought in for UJ problems show bends and knocks to the propshaft and it is quite a common occurrence. Any severe dents or bending and the propshaft should be scrapped.

▲ *PSR1. Remove the lock-nuts or . . .*

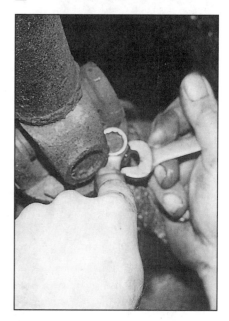

▲ *PSR2. . . . where nuts and bolts are fitted, grip the bolt head with a second spanner to prevent it from turning.*

▲ PSR3. Use a lever, or a strong screwdriver to lever the propeller shaft off the studs by compressing the propeller shaft sliding joint . . .

▼ PSR4. . . . so that the prop. shaft clears the studs and can be lifted away.

PROPELLER SHAFT UNIVERSAL JOINT REPLACEMENT

Wear in the universal joint is usually first identified by a clonk as the drive is taken up. Try levering each UJ with a strong screwdriver and if any wear can be detected, their replacement is called for.

Most workshop manuals seem to give a fairytale method of replacing universal joints. Here's how Liveridge's Andy Piatkowski renews them!

While you have the opportunity to do so, take out the two grease nipples from the sliding joint and check that they are clear by pumping grease through them. If not, fit new replacements.

▼ PSU1. To replace the UJ, take off the propeller shaft and take it to a workbench. Now remove the grease nipple, if fitted. Make a mark (g) on each part of the yoke (h) so that the UJ can be reassembled the same way round as it came apart.
(Illustration © Lindsay Porter)

▲ PSU2. After drifting the end cap firmly downwards to take the pressure off the circlip, a pair of long-nosed pliers are used to extract the circlip. Quite a fiddle!

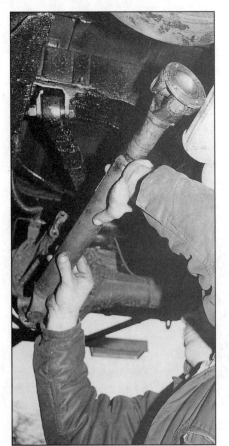

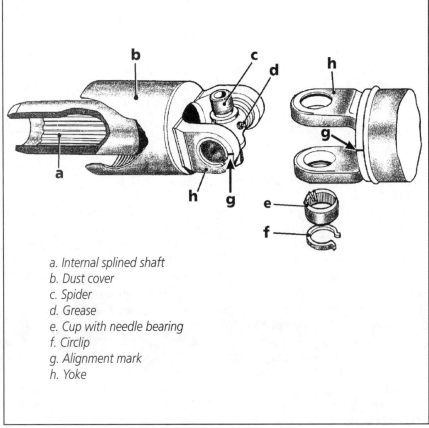

a. Internal splined shaft
b. Dust cover
c. Spider
d. Grease
e. Cup with needle bearing
f. Circlip
g. Alignment mark
h. Yoke

▲ PSU3. With all circlips out, the drive flange is placed on the edge of the vice and the yoke hammered downwards to drift the cap halfway out.

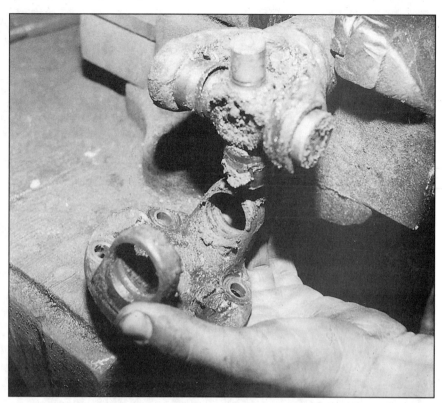

▲ PSU5. The two halves are separated and the other cap drifted out of the yoke. A similar procedure is used to remove the UJ from the other half of the assembly. You can now clean the components to be reassembled removing every trace of grit, dirt and grease.

▲ PSU4. It is then turned over, the cap is grasped with a self-grip wrench and extracted. If the cap refuses to budge, you could use a very narrow drift down the side of the yoke.

▲ PSU6. Take off two of the caps from the new spider with great care so that the needle roller bearings don't spill out onto the floor. Grease will hold them in but don't take chances! Carefully holding down the two caps that are to stay in place at this stage – you could use a rubber band – insert the new caps into the yoke as far as they will go. Then press them home in the vice carefully locating the spider's 'legs' into the caps, using a pair of spanner sockets to get them all the way in.

▲ PSU7. Insert the yoke and spider into the propshaft yoke.

▲ PSU9. . . . pressing them in with the vice, then fit the new circlips. Some circlips have small holes in them and demand the use of a pair of circlip pliers.

▲ PSU8. Fit the two remaining caps . . .

Chapter 5

Running Gear

Working on almost any part of the Land Rover's running gear involves raising the vehicle off the ground. Follow all the usual safety procedures when working beneath the vehicle, as outlined elsewhere in this book.

Also, note that if a halfshaft has to be removed, the handbrake will be ineffective because it operates on the transmission system only. Therefore, it is doubly important that the wheels remaining on the ground are carefully and adequately chocked to prevent movement.

Most work on the running gear can be carried out with the axle housings fitted to the vehicle but if you need to remove the complete axle for any reason, note that at least two people, and preferably three, will be required to handle the axle unit safely.

SAFETY: BRAKING SYSTEM
Do not carry out any work on your Land Rover's braking system unless you are fully competent to do so. If you have not been trained in this work, make sure that you have a garage or qualified mechanic check your vehicle's brakes before using the car on the road. Always replace disc pads and/or shoes in sets of four – never replace them on one wheel only. If friction components are contaminated with oil or grease, replace them – there is no way of cleaning them because the oil or grease will have soaked into the friction materials. If the rear brakes are contaminated with oil, you may need to replace the rear axle oil seal.

SAFETY: HYDRAULIC FLUID
There are several hazards associated with hydraulic fluid, so take careful note of the following: a) Hydraulic fluid is poisonous. Do not ingest, keep away from children and seek immediate medical advice if swallowed. b) Wear gloves when handling hydraulic fluid and if any gets on the skin, wash it off immediately with soap and water. c) Hydraulic fluid deteriorates when exposed to the air. Never re-use old hydraulic fluid and always top-up with fluid from a freshly opened container. Be sure to use the correct, recommended type for your vehicle. d) Most hydraulic fluid is flammable. Keep away from sources of heat, sparks or ignition. e) Hydraulic fluid is a slow but effective paint stripper and will also attack plastics. Wipe up any spills immediately then wash off the residue with washing-up liquid and warm water.

RUNNING GEAR – GENERAL INSTALLATION NOTES

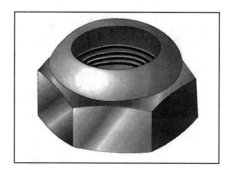

▲ RG1. Whenever you refit components held in place with a lock-nut, the old lock-nut must be discarded and a new one fitted. (Illustration © Lindsay Porter)

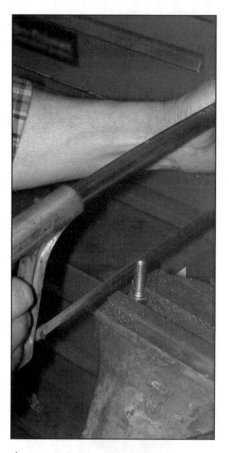

▲ RG2. Before replacing a bolt in a tapped thread, make sure that the female thread has been properly cleaned out. If you have access to a thread tap of the correct size and type, use it to clean out the threads; if you don't have a thread tap, make a hacksaw blade cut part of the way down a spare bolt (of the correct size and type, of course!) and run it through the thread to be cleaned out. This will not re-cut a thread but it will clean out debris such as old thread sealer. You will have to remove the bolt and screw it in again every time the slot clogs up. (Illustration © Lindsay Porter)

▶ *RG3. Most suspension components which are not fitted with lock-nuts should have liquid thread lock applied to the thread before it is refitted. This is how to apply Wurth thread locker: make sure that both male and female threads are clean, dry and free of lubricant. Apply a few drops of thread lock to the bolt or machine screw being fitted immediately before fitting it into place, then tighten up to the recommended torque, using the specified number and positions of washers.*

▶ *RG4. In several leak-prone locations, such as at the swivel hubs, it pays to use a non-setting gasket compound to help ensure that no leaks can occur. Make sure that both mating surfaces are clean, dry and free of lubricants. Wipe a thin but even coating of gasket compound on both sides of the gasket, taking care not to contaminate the compound with grit or dust. Fit and use the gasket in the normal way. Do not use a setting-type of compound because this will make future dismantling extremely difficult.*

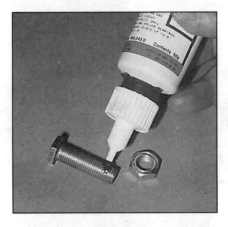

FRONT AXLE REMOVAL

Chock both rear wheels, fore and aft, raise the front of the vehicle and support it on axle stands placed beneath the chassis.

Disconnect the brake hose brackets from the swivel housings (a), then refit the bolts to the swivel housings to prevent oil leakage.

Remove the brake caliper as shown in a later section, and hang the caliper on a piece of wire to the front suspension coil spring but take care not to place any strain on the hydraulic hose.

▼ *FAR1. These are the front axle and suspension components. The numbers and letter in the text in this section refer to this drawing.*

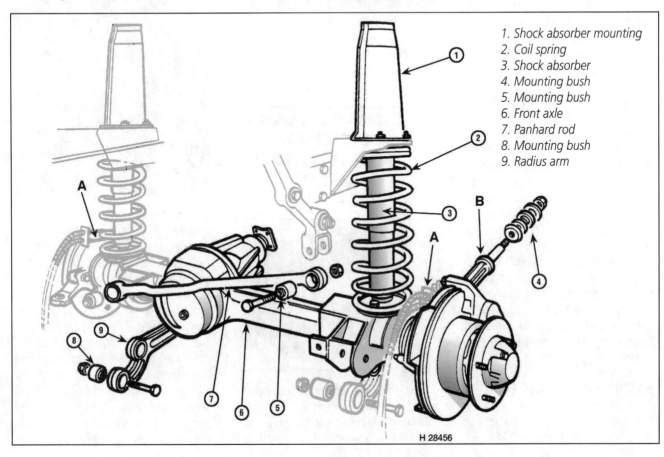

1. Shock absorber mounting
2. Coil spring
3. Shock absorber
4. Mounting bush
5. Mounting bush
6. Front axle
7. Panhard rod
8. Mounting bush
9. Radius arm

H 28456

Take the weight of the front axle on a trolley jack placed beneath the differential housing.

Disconnect the following items as described elsewhere in this book:

A. Disconnect the track rod end from the steering arm.
B. Take the steering drag-link off the swivel pin housing.
C. Disconnect both radius arms (b) . . .
D. . . . and the Panhard rod (7).
E. Disconnect the bottom of the shock absorber from the axle.

Refit the wheels to the axle, lower the axle to the ground. You can now, relatively easily, roll the axle from underneath the vehicle. Note that the front coil springs become unseated as the axle is lowered.

FRONT AXLE REFITTING

Refitting the front axle is essentially the reverse of its removal. Bear in mind the following points:

A. When the axle is raised into position, both coil springs (2) will need to be correctly seated.
B. The upper swivel pin retaining bolts (A) should be cleaned and fitted with locking compound applied to each thread.
C. None of the fixing bolts should be finally tightened up before the road wheels have been refitted to the axle, the vehicle has been lowered to the ground and rocked vigorously, to settle all the components. All the fixings should then be tightened to the correct torque. This does not apply to the brake components, of course. These should have been tightened to the correct torque when reassembled.

▲ *FAR2. Disconnect the propshaft from the front differential and tie it out of the way.*

▼ *FAR3. Disconnect the anti-roll bar connecting links from where they are connected to the axle.*

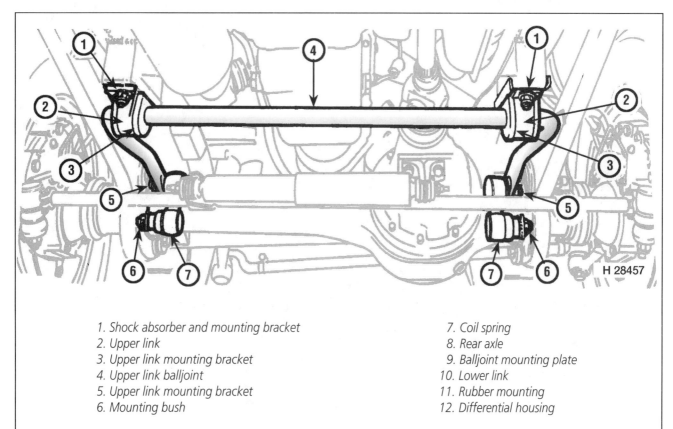

1. Shock absorber and mounting bracket
2. Upper link
3. Upper link mounting bracket
4. Upper link balljoint
5. Upper link mounting bracket
6. Mounting bush

7. Coil spring
8. Rear axle
9. Balljoint mounting plate
10. Lower link
11. Rubber mounting
12. Differential housing

REAR AXLE REMOVAL

Much of the information relating to removal of the front axle also applies to the rear axle, where applicable. The components referred to are shown here and the part numbers are mentioned in the text. Follow the instructions for front axle removal, but note the following main differences:

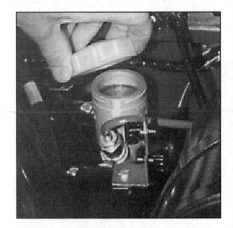

▲ RAR1. Remove the brake master cylinder cap. Refit it with a piece of plastic bag between cap and reservoir. This seals the cap and minimises the amount of brake fluid lost when you carry out the next step.

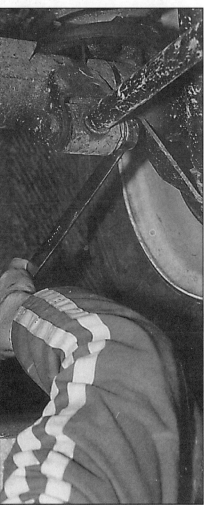

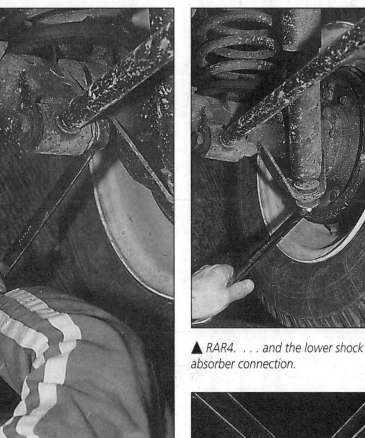

▲ RAR3. Disconnect the lower links from the axle, the anti-roll bar (when fitted) . . .

▲ RAR4. . . . and the lower shock absorber connection.

▲ RAR5. Disconnect the upper link balljoint where it connects to the top of the axle. You have to remove the split-pin before removing the nut at the bottom of the balljoint.

The axle can now be removed as described for the front axle. Bleed the rear brakes – see the relevant section of this manual.

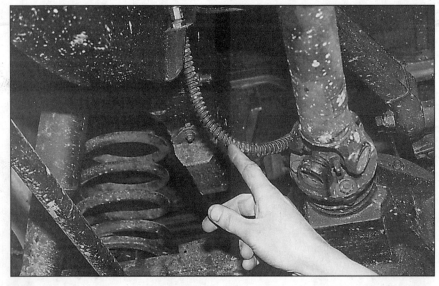

▲ RAR2. Disconnect the brake pipe flexible hose at the point where the pipe which runs under the bodywork is connected to the axle.

DIFFERENTIAL REMOVAL AND OVERHAUL

It simply does not make sense to consider overhauling your own differential unit. The business of rebuilding a differential unit in such a way that it operates satisfactorily and without excessive noise requires a number of special tools and no little experience. You are strongly recommended to have your differential overhauled professionally, or purchase an exchange unit from a reputable specialist.

Differentials are easily removed after draining the oil, pulling out both halfshafts, disconnecting the propshaft, undoing the ring of retaining nuts and lifting out the differential from the axle casing.

BRAKE PADS – RENEWAL

The procedure is the same for both front and rear brake calipers (where rear calipers are fitted) but note that on some models, shims may be fitted to the rear of the brake pads. If so, make sure that the correct shims are replaced in the correct locations.

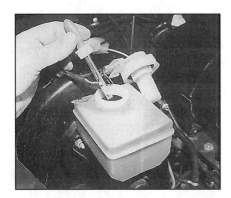

▲ BPR1. Before replacing the brake pads, use a redundant hydrometer (or battery fluid tester) to siphon brake fluid out of the master cylinder. Otherwise, as the pistons are pushed back into the caliper (assuming new pads are to be fitted) brake fluid can spill out of the master cylinder.

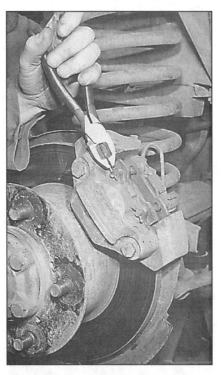

▲ BPR2. There are three different variants to the brake pad retaining system but all are similar in principle. Remove the split pins securing the pad retaining pins in place. This is the wire-type of anti-rattle spring. Remove it but make a careful note of where it goes so that it can be replaced later. Others have plate-type or coil-type anti-rattle springs.

▲ BPR3. Before starting, spray on a proprietary brand of brake cleaner. This Wurth brake cleaner is available from motor factors and washes away excess brake dust.

▲ BPR4. Remove the small split-pins and use pliers to tap or pull out the pad retaining pins (taking care to retain the anti-rattle springs, if this type is fitted to your vehicle) . . .

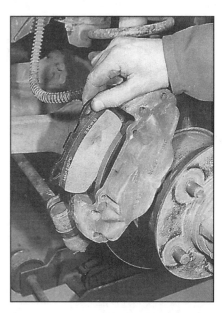

▲ BPR5. . . . and pull out the brake pads. You may need to force the pads back towards the caliper body to push the brake pads away from the disc, which will allow them to come out of the caliper. Note that on some models, the retaining pins may actually be large split pins, which should be replaced each time.

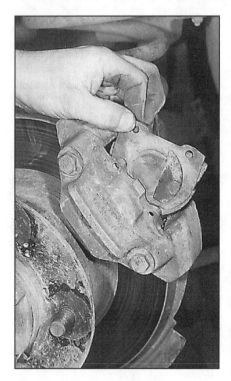

▲ BPR6. If shims are fitted, note their positions so that they can go back in the same place and remove them now. Spray on more of the brake cleaner to clean out the insides of the calipers . . .

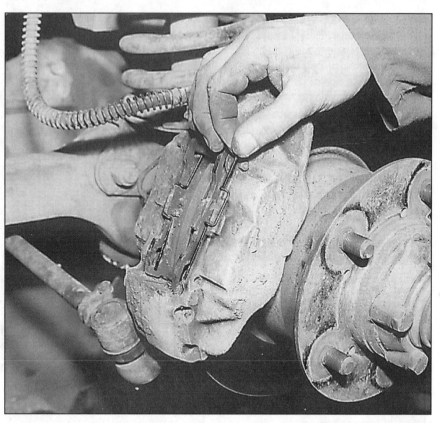

▲ BPR8. These are an example of wire anti-rattle clips – in all other respects the same brakes.

▲ BPR7. . . . before fitting the new pads, bear in mind that the twin pistons may need to be pushed back into the caliper, using a clamp. Before pushing the pistons back in, check the seals on the pistons for damage or deterioration and the housings for corrosion. If necessary, don't risk it – fit replacement calipers!

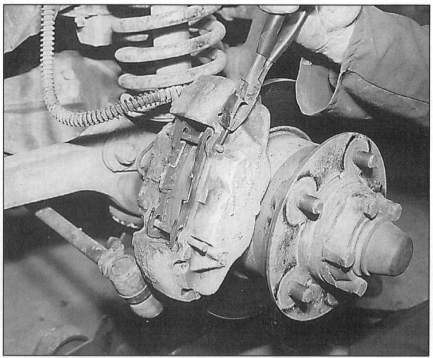

▲ BPR9. Always fit new split pins to the caliper retaining pins on all brake types – DON'T be tempted to re-use the old ones – a false economy that could have catastrophic consequences!

FRONT BRAKE CALIPER REMOVAL AND REPLACEMENT

You can remove the front brake caliper in order to overhaul the front suspension without having to disturb the hydraulic connections, or the caliper can be taken right away from the vehicle, if preferred. We do not recommend that you overhaul the brake caliper yourself, for safety reasons. It might also be difficult to obtain spares for the caliper from your Land Rover dealer so you are advised to purchase an exchange unit from a reputable specialist.

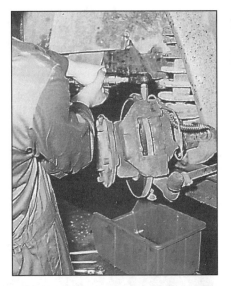

◄ *FBC3. As the top bolts are removed, oil runs out of the swivels – so a catch tank is needed! Note that from chassis No. LD104957 Land Rover recommend that you use Molytex grease type EP00 in place of the usual lubricating oil.*

Take out the two bolts fixing the caliper in place and lift it away. It may be necessary to push the brake pads away from the disc with a screwdriver if the disc is worn, so that the pads and caliper can be lifted away from the disc. Make sure that you don't cause brake fluid to spill out of the top of the master cylinder.

▲ *FBC4. If the caliper is to remain connected to the hydraulic pipe, rest it on the suspension tie bar taking care not to put strain on the hydraulic flexible hose.*

If the caliper is to be removed, clamp the hydraulic hose – just enough to seal it but not so much that you damage it – and unscrew the caliper from it.

When the caliper, or a replacement, is refitted, it will be necessary to bleed the front brakes as described elsewhere in this manual.

▲ *FBC1. Start by removing the pads. Here the split pin holding the retainer in place is removed before tapping out the retainer pin, but retaining the anti-rattle springs over the retainers. Two different types of retainer are also used, but the principle remains the same. Always use a new split pin.*

▶ *FBC2. To remove the caliper without disturbing the hydraulic connections, bend back the brake hose bracket so that you can gain access to the top bolts.*

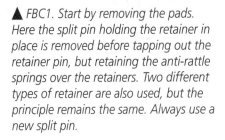

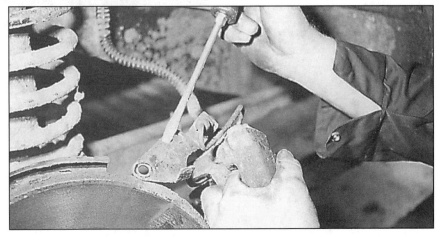

REAR BRAKE CALIPER REMOVAL AND REPLACEMENT

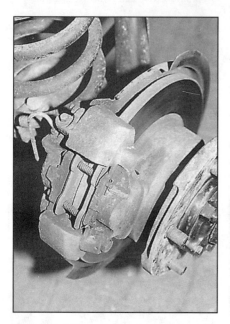

▲ RBC1. When a Defender is fitted with rear disc brakes, the procedure is the same as for the front brake calipers, except that, because there is no flexible hose to the rear calipers, they cannot be removed while still connected to the hydraulic system.

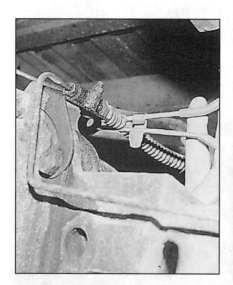

▲ RBC2. You can minimise the amount of brake bleeding required by clamping the flexible hose where the hydraulic pipework connects to the axle.

REAR BRAKE SHOE REPLACEMENT

Land Rover 90s, 110s and Defenders up to the 1994 model year were fitted with rear drum brakes. These were very similar to the units fitted to Series III vehicles. Note that the rear drums can easily fill with mud if you do a lot of off-roading.

The drum brakes on 90 and 110 models are similar but not identical.

▲ RBS1. Before attempting to remove the brake drum, slacken the brake adjuster or adjusters on the rear of the back-plate. There is one on 90 models and there are two on 110s.

▲ RBS2. Remove the single drum retaining screw . . .

▲ RBS3. . . . and the drum should now, in theory, pull straight off. In practice, it may stick, in which case you can use a UNC bolt, screwing it into the threaded hole in the drum, and easing the drum away gradually.

▲ RBS4. If you have to tap the drum to encourage it to come off, only use a soft-faced mallet, never a hammer.

▲ *RBS5. Check each drum for excessive scoring, cracks or other damage. Hang up each one in turn by a piece of string and tap the drum with the end of a spanner. If it rings clearly, the drum is unlikely to be cracked. If it gives a dull tone, the drum is cracked and should be scrapped and replaced.*

▲ *RBS9. Check inside the dust cover on each rear brake cylinder and if there is any evidence of escaping brake fluid, scrap the wheel cylinder and fit a new one.*

▲ *RBS6. 90 MODELS. Knock back the tab washer . . .*

▲ *RBS8. Grip the bottom of one of the brake shoes with a self-grip wrench and pull the bottom of the brake shoe away from the bottom pivot, anchoring it just outside the pivot. Do the same to the other shoe so that the tension has now been removed from the bottom pull-off spring. Remove the bottom spring. The top spring can be disconnected when the pressure has been taken off the tops of the shoes in a similar way. Both shoes and springs can now be removed.*

▲ *RBS10. Wheel cylinder pistons will often pop themselves out of their cylinders of their own volition, because of the pressure of the fluid in the braking system. To prevent them from doing so (and so that you don't have to bleed the brakes) wrap a piece of wire around the wheel cylinder to keep the pistons in place.*

▲ *RBS7. . . . and remove the two bolts and remove the anchor plate from the lower edges of the brake shoes.*

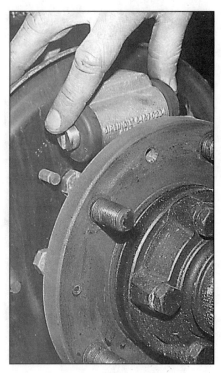

▲ *RBS11. If the wheel cylinder needs to be replaced, it is removed by simply taking off the two nuts and spring washers from the rear of the back plate.*

▲ *RBS12. Make sure that the snail-cam adjuster is free and is not corroded. If necessary, dismantle it, clean it and grease the assembly before refitting.*

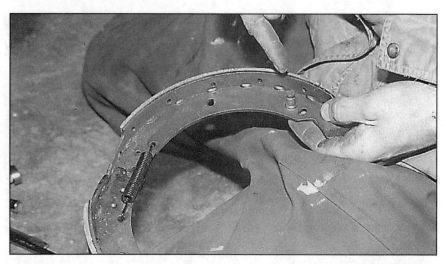

▲ *RBS13. When fitting the brake shoes, it is absolutely essential that the pull-off springs are fitted in their correct locations. Note that the springs are on the insides of the shoes (when fitted) and that there is a groove in the peg, around which the end of the spring is hooked on 90 models. These are the correct location points for the 90 model pull-off springs . . .*

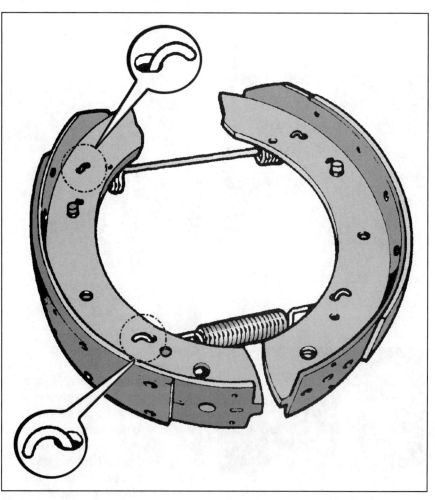

▲ *RBS14. . . . and these are the correct locations for 110 springs. (Illustration © Lindsay Porter)*

▲ RBS15. Assemble the brake shoes, allowing the surfaces which bear on the wheel cylinder and the pivot points to remain to one side of the wheel cylinder or pivot point so that the springs can be fitted without applying too much tension.

▲ RBS16. Use a pair of long-nosed pliers to locate the springs, then pull the shoes into position as you did when you were removing them.

90 MODELS. Replace the anchor plate and tab washer, tighten the two bolts and then bend over the locking tab.

▲ RBS17. Replace the drum and refit the retaining screw. Before fully tightening the screw, tap all the way around the drum with a soft-faced mallet to make sure that the drum is seated correctly before finally tightening the retaining screw.

Use the adjuster or adjusters on the rear of the back plates to adjust the rear brakes.

▲ RBS18. What, you may ask, has the axle breather being pointed to here got to do with rear brakes? Well, if the brakes have been spoiled by oiling, it could be a failed oil seal, which will need replacing, or it could be a blocked breather, allowing the axle to be pressurised. Unscrew and free off – or replace – the breather if necessary.

BRAKE PIPES AND HOSES

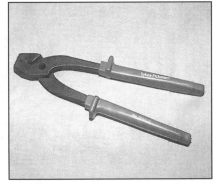

▲ BPH1. It can be very difficult to bend steel piping near to its end. This Sykes-Pickavant bending tool makes the job much easier than trying to carry it out with your bare fingers and greatly reduces the risk of kinking the pipe.

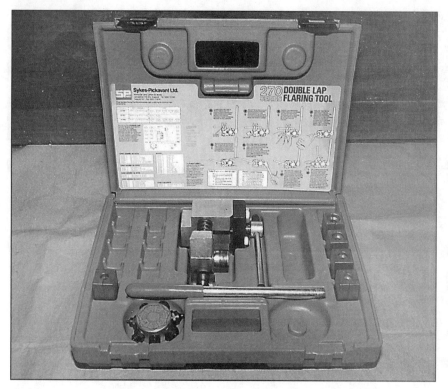

▲ BPH2. For making up your own brake pipes, you will need a flaring tool. This is the sort of Sykes-Pickavant professional equipment that Liveridge use and, if you don't have access to this level of equipment, it would be best having brake pipes made up for you.

▲ BPH4. Here, Liveridge have also fitted a new T-piece to this 'refurbish' project vehicle – a sensible step if all else is being replaced.

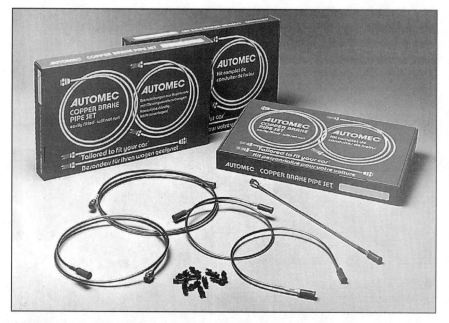

▲ BPH3. A solution to both the previous problems and the risk of brake pipes corroding is to use copper brake pipes, which are available in made-up sets from Automec. They come ready to fit and, in theory, require no more effort than to screw both ends in place although we have found that, in practice, pipes occasionally need to be cut to length and the ends flared before they can be made to fit neatly. Copper has the enormous advantage that it will never corrode and it is also easy to bend to shape. Also available, and just as useful, are Automec's copper fuel lines.

▲ BPH5. Flexible hoses invariably screw into a union at one end and are held to a bracket at the other end with a nut passed over the end of the flexible hose fitting. After the flexible hose has been fitted into place, a piece of rigid hose is screwed into the bracket-end of the flexible hose. To remove the flexible hose, you reverse the order: remove the rigid pipe; detach from bracket and unscrew from union.

▲ *BPH6. Take care when running a new brake line that it is well clipped in place, cannot foul on any suspension or steering components, wheels or tyres, and cannot be snagged by any passing undergrowth.*

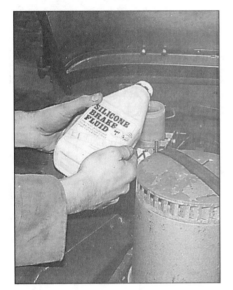

▲ *BPH7. Earlier, we explained how brake calipers and wheel cylinders should be checked for leaks and corrosion. By far the major cause of corrosion is the brake fluid itself. Conventional brake fluid is hygroscopic, which means that it takes in moisture from the air. This absorbed water vapour causes corrosion to take place in caliper and wheel cylinder bores. It can also be the cause of catastrophic brake failure. When you apply the brakes hard and over a long period, the temperature of your brake fluid can exceed 100° Celsius. If there is a significant amount of water in the fluid, it will boil, turn to steam and form a pocket of vapour in the brake fluid where only brake fluid should be. The 'solid' nature of the brake fluid will thus be replaced by 'spongy' water vapour and your right foot will push the brake pedal to the*

floor even though the brakes will fail to stop the vehicle. Nowadays, most vehicle manufacturers recommend changing the brake fluid every two years, but there is another way. Automec (and other manufacturers) produce silicone brake fluid which is non-hygroscopic and which also has the beneficial side-effect of not stripping paint if it is spilled on it. You can use silicone brake fluid by draining down the old system, although the benefits will be felt most strongly when the braking system has been overhauled and the major components replaced. Silicone fluid can be mixed with conventional fluid but you then lose the silicone brake fluid's primary benefit, of course!

MASTER CYLINDER REMOVAL – EARLY MODELS

We strongly recommend that you do not attempt to overhaul the brake master cylinder yourself. It is such an important component of the braking system, and its replacement cost is so relatively low, that if the master cylinder is faulty you are strongly advised to replace it with a new one from a reputable company. The following instructions show how to remove and replace a master cylinder unit.

A. Start by connecting a piece of plastic tube to one of the brake bleeding screws, slacken the screw, place the other end of the tube in a glass container and gently pump the brake pedal until all of the brake fluid has been pumped out of the reservoir.

B. Unscrew and remove the two brake pipes from the master cylinder body. Be sure to mop up any drips of brake fluid and blank off the brake fluid openings so that no dirt can get in.

C. Take off the two nuts and washers holding the master cylinder to the servo unit and pull off the master cylinder assembly. Be sure to hold onto the 'O' ring from the end of the master cylinder.

The numbers in the following instructions relate to the drawings shown here.

The following section relates to 90 models up to VIN HA701009 and 110 models up to HA901220.

▼ *MCR1. On the early type of master cylinder, the reservoir (1) is held to the top of the master cylinder with two roll pins (5). Tap them out with a suitable drift and ease the reservoir out of the two seals (6) in the top of the master cylinder.*

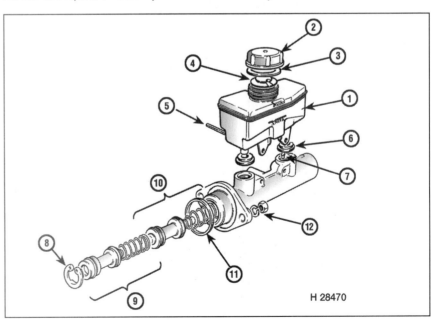

H 28470

When purchasing the new master cylinder, make sure that the seals for mounting the reservoir are supplied with the replacement master cylinder. Wipe a very small amount of brake fluid around the 'O' ring (11) before inserting the new master cylinder into the servo unit and take great care not to damage the 'O' ring.

The following section relates to later 90 models from VIN HA701010 and 110 models from HA901221.

▶ MCR2. *With the later type of master cylinder, there are no roll pins holding the reservoir (2) into the master cylinder body (3) but the seals (4) are more substantial in size. Carefully ease the reservoir up and away from the master cylinder body and note which seal goes where. When refitting the reservoir to the master cylinder body, wipe a very small amount of brake fluid around the seals to help everything to slip into place. Note the above advice regarding the 'O' ring (18) when refitting.*

Bleed the system as described in a later section. Take this opportunity to eject all of the old brake fluid from each of the brake lines, replacing it with new.

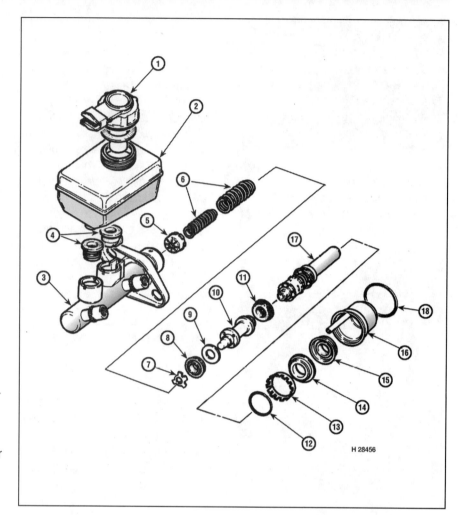

BRAKE SERVO REPLACEMENT

▶ BSR1. *It is not recommended that you attempt to overhaul the brake servo unit yourself. If it fails, check first that the vacuum hose is connected properly and has no splits in it. Then, remove and check the check valve. See if there is any damage to the rubber sealing grommet and try both blowing and sucking through the check valve. Air should pass through it in one direction only. The check valve can be removed from the front of the servo unit by removing the vacuum hose then pulling and twisting the check valve until it comes free. If the servo unit is found to be faulty, replace it with a new unit purchased from a good quality source.*
(Illustration © Lindsay Porter)

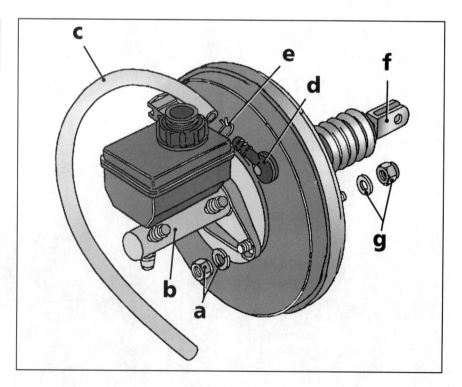

A. Remove the retaining nuts and bolts (a) and take off the master cylinder (b), as shown in an earlier section.

B. Disconnect the vacuum hose (c) from the check valve (d), taking off the spring clip (e) from later models.

C. Working from inside the vehicle, lever out the rubber sealing grommets from the brake pedal mounting box and, inside the aperture, take out the split pin, remove the washer and pull out the clevis pin holding the pedal to the servo unit pushrod (f).

D. Take off the four nuts and washers (g) holding the servo unit to the pedal mounting bracket . . .

E. . . . and lift out the servo unit from inside the engine bay. Be sure to hang on to the rubber seal which is fitted between the servo and the bracket but be prepared to replace it if it shows signs of deterioration.

F. Installation is the reverse of removal but make sure that you grease the brake pedal lever where it connects to the fork on the back of the servo, and make sure that the fixing nuts have their spring washers under them and that they are tightened to the correct torque.

DIESEL ENGINE VACUUM PUMP

Because there is no vacuum in the inlet manifold of a diesel engine, diesel engines are fitted with a vacuum pump to supply the necessary vacuum for the servo unit.

A. On the 300 Tdi engine, position No. 1 cylinder at top-dead-centre to release the tension from the pump operating plunger.

B. Disconnect the battery and remove any ancillary hoses or clips which might be in the way of the pump.

C. Use a felt pen to make a mark on the pump and the cylinder block (where appropriate) so that the pump can be refitted in exactly the same position it came from.

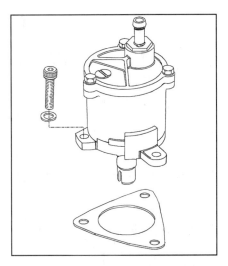

▲ *DEV1. On all engines, the vacuum pump is mounted on the right-hand of the cylinder block. On 2¼-litre engines, it is belt driven. On all other engines, the drive is direct.*
(Illustration © Lindsay Porter)

D. Unbolt and remove the pump, taking great care that the drivegear assembly in the cylinder block is not disturbed, where appropriate.

E. When refitting the pump to the 2¼-litre engine, ensure that the drivebelt has 12mm of movement in the longest run of the belt and that the oil level is topped up to the level of the plug hole with SAE 15/50W engine oil.

F. When you refit the pump to the cylinder block, always use a new gasket, and make sure that the driveshaft is correctly aligned and that the alignment marks made earlier line up perfectly.

BRAKE BLEEDING

You can buy various gadgets to assist with the process of brake bleeding but the basic procedure is the one described here. The idea is to push fresh fluid through each part of the system, expelling any trapped bubbles of air. Any air caught in the system will make the pedal feel spongy and could even leave you with no brakes when you need them most. Don't re-use brake fluid, and don't

be afraid to 'waste' fresh fluid in the interests of expelling all the air. It's a lot cheaper than a life! If you are not qualified in carrying out this work, have the vehicle checked before using it again.

You will need the following items: lots of fresh brake fluid; a clean glass jar; a piece of clear plastic which fits tightly over the bleed screw and is long enough to reach the bottom of the jar when it is on the ground; a ring spanner to fit the bleed screw; a willing assistant.

▲ *BB1. Take the cap off the master cylinder reservoir and top it up. It is most important that the level in the reservoir does not drop below the MIN mark at any time. If you draw more air into the system, you will have to start again from scratch.*

▲ *BB2. Take off the dust cap from the bleed screw which is furthest away from the master cylinder. This will be at one of the rear brakes but it all depends whether your vehicle is left-hand or right-hand drive. Fit the spanner to the screw, push one end of the tube over the end of the screw and place the other end in the jar. Pour in sufficient fluid to cover the end of the tube.*

A. Unscrew the bleed screw about one turn while your assistant inside the car pushes down on the brake pedal. The push should be firm and steady but not too vigorous. When the pedal reaches the bottom of the stroke, the person inside the car shouts out the word 'Down!' and holds the pedal down until the bleed screw has been re-tightened.

B. The person at the bleed screw shouts out the instruction 'Up!' and the person inside the car lets the brake pedal rise again.

C. The bleed screw is loosened once more and the person inside the car pushes the brake pedal 'Down . . .', the process being repeated over and again until no more air can be seen coming down the plastic tube or out of the end of the pipe.

D. It is important that, after every few strokes, the level of the fluid in the master cylinder is checked, as described earlier.

E. The other rear bleed point is then bled, followed by the front wheel furthest away from the master cylinder and then the fourth wheel. If the pedal still feels spongy, or sinks too close to the floorboards when the brake is applied with the vehicle stationary and the engine running, you may have to repeat the entire sequence again.

TRANSMISSION BRAKE OVERHAUL

▲ HSR1. Slacken the adjuster screw on the back of the backplate, as far as it will go.

▲ HSR2. With the vehicle correctly supported off the ground, disconnect the propeller shaft from the rear of the transfer box . . .

▲ HSR3. . . . levering it off the flange to compress the sliding splines and clear the threaded studs . . .

▼ HSR4. . . . and tie it well out of the way, or remove it completely.

EARLY MODELS – ROD-OPERATED BRAKE

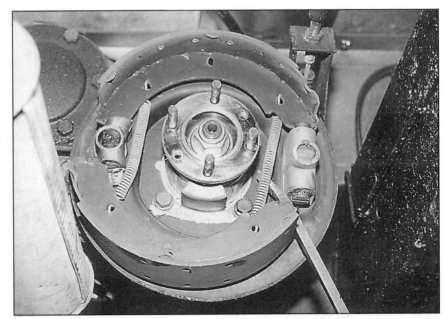

▲ HSR5. With the handbrake fully off, remove the brake drum retaining screw or screws (use an impact screwdriver, as here, if necessary) . . .

▲ HSR7. Make a careful written note of where each return spring is fitted to each brake shoe. Take the pressure off the return springs as described for the rear brake shoes . . .

▲ HSR6. . . . and attempt to remove the brake drum. If it is reluctant to come off on cable-operated versions, try slackening the handbrake cable adjuster nut and turn the adjuster bolt anti-clockwise, moving the shoes away from the drum.

If you see any oil on the shoes or in the drum assembly, the transfer box output shaft oil seal has almost certainly failed and this should be renewed before fitting new shoes.

▲ HSR8. . . . and remove the springs and shoes.

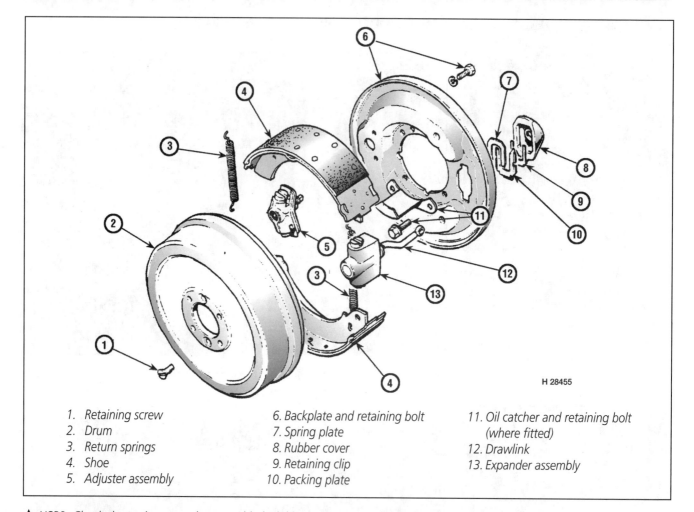

1. Retaining screw
2. Drum
3. Return springs
4. Shoe
5. Adjuster assembly
6. Backplate and retaining bolt
7. Spring plate
8. Rubber cover
9. Retaining clip
10. Packing plate
11. Oil catcher and retaining bolt (where fitted)
12. Drawlink
13. Expander assembly

H 28455

▲ HSR9. Check the entire expander assembly (13) (the equivalent of the wheel cylinder in a hydraulic system) for free movement and if necessary, remove the assembly, strip it down, grease and reassemble. To remove the expander from the backplate pull back the grommet (8), pull out the retaining clips and packing plate (7, 9 and 10).

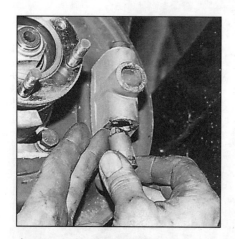

▲ HSR10. Similarly, check the adjuster assembly (5) and, once again, strip clean and grease, as necessary. To remove the adjuster, take off the two bolts (6) and spring washers from the rear of the backplate.

LATER MODELS – CABLE-OPERATED BRAKE

Start by removing the two shoe retainer spring clips. Push in the cup, turn it through 90°, lift off the cup and spring and pull out the retainer pin from the rear of the backplate. There is one on each shoe.

Make a careful written note of where all the brake springs go and take off the shoes and springs, as described for the earlier models.

When you take off the left-hand shoe, note the strut which fits between the shoe upper ends and make a written note of which way around it is fitted.

The right-hand shoe has to be detached from the handbrake cable.

If the operating lever to which the handbrake cable fits is not supplied fitted to the new right-hand shoe, you will have to transfer it from the old one to the new one – so don't throw those old shoes away until you have fitted the new ones!

Check, clean and grease the adjuster, as described for early models.

Refit the shoes in the following order:
a) Fit the handbrake cable to the right-hand shoe, place the shoe on the backplate and hold it in position with the retaining pin, spring and cup. b) Fit the strut to the upper end of the right-hand shoe – the right way up, of course! c) Fit the lower return spring to the right-hand shoe, hook it onto the left-hand shoe and pull the left-hand shoe into position on the backplate. d) Put the top spring in position on both shoes and then, using a self-grip wrench, pull the shoes into their final positions on the backplate.

FRONT WHEEL BEARING/HUB ASSEMBLY

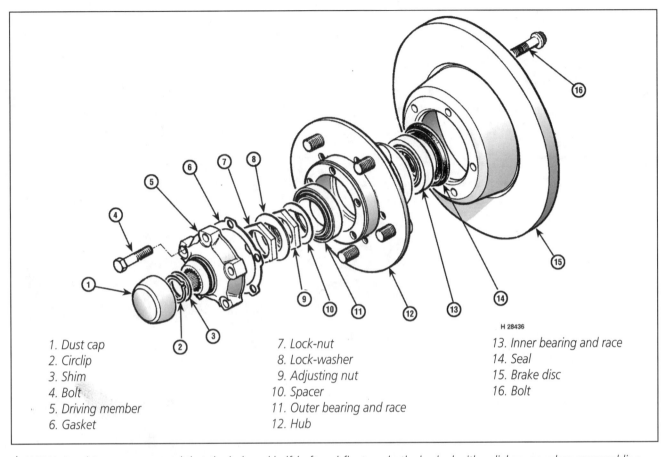

1. Dust cap
2. Circlip
3. Shim
4. Bolt
5. Driving member
6. Gasket
7. Lock-nut
8. Lock-washer
9. Adjusting nut
10. Spacer
11. Outer bearing and race
12. Hub
13. Inner bearing and race
14. Seal
15. Brake disc
16. Bolt

H 28436

▲ *WBH1. Land Rover recommend that the hub and halfshaft end-float are both checked with a dial gauge when reassembling the hub. If you don't own a dial gauge, you could carry out the work as described here by Liveridge – the way they do it – and then take the vehicle to your Land Rover dealer for final adjustment. These are the components of the hub assembly.*

After supporting the front of the vehicle on an axle stand and removing the road wheel, (remembering to chock the wheels remaining on the ground, fore and aft) disconnect the brake hose bracket from the swivel housing. Refit the bracket retaining bolts to prevent oil leakage. Remove the brake caliper, as described earlier.

ALTERNATIVE METHODS

In some of these illustrations the wheel is shown as still on the hub (and is *just* touching the ground, to take some of the weight) and is used to help pull off the hub itself. The views taken *without* the wheel in place illustrate the method recommended by Liveridge.

Remove the brake caliper and support it on the suspension, as described in an earlier section.

▲ *WBH2. Lever and remove the dust cap from the centre of the hub . . .*

▲ *WBH3. . . . and take off the circlip from the end of the halfshaft, using circlip pliers.*

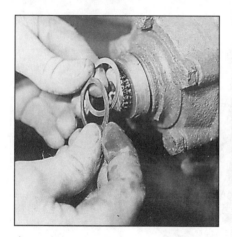

▲ WBH4. You can now take off the thrust washer or washers from beneath the circlip.

▲ WBH5. Take out the five bolts which connect the halfshaft to the hub and slide the driving member off the end of the halfshaft. (If the bolt heads have become very rusty use an ¹¹⁄₁₆ AF socket on 17mm bolts but the socket must be tight, advises Rob at Liveridge.)

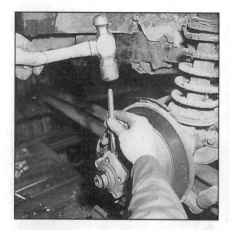

▲ WBH6. Use a chisel to get the member to move.

▲ WBH7. There is a lock-nut on the outside of the hub-nut and a bent over tab washer holding the lock-nut in place. Knock back the tab washer . . .

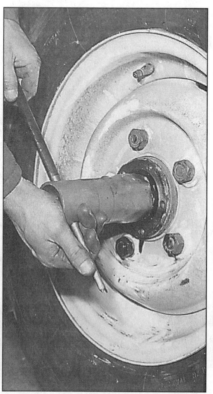

▲ WBH8. . . . unscrew the lock-nut . . .

▲ WBH9. . . . and take off the tab washer . . .

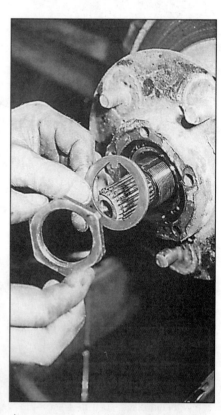

▲ WBH10. . . . then unscrew the hub-nut and remove the spacer from beneath it, although it will come off with the outer bearing – see WBH11 and 12.

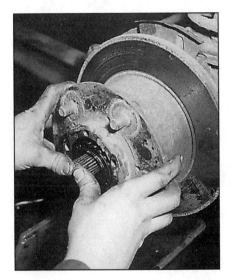

▲ WBH11. The front hub assembly can now be slid a little way off the stub axle but NOT right off yet. With the hub loose on the stub axle, extract the outer bearing rollers . . .

▲ WHB12. . . . and then remove the rest of the hub assembly.

▲ WBH13. Lever the oil seal from the rear of the hub . . .

▲ WBH14. . . . lift out the inner bearing rollers . . .

▲ WBH15. . . . and use a suitable punch to drift the inner and outer bearing races from the hub assembly. Apply the punch only to the outer section of each one and take very great care not to damage the hub bore.

Thoroughly clean both the stub axle and the hub bore and if the hub is cracked or badly damaged, or if the disc is cracked, it will have to be renewed.

Very lightly grease the hub bore and start by fitting the new bearing outer races. Ideally, they should be pressed home using a large vice and a suitable distance piece, such as a large socket spanner but it is possible to *very* carefully drift the race home, provided that it is kept perfectly square at all times.

Use a thread tap (or failing that, a spare bolt with a hacksaw slot cut down the length of its thread) to chase out the bolt threads in the hub for the driving member bolts.

▲ WBH16. Work some suitable high melting point grease into the inner bearing rollers and fit the inner bearings to the hub assembly. Grease the new inner oil seal and press it into position with its sealing lip facing inwards and making absolutely certain that it is fitted square and flush with the hub surface. Double check that the inner oil seal has a smear of oil on it and slide the hub on to the stub axle, taking care not to damage the seals on the halfshaft splines.

▲ WBH17. Refit the hub and fit the outer bearing in-situ, as shown. Note the use of lots of grease!

▲ WBH18. Refit the spacer and hand-tighten the hub-nut . . .

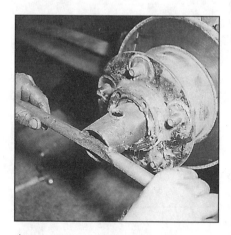

▲ WBH19. . . . then tighten the nut with a spanner while rotating the hub until the bearing starts to tighten up and the hub cannot be turned. This will check that the bearings are properly seated. Slacken the nut off again then re-tighten it until there is no free play in the hub. Slacken off again by a quarter of a turn. Make certain that the bearing does not 'bind' when turned and, if so, slacken off until it just ceases to do so.

IMPORTANT: In order to follow Land Rover's assembly instructions, the hub end-float must now be measured using a dial gauge and moving the hub in and out in the direction of the halfshaft. The end-float must be between 0.05 to 0.10mm. If you don't own a dial gauge, or the expertise to use one, take the vehicle to your Land Rover dealer or specialist before putting the vehicle back into use, and have the work carried out for you. Be sure to refit the lockwasher and outer locknut to the correct torque before driving the vehicle.

When the end-float is correct, fit a new lock-washer and then the (outer) lock-nut. Tighten the hub (outer) lock-nut to 65Nm (48lbf/ft) and check the end-float once again.

▲ WBH20. When you are satisfied that the end-float is correct, bend one side of the lock-washer inwards, to stop the inner nut from turning, and the opposite side of the lock-washer outwards to stop the outer nut from turning, bending the lock-washer over the flats of the nuts.

▲ WBH21. Clean the mating surfaces of both the hub and the driving member, fit a new gasket . . .

▲ WBH22. . . . and bolt the driving member back into position.

Clean the bolt threads and, immediately prior to installation, apply locking fluid to each bolt thread.

▲ WBH23. Refit the thrust washer or washers onto the halfshaft, followed by the circlip.

▲ WBH24. Now use a dial gauge to check the end-float on the halfshaft, moving the halfshaft in and out. The end-float should be between 0.12 and 0.25mm.

It may be helpful to screw a bolt into the thread in the end of the halfshaft to give the dial gauge something to 'lean' on. If the end-float is not within the necessary tolerances, you will have to buy additional or replacement thrust washer/s from your Land Rover dealer. Again, if you don't have a dial gauge, have this work carried out by your dealer when the hub end-float is checked.

Follow the instructions given in an earlier section for refitting the brake caliper assembly.

Remove the two brake hose clip retaining bolts – also the upper swivel pin retaining bolt – clean each thread and apply a drop of locking fluid immediately before refitting each bolt. They must be tightened to 65Nm (48lbf/ft).

After lowering the vehicle to the ground, check that the oil in the swivel pin housing is at the correct level, as described in a later section.

FRONT STUB AXLE REMOVAL AND REPLACEMENT

▼ FSA1. This, for reference, is a cross-sectional view of the front hub and stub axle components.

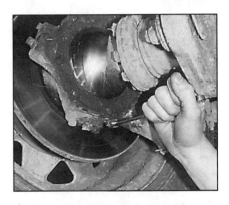

▲ FSA2. Take off the hub assembly, as described in the previous section and drain the swivel pin housing oil – it's going to come out anyway – it's just tidier this way!

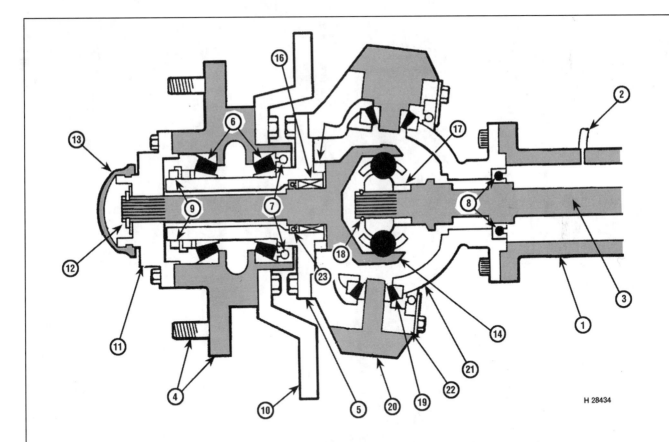

H 28434

1. Axle tube
2. Breather
3. Inner halfshaft section
4. Hub
5. Stub axle
6. Hub bearings
7. Inner hub seal
8. Circlip

9. Hub assembly washer, adjusting nut, lock-nut and lock-washer
10. Brake disc
11. Driving member
12. Shim and circlip
13. Hub cap
14. Outer halfshaft section
15. Bush

16. Needle roller bearing
17. Spacer
18. Circlip
19. Swivel pin bearing
20. Swivel pin
21. Swivel ball
22. Swivel pin housing
23. Seal

▲ FSA3. So that the stub axle and housing can be refitted in the same place, make an alignment mark between the two. Take out the six retaining bolts and washers . . .

▲ FSA5. You can now remove the stub axle from the swivel pin housing.

▲ FSA4. . . . take off the large steel washer (when fitted) and then crack the joint with a mallet.

▲ FSA6. Check the land – on the stub axle, where the oil seal runs, and replace the complete axle stub if necessary – available from specialists at a lower price than a genuine part!

▲ FSA7. At the rear of the stub axle is a bearing. On early models it is a bush but on later models there is a thrust ring fitted to the rear of the axle flange and a needle roller bearing and oil seal fitted to the inside of the stub axle. If any of these components need renewing, take them to your Land Rover dealer or specialist. (But Liveridge say that they have never known one fail!)

▲ FSA8. Before refitting, clean all traces of gasket or locking compound from the mating surfaces and clean out the threads in the swivel housing. If you don't own a thread tap of the correct size, cut a slot in the threads of a spare bolt, from end to end, and run the bolt through each of the threads.

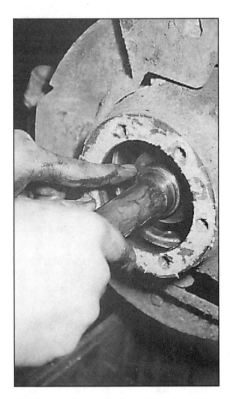

▲ FSA9. Before refitting the stub axle, make sure that the halfshaft splines are correctly engaged in the differential: you can tell when it's in because it will be difficult to turn! Always use a new gasket on the swivel housing.

▲ FSA10. Wipe oil or grease on to the stub axle bush or bearing and seal (as appropriate) and refit the stub axle, with the keyway at the top (12 o'clock). You must always use a new gasket and Liveridge recommend strongly that you also use an RTV silicone gasket sealer, such as the Wurth type shown here. If a mud shield was fitted to the stub axle, refit it.

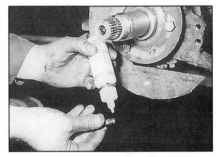

▲ FSA11. Clean the retaining bolt threads, put a drop of Wurth locking fluid on each one and refit the bolts and washers.

You can now refit the hub assembly, as described earlier.

FRONT AXLE HALFSHAFT AND CONSTANT VELOCITY JOINT REMOVAL AND REPLACEMENT

Remove the stub axle and hub assembly as described in earlier sections. Note that from chassis No. LD104957 Land Rover, recommend that Molytex grease type EP00 is used to replace oil in the constant velocity joint housing. No more leaks!

▼ HCV1. The halfshaft can now be pulled out from the axle, complete with the constant velocity joint.

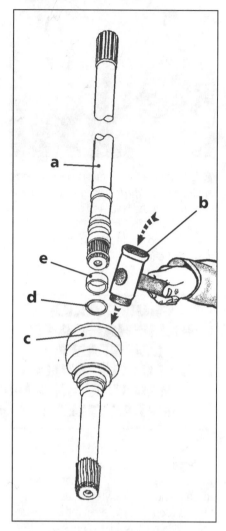

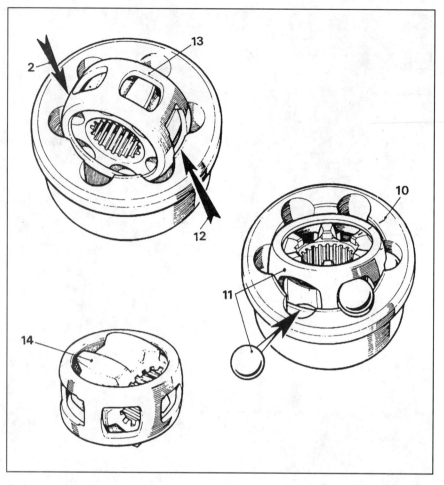

▲ HCV3. CONSTANT VELOCITY JOINT INSPECTION. A. Make marks on the inner and outer races of the constant velocity joint (10) so that they can be reassembled correctly. (Illustration courtesy Land Rover)

▲ HCV2. With the main body of the halfshaft (a) clamped in the vice, use a soft-faced mallet (b) to tap the constant velocity joint (c) off the end of the halfshaft. Take the circlip (d) from the end of the halfshaft and slide off the spacer (e). Use paraffin (kerosene) or a proprietary degreaser to clean all of the constant velocity joint and halfshaft components. (Illustration © Lindsay Porter)

B. Tilt the cage and inner race until each of the balls (11) can be removed.

C. Tilt the cage further so that it is 90° off its original axis (12). If you now turn the cage until two of the opposite windows coincide with two of the protruding sections of the outer cage (see arrows), you will be able to lift the cage (13) out.

D. Turn the inner (splined) track (14) at right angles to the cage, into the position shown, and lift out the inner race.

E. Check the following items for pitting, cracking, excessive looseness or wear: a) each ball in the CV joint in a member, b) the ball cage windows, c) the ball tracks, d) the halfshaft splines.

Before reassembling, make sure all traces of paraffin (kerosene) or degreaser have been removed and make sure that all bearings and splines are packed with a suitable grade of high melting point grease.

Push the spacer on to its seating on the halfshaft and fit a new circlip (it is *important* that the old circlip is not re-used), seating it correctly in the groove.

Push the constant velocity joint on to the halfshaft and tap it until the circlip engages in its groove. Make *sure* that the joint is properly retained by the circlip! Lubricate the C.V. joint with EP axle/gear oil.

When pushing the halfshaft back into the axle, make sure that the splines on the inner end of the halfshaft are located in the differential. The remainder of the re-assembly is the reverse of the dismantling process.

SWIVEL PIN HOUSING
DISMANTLING AND OVERHAUL

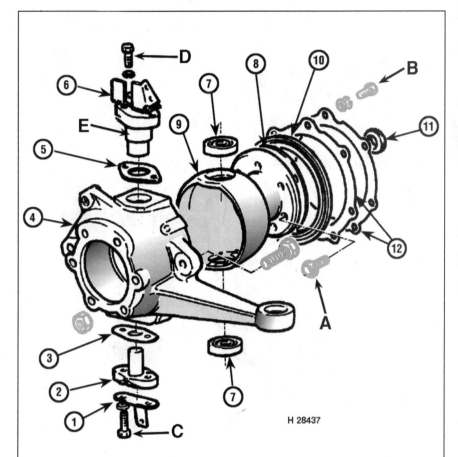

H 28437

1. Mudshield bracket
2. Lower swivel pin
3. Gasket
4. Swivel pin housing
5. Gasket
6. Upper swivel pin and brake hose bracket
7. MODELS WITH REAR DISC BRAKES. Swivel pin bearing and race
7. EARLIER MODELS. A bush and thrust washer
8. Shim
9. Swivel ball
10. Oil seal
11. Oil seal
12. Retaining plate and gasket

▲ SPH2. Remove the hub assembly, stub axle and halfshaft, as described in earlier sections. Also, disconnect the track rod end and (where necessary) the drag-link from the swivel pin housing, as described in later sections.

▲ SPH1. The swivel pin assembly is essentially the same as the one that has always been fitted to Land Rovers. However, a minor modification has taken place part way through the production sequence (probably when rear disc brakes were also introduced), when the top bush was replaced by a roller bearing. This means that there is a small difference involved in dismantling and reassembling the swivel pin.

Note that in the following instructions, EARLY MODELS means 90 versions up to VIN LA930455 and 110 versions up to LA930434, while LATER MODELS means all models with VINs higher than these numbers.

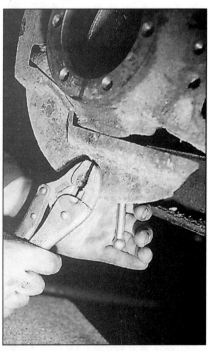

▲ SPH3. Also, remove the dust shield. Grip the (usually rusty) bolt heads with a self-grip wrench.

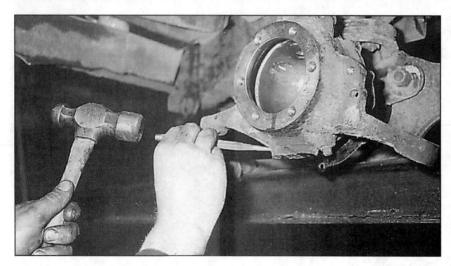

▲ SPH4. Remove the bolts holding the lower swivel pin and drift the pin first around, then out.

▲ SPH8. Take out the bolts and washers . . .

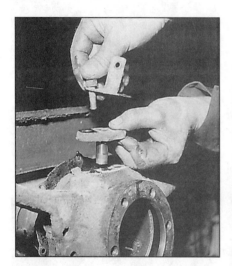

▲ SPH5. Remove the top pin and brake hose bracket . . .

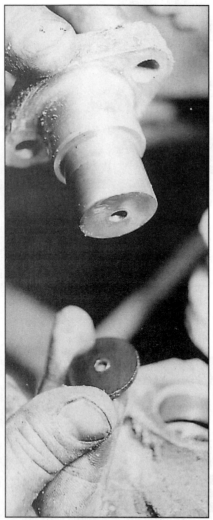

▲ SPH7. Don't forget the washer located at the bottom of the top pin, when fitted.

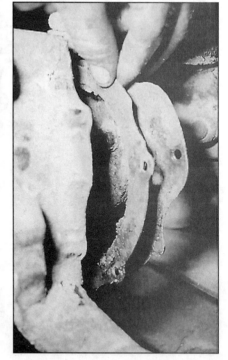

▲ SPH9. . . . holding the swivel pin housing oil seal and retaining plate from the rear of the swivel housing and take careful note of which way round the seal is fitted. If a bolt shears (usually the top one because there is no oil there) you will need to drill out and tap. Use plenty of releasing fluid and try to avoid the problem.

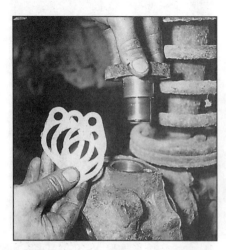

▲ SPH6. . . . and take out and retain the shims.

▶ *SPH10. You can now remove the housing. Wash the outside of the housing in paraffin (kerosene) or a proprietary brand of degreaser.*

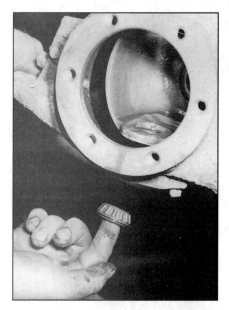

▲ *SPH11. Note that, as the housing is removed, the bottom bearing will drop free.*

▲ *SPH12. Remove the bolts holding the swivel assembly to the axle.*

Before refitting, lever out the old oil seal from the end of the axle tube. Clean the mating surfaces between the swivel ball and the axle, fit the new seal evenly and lubricate it. Coat both sides of the gasket with non-setting gasket compound and, when reassembling, refit the bolts and washers, tightening them evenly to 65 to 80Nm (48 to 59lbf/ft). Note that each of the bolts should have a drop of thread locking fluid applied immediately before fitting.

EARLY MODELS – refer to illustration SPH1: After taking the swivel ball (9) from its housing (4), you can remove the thrust washers and bearing from the upper pin bush and the lower swivel pin bearing.

Working through the swivel ball (9) from one side to the other, drift the lower bearing race (7) and then the top bush out of the swivel ball.

LATER MODELS – refer to illustration SPH1: Remove the swivel ball (9) from the housing (4), take out both swivel pin bearings (7) and, working from the opposite side of the swivel ball, drift out both bearing races from the swivel ball.

ALL MODELS. A sure sign of a swivel ball in need of replacement is missing chrome plating or other obvious signs of wear – but you would have known this before you stripped it down, of course! However, you can check the bushes and bearings (as appropriate) and if there are any signs of roughness in the bearings, replace them. You should fit all new oil seals and gaskets when reassembling the swivel pin housing.

▲ *SPH13. Fit the upper bearing or bush (as appropriate) to the swivel ball, making sure that each is perfectly square and that bearings are tapped or pressed into place with a suitable drift which pushes only against the outer bearing race. This is the early, bush-type.*

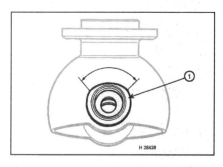

▲ *SPH14. EARLY MODELS: Make sure that the cut-away area on the lip of the upper swivel bush (1) is towards the back of the housing . . .*

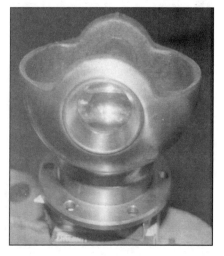

▲ *SPH15. . . . as also shown here. Lever out the oil seal from the back of the housing, fitting a new one with the sealing lip facing away from the ball. Make sure that all the bearings and the oil seal are lubricated with grease, and also apply lubricant to the bearing and thrust washers for the upper and lower swivel pins which go into the main swivel pin housing.*

REASSEMBLY

▲ SPH16. This is the halfshaft bearing, a sliding roller bearing, which is often overlooked but must be put in fairly early on in the reassembly process.

▲ SPH19. The aperture for receiving the oil seal has been cleaned and must now be sealed. The bottom bearing has been fitted, prior to . . .

▲ SPH17. Likewise, carefully grease the big oil seal (a twin track seal so grease must be put between both tracks). The aperture in the swivel housing carrier must be meticulously clean or the seal won't be seated properly.

▲ SPH20. . . . 'sticking' the lower bearing in place with grease, after which . . .

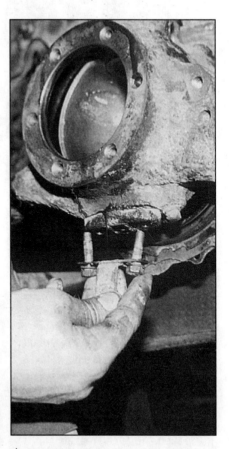

▲ SPH18. Don't forget the retainer at this stage, shown here going into place. On later models, Land Rover recommend replacing oil with grease. See Front Axle Halfshaft section.

▲ SPH21. . . . the housing can be carefully offered up to the swivel ball.

▲ SPH22. It is important to remember that the lower swivel pin is fitted with its lug facing outwards, followed later by the disc shield bracket and the retaining bolts, tightened only loosely.

▲ SPH23. Also, remember that the new gasket must be coated on both sides with non-setting gasket sealant, such as Wurth silicone RTV . . .

▲ SPH24. . . . and the bolts (before they are fully tightened, later) must first be removed, the threads cleaned and a drop of thread locking fluid applied to each bolt.

▲ SPH25. You can now fit the upper swivel pin and shim or shims to the top of the housing, with the bolts fitted loosely and the hose bracket in place. These bolts will also need thread locker applying when they are properly tightened down.

IMPORTANT. Re-shim and fit the top swivel before fitting the oil seal – a new seal creates its own drag and should only be fitted after the shims have been set – see SPH26.

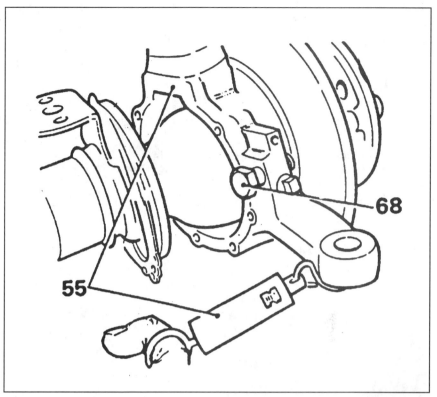

▲ SPH26. Before making any further connections, the swivel pin bearing preload must be checked. (This Land Rover drawing shows the check being carried out before the oil seal and retainer have been fitted.) Use a spring balance (55 – lower) on the track rod end hole on the swivel housing to pull the swivel housing towards you. Note the loading necessary on the spring balance to do so. The correct force will be between 3.6 to 4.5kg (approximately 8 to 10lb). If the force required to swivel the housing is higher than this figure, more or thicker shims will be required; if the force required is lower, fewer or thinner shims will be required. They are available from your Land Rover specialist and finding the correct thickness is a matter of trial and error. If you take the settings you have obtained to your specialist, they should be able to advise the best thickness to try next. You can now refit the oil seal to the rear of the housing.
(Illustration courtesy Land Rover)

◀ SPH27. With the swivel housing bearing preload correctly set, remove the upper and lower swivel bolts, one at a time, clean the threads, apply a drop of thread locking compound to each one and then refit them to the correct torque: LOWER BOLTS – 22 to 28Nm (16 to 21lbf/ft); UPPER BOLTS – 60 to 70Nm (44 to 52lbf/ft).

Refit the track rod end, the drag-link (if appropriate), the halfshaft, hub assembly and stub axle as described earlier. When the wheels and tyres have been refitted, check the steering lock stop position.

REAR AXLE HALFSHAFT REMOVAL AND REPLACEMENT

With the rear of the vehicle raised off the ground and the front wheels chocked, drain the differential oil. Alternatively, if you raise just the side of the vehicle you are working on and support it on axle stands, you may be able to avoid having to drain the oil out of the axle.

SPLINED HALF-SHAFT MODELS

▲ RAH1. Take off the dust cap from the end of the shaft . . .

▲ RAH2. . . . remove the circlip . . .

▲ RAH3. . . . and separate the driving member from the halfshaft.

▲ RAH4. Screw a bolt into the end of the halfshaft, take off the driving member and pull out the halfshaft.

MODELS WITH COMBINED DRIVING MEMBER AND HALFSHAFT

▼ RAH5. Take out the five bolts and washers holding the halfshaft to the hub and pull out the halfshaft.

REASSEMBLY

▲ RAH6. After cleaning all the surfaces and threads, make sure that the retaining bolts have a spot of locking fluid applied to their threads immediately before refitting, and coat each side of the new gasket with non-setting gasket compound.

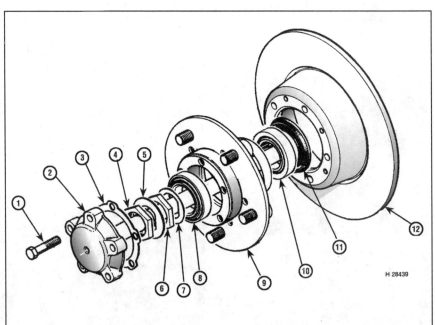

1. Retaining bolt	6. Adjusting nut	10. Inner bearing and race
2. Halfshaft	7. Spacer	11. Seal
3. Gasket	8. Outer bearing and race	12. Brake disc
4. Locknut	9. Hub	
5. Lockwasher		

REAR HUB AND BEARING OVERHAUL

▼ *RHB1. Some later Defenders use the halfshaft arrangement shown here...* (Illustration © Lindsay Porter)

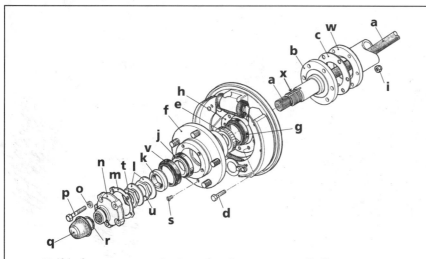

a. Halfshaft
b. Stub axle
c. Gasket
d. Stub axle to axle casing, bolt
e. Inner bearing
f. Hub
g. Inner oil seal
h. Oilcatcher (110 only)
i. Stub axle to axle casing, locknut

j. Outer bearing
k. Seal track spacer
l. Lock-washer (only one – between nuts, some models)
m. Gasket
n. Hub driving member
o. Spring washer
p. Hub driving member bolts
q. Dust cap

r. Circlip
s. Brake drum retaining screws
t. Locknut
u. End-float adjusting nut
v. Outer oil seal
w. Axle casing
x. Keyway

▲ *RHB3. Remove the brake drum or caliper, as appropriate. These jobs are described in other sections. It's a good idea to lock the hub and prevent it from turning with a long lever, as shown here.*

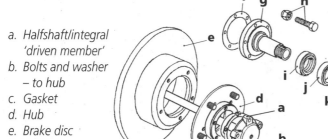

a. Halfshaft/integral 'driven member'
b. Bolts and washer – to hub
c. Gasket
d. Hub
e. Brake disc
f. Gasket
g. Stub axle
h. Bolts and washer – to axle case
i. Seal
j. Inner bearing
k. Outer bearing
l. Seal track spacer
m. Hub nut
n. Tab washer
o. Lock nut

▲ *RHB4. The two large locking nuts retaining the hub bearings are now exposed. There is a lock plate which is bent over both of the nuts – this must be straightened before you can undo them. The inner nut shouldn't be too tight on its thread, so a tommy bar probably won't be needed. Behind the inner nut is a thrust washer or spacer washer. Unscrew the hub-nut and slide off the seal track spacer from beneath it, noting which way round it goes.*

▲ *RHB2. . . . while others use the type shown here. The following instructions refer separately to the two types, where necessary.* (Illustration © Lindsay Porter)

▲ RHB5. The whole hub can now start to be removed. The trick is to pull it away without dropping the inner bearing on the floor or in any dirt!

▲ RHB6. Before taking out the oil seals, make a note of which way round they go. Use a screwdriver to lever out both seals.

▲ RHB7. Take out both seals and inner bearing inner races . . .

▲ RHB8. Both races must be minutely examined for the smallest trace of scoring, shiny stripes, swarf and pitting, assuming that you have stripped the hub for a purpose other than replacing the bearings . . .

▲ RHB9. . . . and if damaged, they can be drifted out, working around with the drift so that they don't jam as they come out. Also, look closely at the oil seal housings in the hub and if there are any burrs that could damage the seal, remove them.

▲ RHB10. Tap or press the new bearings into place, taking very great care to only bear on the outer races and to ensure that the bearings go in completely square.

▲ RHB11. Make sure that the inner bearing is packed with high melting point grease . . .

▲ RHB12. . . . and put a liberal smear (in other words, do not pack!) in the cavity between the seal lips.

re-tighten the nut to give the correct hub end-float of 0.05 to 0.1mm (0.002 to 0.004in), compressing the rubber on the new seal track spacer by the correct amount.

NOT USING NEW RUBBERS. Check and set the end-float with a dial gauge as described in section 'Front Wheel Bearing/Hub Assembly', earlier in this chapter.

▲ RHB13. Each seal – whether there is just an inner or both an inner and an outer seal – must be fitted perfectly square into the housing and for that reason, once it has been started, it must be pushed in with a large tube that bears on the four pads in the channel around the seal.

▲ RHB15. The lips of both seals must be smeared with high melting point grease, otherwise the new seal will be destroyed within a few seconds of use.

When refitting the hub, take care not to allow the weight of the hub to rest, even momentarily, on the seals otherwise damage could well occur.

With the hub in place and the seal held clear of the stub axle, fit a new seal track spacer, with the seal lip leading.
WITH ALL NEW SEALS FITTED. Refit the hub-nut and tighten it while slowly turning the hub until all end-float has been removed. Back off the nut by half a turn and then, with a torque wrench,

▲ RHB14. Both the inner and outer seals are fitted with the lip-side facing the outside of the vehicle. Both seals must be square and recessed between 4.8 to 5.3mm (0.19 to 0.21in) from the outer faces of the hub.

▲ RHB16. ALL VEHICLES. Fit a new lock-washer and refit the lock-nut. Drift one section of the lock-washer over a flat of the hub-nut and then, gripping the hub-nut so that it cannot turn, tighten the outer lock-nut to 95 to 108Nm (70 to 80lb/ft). Rotate the hub several times to settle the bearings and recheck the end-float. Now a section of the lock-washer opposite the one that has already been bent over the hub-nut can be bent forwards and over one flat of the lock-nut.

Use a new gasket with non-setting gasket compound thinly spread over each side of it.
SEPARATE DRIVING FLANGE MODELS: Refit the halfshaft, driving member and circlip and five or six bolts, as appropriate.
INTEGRAL DRIVING FLANGE MODELS: Refit the halfshaft.
ALL VEHICLES:
Use a drop of thread lock fluid on each bolt immediately before fitting.

REAR STUB AXLE REMOVAL AND REFITTING

FRONT SHOCK ABSORBER REPLACEMENT

Refer to the illustrations RHB1 and RHB2, in the previous section.

A. Remove the rear hub as described in the previous section.
B. Take out the six stub axle retaining bolts and nuts.
C. In order to remove the backplate, you will first have to disconnect the hydraulic pipe to the wheel cylinder. So that you cut down on fluid loss, clamp the flexible hose before disconnecting.
D. 110 MODELS ONLY. You will also have to remove the oil catcher, as Land Rover call it – what appears to be a retaining plate which fits on top of the brake backplate.
E. Take off the brake backplate (drum brake models) or dust shield (disc brake models).
F. If fitted, lever out the old oil seal from the back of the axle casing and fit a new one with a smear of grease around the seal lip so that you don't ruin the seal the first time the vehicle is used. Press the new seal into position as described in the previous section, for hub seals.
G. Refit the components, using a new gasket between stub axle and axle. Make sure that the keyway in the end of the stub axle is facing upwards, at 12 o'clock.
H. Fit new lock-nuts to the stub axle retaining bolts, reassemble all the other components in the reverse of their removal process and bleed the brakes as described in an earlier section.

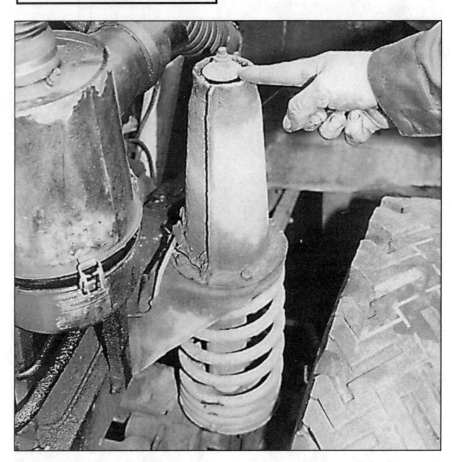

▲ *FSA1. This is the arrangement of the front shock absorber and spring seen clearly with X-ray specs.*

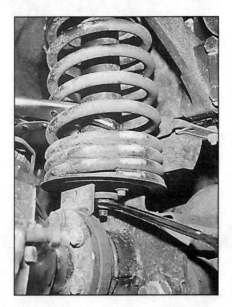

Support the front of the vehicle off the ground on axle stands placed beneath the front axle so that the front suspension is compressed by the normal weight of the vehicle. Make sure that the rear wheels are *very firmly* chocked in both directions and that the supports are solid.

◀ *FSA2. With the road wheels removed, and the shock absorber body locked with a large self-grip wrench so that it can't turn, take off the shock absorber lower mounting nut . . .*

▲ FSA3. . . . and remove the outer washer and rubber bushing. It is important to note that the washers must be fitted where they came from and must not be interchanged, but when fitting new shock absorbers, new mounting lock-nuts should be used every time. (Illustration © Lindsay Porter)

▲ FSA4. From inside the engine bay, there is an access cover which must now be removed . . .

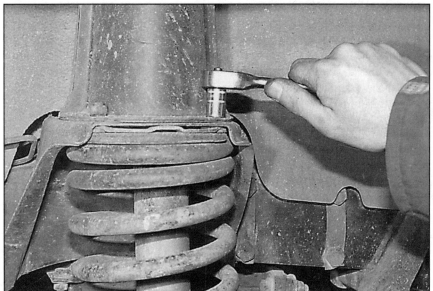

▲ FSA5. . . . giving access to two of the four shock absorber top mounting nuts and washers. The other two can be seen here, under the wing. You can now lift the shock absorber and upper mounting assembly out of the vehicle, leaving the coil spring in place, still compressed by the weight of the vehicle.

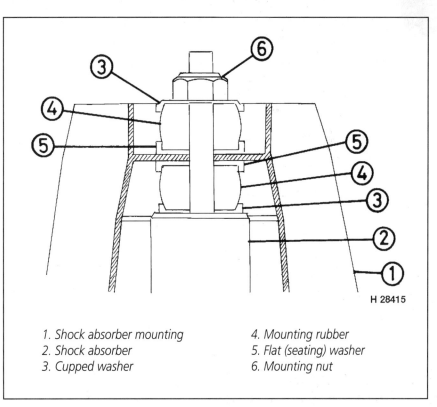

H 28415

1. Shock absorber mounting
2. Shock absorber
3. Cupped washer
4. Mounting rubber
5. Flat (seating) washer
6. Mounting nut

▲ FSA6. It is now possible to remove the upper mounting nut, the upper top bushing and the lower top bushing, and to take the shock absorber from inside the mounting assembly. It's a good idea to temporarily reassemble the components onto the shock absorber, or to immediately fit them to the new shock absorber (as appropriate) so that you don't confuse the order they go in. These are the lower washers and mounting rubber.

TESTING.

The weight and stiffness of a Land Rover's suspension means that it is extremely difficult – if not impossible! – to carry out the conventional bounce test for shock absorbers. You can really only test them properly in this way: place one end in the vice (taking great care not to damage the threads) and, with the shock absorber in a vertical position, try moving the piston both through complete strokes and through short up and down movements. If the movement feels uneven or jerky, or if there are any signs of fluid leaks, or if there is any damage or corrosion evident on the strut, the shock absorber will have to be replaced.

▼ *FSA7. REFITTING. When refitting, make certain that all of the washers and bushings go back in the correct locations, use new lock-nuts, and always replace shock absorbers in axle-pairs. To replace just one shock absorber on an axle can produce a dangerous imbalance in the suspension. This drawing also relates to several of the following sections. (Illustration courtesy Land Rover)*

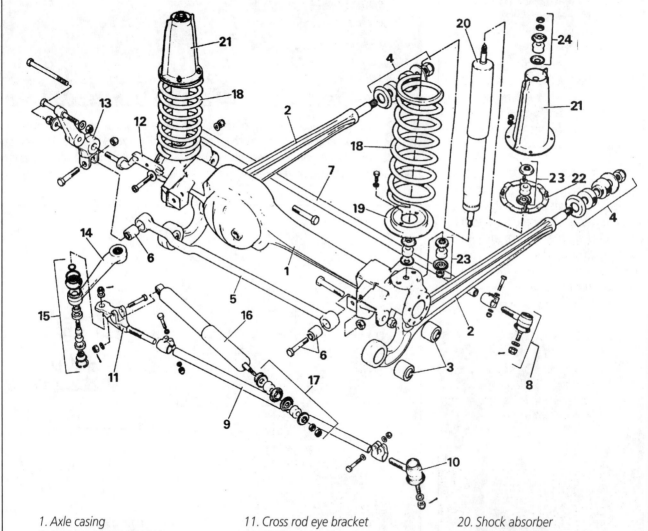

1. Axle casing
2. Radius arm LH and RH
3. Radius arm front bushes
4. Radius arm rear bushes
5. Panhard rod
6. Panhard bushes and bolts
7. Track rod
8. Track rod ball joint
9. Cross rod assembly
10. Cross rod ball joint

11. Cross rod eye bracket
12. Tie bar
13. Tie bar and cross rod mounting bracket
14. Drop arm
15. Drop arm ball joint assembly
16. Steering damper
17. Steering damper bush assembly
18. Coil spring
19. Coil spring seat

20. Shock absorber
21. Shock absorber mounting (shown twice!)
22. Spring seat (top)
23. Shock absorber lower bush assembly
24. Shock absorber upper bush assembly

FRONT COIL SPRING REPLACEMENT

Refer to the drawing FSA7.

A. Disconnect the shock absorber lower mounting (23) and detach the shock absorber complete with upper mounting bracket (21), as described in the previous section.

B. As well as leaving the axle stands in place underneath the front axle, you must now support the weight of the front of the vehicle on axle stands, as well. This is because, when you remove the spring, there will be nothing to hold the vehicle up!

C. Use a trolley jack to take the weight of the axle on the side from which you are removing the spring, take out the stand from underneath the axle and lower the axle *slowly* and *carefully* towards the ground, taking very great care that you don't place any strain on the brake hoses and that the axle does not slip off the jack.

D. Take out the spring and put a dab of paint on the top face so that you know which way round it goes, if it is going to be re-used.

E. ▼ *FCS1. The upper spring mounting only needs to be replaced if it has corroded badly, as in the case of this one, but note where it goes if it happens to be taken out when the spring is removed.*

F. Fitting a spring is essentially the reverse of the removal process but note that the upper spring seat (23) must be in place between the spring and the mounting position on the chassis as the axle is jacked back up into position. If necessary, use a couple of the strut nuts to hold it in position as the spring is fitted.

PANHARD ROD REPLACEMENT

Refer to the illustration FSA7.

The Panhard rod (5) prevents the front axle from moving sideways.

▼ *PHR1. The Panhard rod would only need to be replaced if it was physically damaged or if the mounting bushes have become soft or deteriorated in any other way. Check the bushes by levering them. This is the right-hand end, where the rod is fitted to the mounting bracket (13).*

▲ *PHR2. The rod is simply unbolted from its two mountings and the bushes can be pressed out, if necessary, using a vice and spacers (such as suitably-sized socket spanners), making sure that the spacer which presses out the bush bears only on the hard outer edge, and not on the bush rubber. Note that new lock-washers must be used each time they are removed.*

FRONT RADIUS ARMS AND BUSHES

Refer to the illustration FSA7.

The two radius arms (2) prevent the axle from moving backwards and forwards. If the radius arm itself is damaged or bent or (more likely) any of the bushes (3) are soft or deteriorated, it will have to be removed.

A. Support the front of the vehicle off the ground with axle stands placed underneath the axle, holding the suspension in its normal compressed position. Chock the rear wheels in front and behind.

B. ▼ *FRA1. Disconnect the radius arm from the axle by taking out the retaining bolts and washers . . .*

C. ▼ *FRA2. . . . and disconnect the rear of the radius arm from the chassis by removing the lock-nut, washer and rear bush (4) from the back of the chassis member. Support the front of the radius arm while doing so.*

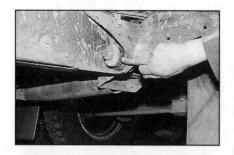

D. If the front bushes need to be replaced, follow the instructions for the Panhard rod bushes in the previous section. When refitting the radius arm, make sure that the rear washers and bushes are replaced in their correct positions and use a new lock-nut.

REAR SUSPENSION AXLE LINK

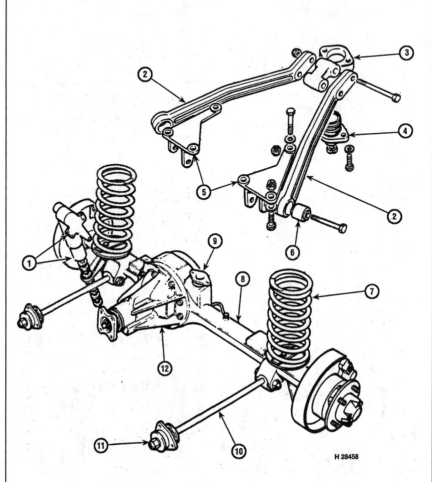

1. Shock absorber and mounting bracket
2. Upper link
3. Upper link mounting bracket
4. Upper link balljoint
5. Upper link mounting bracket
6. Mounting bush
7. Coil spring
8. Rear axle
9. Balljoint mounting plate
10. Lower link
11. Rubber mounting
12. Differential housing

▲ *RSL1. Take out the two nuts and bolts securing the anti-roll bar to the axle link and the anti-roll bar can now be removed from the vehicle. If the rubber bushes have become worn, spongy or deteriorated, they must be renewed. Note: This drawing will be useful for reference in later sections on the rear suspension. You can remove the axle link by taking out the split pin, unscrewing the castle-nut (6), removing the washer, and taking the balljoint and link from the axle location. If the balljoint shows wear or excessive stiffness, or if the rubber is split, the balljoint itself cannot be renewed; the complete link must be replaced.*

FRONT AND REAR ANTI-ROLL BAR BUSHES AND BALLJOINTS

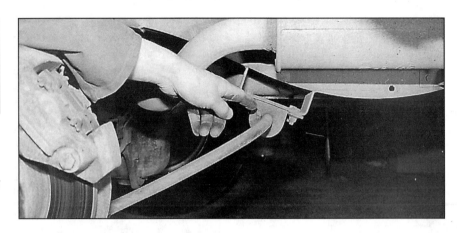

▶ *ARB1. REAR ANTI-ROLL BAR. Four nuts and bolts on each side hold the rear anti-roll bar to the chassis – remove them.*

a. Anti-roll bar
b. Rubber bush
c. Nut and washers
d. Bracket
e. Bolt
f. Anti-roll bar pin
g. Washer
h. Rubber bush
i. Lock-nut
j. Ball joint and link assembly
k. Castle nut
l. Split pin

▶ *ARB2. FRONT ANTI-ROLL BAR. When refitting, Land Rover recommend that new lock-nuts (where fitted) and a new split pin for the castle-nut should always be used. Note that the split in each of the two large bushes (b) should face the axle.*
(Illustration © Lindsay Porter)

REAR SHOCK ABSORBER REPLACEMENT

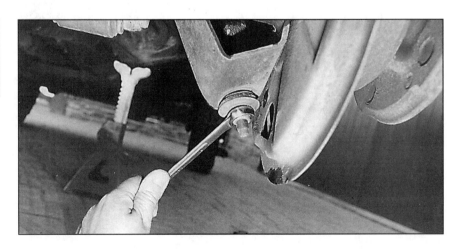

▶ *RSA1. The rear shock absorber is simply held at the bottom with a lock-nut and washers . . .*

▲ RSA2. . . . and at the top with another lock-nut and washers. When refitting, make sure that the correct order of reassembly is carried out, with a washer on each side of the rubber bush.

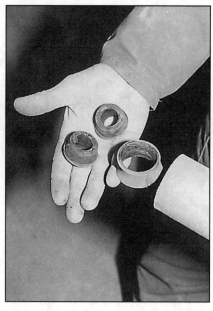

◄ RSA3. An old, worn top bush will probably be easy to remove but fitting a new one will require some lubrication, such as a spot of brake fluid or washing-up liquid – NOT oil, because that would cause the rubber to deteriorate.

TESTING

As with the front shock absorber, the rear shockers can only be properly tested off the vehicle. See details under Front Shock Absorber Replacement.

▼ RSA4. The shock absorber lower bush assembly (18) consists of a single rubber bush compressed between two shaped washers. Make sure they are refitted just as they were removed.
(Illustration courtesy Land Rover)

1. Salisbury axle casing
2. Anti-roll bar
3. Boge self levelling unit
4. Levelling unit upper balljoint assembly
5. Levelling unit lower balljoint assembly
6. Fulcrum bracket
7. Fulcrum bracket balljoint assembly
8. Suspension top links
9. Top link mounting brackets
10. Top link bushes
11. Lower links
12. Lower link flexible bush assembly
13. Lower link bush and bolt assembly
14. Coil spring assembly
15. Bump stop
16. Shock absorber
17. Shock absorber top bush assembly
18. Shock absorber lower bush assembly
19. Anti-roll bar bush and strap assembly
20. Anti-roll bar balljoint and link assembly
21. Heavy duty Rover axle casing

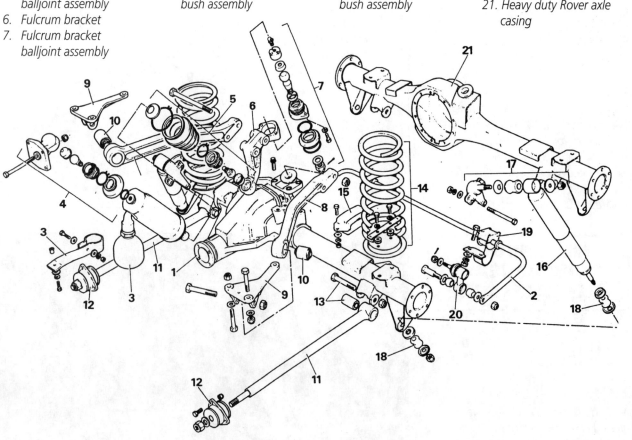

REAR COIL SPRING REPLACEMENT

Refer to the illustration RSA4.

Support the rear of the vehicle on strong axle stands, beneath the chassis (NOT the axle!) and *very firmly* chock the front wheels, in front and behind.

The procedure for replacing the rear coil spring is very much the same as that for the front, except for the following points:

▲ *RCS1. The bottom of the coil spring is held to the spring mounting plate and the axle with a steel strap, washers and bolts (14). You may need to raise the vehicle and support it with axle stands beneath the chassis, with the wheels hanging free to give yourself enough room between the coil springs to undo the retaining bolts and remove the strap.*

You then have to support the axle underneath the spring-area with a trolley jack, remove the shock absorber, then slowly and carefully lower the axle until the force of the coil spring is removed and the spring can be lifted free.

ALTERNATIVE – RETAINER STRAP LEFT IN POSITION

When removing the spring, start by disconnecting it from the top mounting in the chassis, then disconnect it from the lower spring pan and retainer plate by turning the spring with a rotary motion.

When refitting the spring, reverse the procedure, 'screwing' the bottom of the spring in place in an anti-clockwise direction in order to locate it on the bottom spring pan and retainer plate.

LAND ROVER COIL SPRING SPECIFICATIONS

Coil springs are colour-coded according to their location on the vehicle and the type of vehicle. Each spring should have a colour stripe or stripes on it and you should always make sure that the correct spring is used in the correct location.

Check with your Land Rover dealer or specialist, to find out if there have been any subsequent changes to these specifications.

MODEL	DRIVER'S SIDE	PASSENGER'S SIDE
110 MODELS, FRONT SPRINGS	double white stripes	double yellow stripes
110 MODELS, REAR, WITHOUT SUSPENSION LEVELLING	red stripe	red and green stripes
110 MODELS, REAR, WITH SUSPENSION LEVELLING	blue stripe	green and white stripes
90 MODELS, FRONT SPRINGS	blue and green stripes	blue and yellow stripes
90 MODELS, REAR, BASIC	blue and red stripes	yellow and white stripes
90 MODELS, REAR, HEAVY DUTY	green, yellow and red stripes	green, yellow and white stripes

REAR SUSPENSION UPPER LINK AND BALLJOINT

Refer to the illustration RSA4.

Before starting any dismantling, remember that you will need new lock-nuts and also a new upper link pivot bolt if they are being removed.

Raise the vehicle off the ground and

▶ *SUL1. If the vehicle is fitted with a self-levelling unit (3), this will first have to be removed. Remove the split pin, castle-nut and washer which holds the balljoint to the fulcrum bracket (6), from beneath the chassis (direction of arrow). The two bolts being pointed out here hold the balljoint retainer (7) to the fulcrum bracket.*

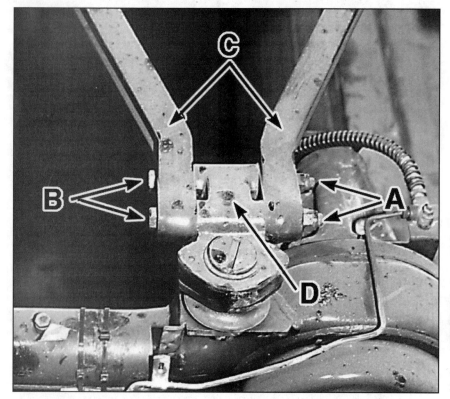

Refer to the illustration RSA4.

▲ LLR1. To replace the lower link/radius arm rear bush at the chassis (13), you will need to remove the lock-nut and pivot bolt from the chassis bracket . . .

▲ SUL2. You can now take off the top link arms (C) from the fulcrum bracket (D), complete with the self-levelling unit's lower balljoint if fitted. After taking out the two nuts (A) and bolts (B) the arms are removed and the fulcrum bracket is lifted away. The balljoint can be taken from the axle bracket using a balljoint extractor.

The replacement balljoint will be supplied complete and ready packed with grease. Use two bolts as a guide to alignment and press the knurled balljoint into the pivot bracket. You can now hold it in place with the two nuts and bolts.

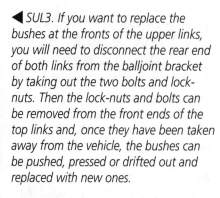

◀ SUL3. If you want to replace the bushes at the fronts of the upper links, you will need to disconnect the rear end of both links from the balljoint bracket by taking out the two bolts and lock-nuts. Then the lock-nuts and bolts can be removed from the front ends of the top links and, once they have been taken away from the vehicle, the bushes can be pushed, pressed or drifted out and replaced with new ones.

When fitting the upper links (8) to the pivot bracket (6), fit the two bolts and nuts but do not tighten until the vehicle has been lowered to the ground and allowed to settle under its own weight. You can now tighten the two bolts and nuts fixing the upper links to the pivot bracket, to the correct torque.

▲ LLR2. . . . and take off the lock-nut and washer from the front end of the radius arm. It can now be lifted away from the vehicle. If it shows any signs of damage or distortion, the arm itself must be replaced. New bushes can be fitted after the old ones have been pushed, drifted or pressed from the eye in the radius arm.

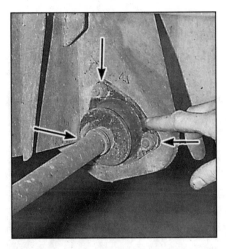

▲ *LLR3. New front-end bushes (12) are built-in to the mounting on the chassis. With the arm taken off, remove the three nuts and bolts (arrowed) and bolt on a new mounting and bush assembly in its place.*

Remember to use all new lock-nuts and, where necessary, a new pivot bolt at the chassis bracket.

SELF-LEVELLING UNIT (WHEN FITTED)

Refer to the illustration RSA4.

When fitted, the Boge Hydromat self-levelling unit is fitted in the centre of the rear axle. It only works as the vehicle is being driven and so, to check it, you have to carry out the following procedure.

A. Make sure that the vehicle is unladen.
B. Measure the distance between the bottom of the rubber bump-stop and the bump-stop plate on the rear axle on both sides of the vehicle. The clearance should be more than 67mm (2.8in). If the clearance is less, it could be because of weak or sagged springs, or it could be because of a faulty self-levelling unit.
C. The first step is to remove the springs and have them checked by your Land Rover dealer or specialist, preferably against the correct colour coding type of replacement springs.

D. If the springs are okay and the clearance is still less than the above figure, Land Rover recommend that you renew the self-levelling unit, as follows:
i) Place 650kg (1143lb) of weights over the rear load area of the vehicle and leave it to settle for at least half an hour.
ii) Place a weight (such as a person!) weighing around 75kg (165lb) in the driving seat and check the bump-stop clearance as described above.
iii) Drive the vehicle for 3 miles (5km) over some bumpy roads and then bring the vehicle to a halt very gently and gradually so that you don't disturb the vehicle loading.
iv) With the weight (or person) placed in the driver's seat as before, check the bump-stop clearance again. It should be 45mm (1.75in) minimum.
v) Now you should subtract this latest measurement from the one you took just before driving the vehicle and if the change in clearance is 10mm (0.4in) or more, the levelling unit is working satisfactorily. If not, the self-levelling unit will need to be replaced. We recommend that before doing so, you have your Land Rover dealer or specialist double-check for you – it could be an expensive mistake to make!

SAFETY NOTE: The self-levelling unit contains gas under pressure and must not under any circumstances be dismantled and the casing screws should not be removed. The unit cannot be repaired but it can be replaced, as follows:

A. Raise the rear of the vehicle off the ground, chock both front wheels in front and behind and support the vehicle on axle stands placed under the chassis. Use a trolley jack to support the weight of the axle.
B. Disconnect the ends of the top-links (8) at the pivot brackets on the chassis (6).
C. Ease up the lower gaiter (5) on the levelling unit and use thin-jawed

spanners to unscrew the lower balljoint at the pushrod.
D. Disconnect the webbing strap (3) from the chassis.
E. The self-levelling unit (3) can now be removed complete with its bracket (4) once the four nuts holding the top bracket to the chassis have been removed.
F. The lower balljoint can be unscrewed from the pivot bracket . . .
G. . . . and the top balljoint (4) unscrewed from its bracket.
H. If the balljoints are worn, they will have to be renewed, and you should also check the condition of the gaiters.
I. On reassembling the balljoints, pack the joints with suitable grease.
J. Reassembly is the reverse of the removal procedure, but remember that the ballpin threads should be cleaned and then used with thread locker.
K. The levelling unit complete with chassis bracket should be secured to the chassis with the four nuts tightened to 47Nm (35lbf/ft).
L. When fitting the upper links (8) to the pivot bracket (6), fit the two bolts and nuts but do not tighten until the vehicle has been lowered to the ground and allowed to settle under its own weight. You can now tighten the two bolts and nuts fixing the upper links to the pivot bracket, to the correct torque.

FRONT AND REAR BUMP-STOPS

Each of the four bump-stops – there is one mounted above each end of each axle – is held in place with nuts, washers and bolts. The biggest difficulty is likely to arise from being able to remove corroded nuts and bolts. If this is the case, you may be well-advised to use a nut splitter or, with a hacksaw, cut through the nut, from top to bottom, fitting a new nut and bolt with the new bump-stop.

STEERING –
INTRODUCTION

▲ S1. It helps to understand how the Land Rover's steering system works! This engine bay, after Liveridge have whipped the engine out, helps you to see the components. The steering column with its two universal joints (A) runs from the bulkhead to the steering box (B). The drop arm (C) connects to the cross rod (D) which joins to the left-hand steering arm on the front of the hub. The track rod (E) connects the steering arms on the rear of the hubs on both wheels.

▲ S2. The balljoint on the end of the cross rod (front of left wheel) . . .

▲ S3. . . . and the track rod balljoint at the rear of the same wheel.

▲ S4. The opposite end of the track rod at the back of the right wheel.

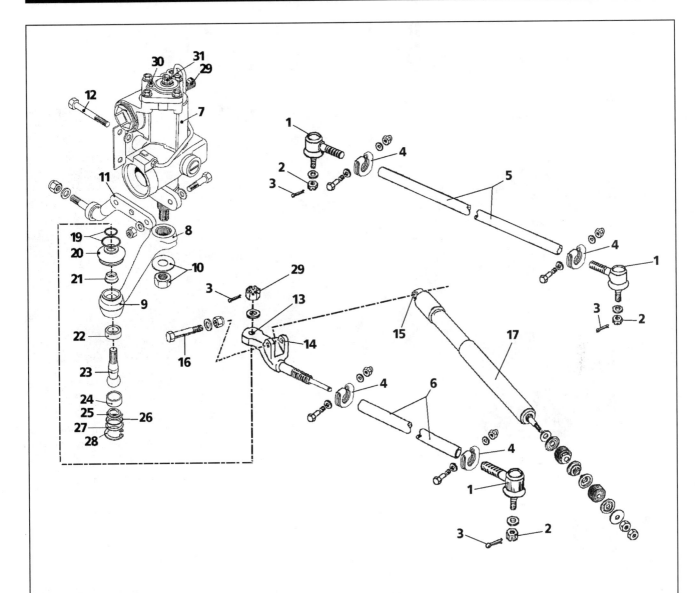

1. Balljoints/track rod ends
2. Balljoint castle-nuts
3. Split pins
4. Clamp (some types have two through-bolts)
5. Track rod
6. Cross rod
7. Steering box
   (Adwest power steering type shown –
   others similar)
8. Drop arm
9. Balljoint eye
10. Plain nut and tab-washer
11. Tie-bar
12. Mounting bolt
13. Eye for mounting to drop arm balljoint

14. Bracket for fitting steering damper
15. Steering damper mounting eye
16. Steering damper mounting bolt, nut and lock-washer
17. Steering damper
18. Drop arm balljoint castle-nut
19. Spring rings
20. Rubber cover
21. Retainer
22. Outer socket
23. Ballpin
24. Inner socket
25. Spring
26. O-ring
27. Cover plate
28. Circlip

▲ S5. These are the components of the steering system and will be referred to in each relevant section. (Illustration © Lindsay Porter)

TRACK ROD AND CROSS ROD BALLJOINT REPLACEMENT

Refer to the illustration S5.

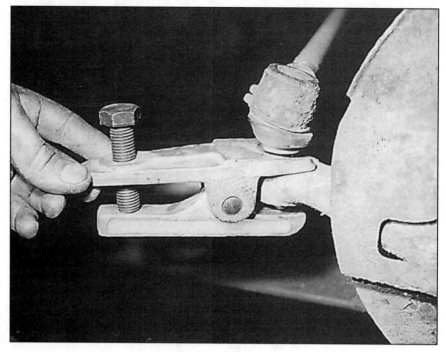

▲ BJ3. Use a balljoint separator to free the balljoint. This is a Sykes-Pickavant tool, available from most auto-accessory stores. Be sure to buy one large enough!

If the taper on the balljoint is particularly stubborn, use a pair of hammers, hit simultaneously on each side of the eye. You stand a strong chance of splitting the balljoint rubber, but if you intend replacing it in any case, that doesn't matter.

▼ BJ4. Each track rod has a left-handed and a right-handed thread balljoint for adjustment to the rod. Make sure you're getting the right one started and make sure the slot in the track rod tube is clear as there is a clamp that goes on to squash the rod tight against the shoulder of the track rod joint. Ensure it is a good fit and use lots of grease. The clip is not shown in the photograph.

▲ BJ1. First, straighten out the split-pin (3) and pull it out of the castle-nut (2) with a pair of pliers.

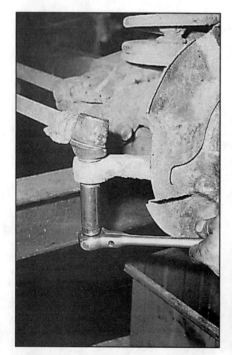

▲ BJ2. Unscrew the castle-nut and remove the washer from beneath it.

▲ BJ5. The steering tube clamp and bolt are seen here, ready to go on to the steering tube. Later models have double clamps, with double bolts, as seen in S2.

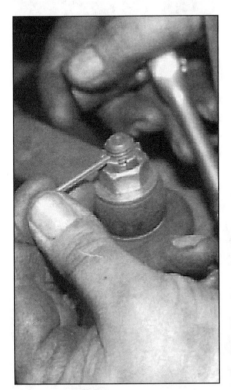

▲ BJ6. A NEW split-pin goes into the castle-nut – a small but vital point to remember. Some non-original track rod ends use self-locking nuts but many experts prefer the split-pin arrangement.

A. Undo the clamp bolt holding the clamp (4) in place . . .
B. . . . and unscrew the balljoint (1) from the track-rod or cross-rod, counting the *exact* number of turns before the balljoint comes free. Write down the number of times so that you won't forget it later!
C. Screw in the replacement balljoint and refit as a reversal of the removal procedure, but note the following important points:
i) The angle of the balljoint must be turned so that the threaded pin, going into the eye, is centralised in the balljoint and is not tipping to one side or the other, otherwise it will wear out quickly.
ii) Be sure to screw the replacement balljoint in by exactly the same number of turns as it took to remove the old one.
iii) Be sure to have the track checked by a garage with track setting equipment before using the vehicle again on the road (other than driving it to the garage) otherwise the steering could be dangerous in use and you could suffer from rapid tyre wear.

STEERING DAMPER REMOVAL AND REPLACEMENT

A. The steering damper (17) is quite simple to remove, by first removing the nut and lock-nut, the washers and bushes from the chassis mounting . . .
B. . . . then taking out the retaining bolt (16) from where the eye on the damper (15) fits into the bracket (14) on the end of the cross rod. When removing the damper, be sure to retrieve all of the nuts, washers and bushes in the correct order. It's a good idea to fit them to the pin on the end of the damper, temporarily, so that their order doesn't become confused.

▼ SDR1. The steering damper locates on the chassis at one end, and on the steering cross-rod, near the steering box at the other. Refer to the illustration S5.

DROP ARM BALLJOINT OVERHAUL

Refer to the illustration S5.

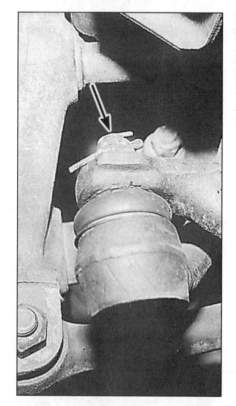

A. ▲ *DAB1. Take out the split pin (3) and remove the castle-nut (29) from the top (arrowed) of the drop arm balljoint (23).*

B. Use a balljoint separator, as described for track rod and cross rod balljoints, to free the drag link (13) from the drop arm (9).

C. Knock back the tab on the lock-washer and remove the drop arm retaining nut. Make an alignment mark on the bottom of the splined shaft, and on the drop arm (8), so that the drop arm can be replaced in exactly the same location. Pull the drop arm off the splines on the bottom of the steering box.

D. You will now have the drop arm off the vehicle, complete with the balljoint mounted in it. Clean it all off ready for dismantling. Take off the spring rings (19) and lever off the dust cover (20).

E. ▲ *DAB2. You now have to compress the cover plate (27) with a clamp and remove the circlip (28) from the underside of the balljoint (9).*

SAFETY NOTE: It is important that the cover plate is compressed, otherwise as the circlip is removed the force of the spring beneath could cause injury.

F. You can now remove the spring (25), socket (24) and O-ring (26).

G. Use a soft-faced mallet to tap the balljoint (23) out of the drop arm.

H. You can now drive the cup socket (22) from the housing but note that you may have to heat the housing in boiling water to expand it before the housing will come out.

▲ *DAB4. Note the following important points:*

i) When refitting the spring, the small diameter must be towards the ball.

ii) When refitting the circlip, you will have to compress the cover plate with a clamp.

iii) When refitting the components to the vehicle, use new lock-washers, lock-nuts and split pins, as appropriate.

I. ▼ *DAB3. The overhaul kit will include a new ballpin and sockets, and all of the other minor components which you removed from the drop arm. After cleaning out all the old grease from the socket, fit the components in the reverse order of removal but pack the inside of the socket with grease after fitting the cup socket.*

STEERING BOX ADJUSTMENT

A small amount of adjustment can be made to the steering box to compensate for wear. However, the problem is that most wear takes place in the straight-ahead position with very little wear at the outer 'edges'. Therefore, when you adjust out the wear in the straight-ahead position, you are likely to end up with stiff steering the more you turn the wheel – an extremely dangerous condition if the steering is reluctant to self-centre, or even jams(!) – when turning a corner. So, take very great care to check the steering very carefully at the two locks before driving the vehicle on the road, and if in doubt have a specialist carry out this work for you.

It is MOST IMPORTANT that there is no free-play in any of the joints in the steering system before attempting to adjust the steering box. Wear is more likely to take place in steering joints than in the box itself, so check these first!

Raise the front of the vehicle off the ground and chock the rear wheels in front and behind. Gently rock the steering wheel at the straight-ahead position and feel the amount of free-play in the steering wheel. This should not be more than 1/8in (9.5mm) at the rim of the steering wheel.

However, you must now check that there is no tightness whatsoever in the steering when it is turned from lock to lock. If it is, you will have to compromise by backing off the adjuster screw, because the first priority is not to have stiff steering! This is so, even if you have too much free-play in the steering wheel. If the problem cannot be overcome through adjustment, and if you have checked that there are no loose or worn joints in the steering system, have a specialist check the system for you and, if necessary, renew the steering box.

When the free-play has been satisfactorily adjusted, re-tighten the lock-nut and check once again that there is no excessive tightness at either lock. As a final check, take the vehicle to a safe, open space, such as a deserted car

▲ *SBA1. If necessary, have an assistant slacken the (outer) lock-nut on the adjuster on the top of the steering box and, while continuing to rock the steering wheel, have the (inner) adjuster screw gradually tightened until the free-play in the rim of the steering wheel is no more than the prescribed amount.*

park and drive the vehicle slowly, turning from lock to lock. The steering should self-centre; in other words, it must be free enough to return to the straight-ahead position without any stiffness and of its own volition.

STEERING COLUMN UNIVERSAL JOINTS

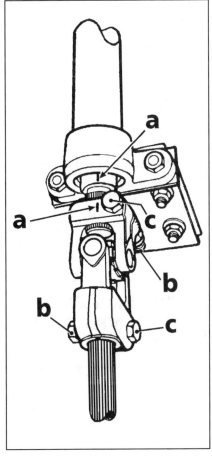

▲ *SCU2. Use typists' correction fluid or something similar to mark the position of the top universal joint (a) relative to the upper steering column (a). Do the same on all UJs to be removed.*
(Illustration © Lindsay Porter)

▼ *SCU1. The two steering column universal joints (UJs) (A) are both in the engine bay, on the intermediate shaft, which also includes the collapsible joint (B).*

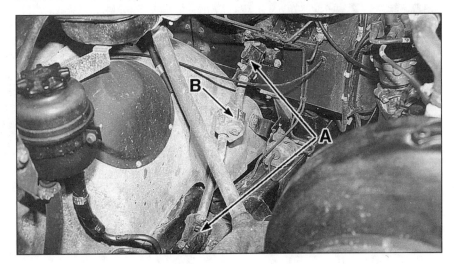

▶ *SCU3. Take off the lock-nuts (30) and remove the clamp bolts from the top universal joint (26). Also, remove the lower bolt from the bottom universal joint and slacken the other bolt. You can now remove the intermediate shaft complete with UJs. If there is free-play in a UJ or roughness in its movement, you will have to fit a replacement.*
(Illustration courtesy Land Rover)

When fitting a universal joint, make sure that the upper column, intermediate shaft and steering box pinion are all aligned as when they were dismantled.

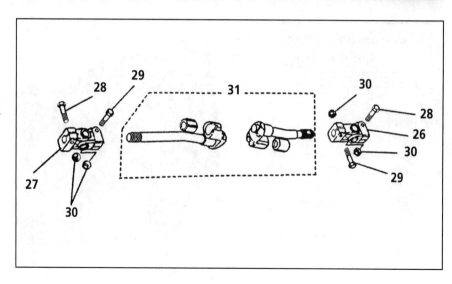

STEERING WHEEL REMOVAL AND REFITTING

With the ignition key removed, turn the steering wheel so that the steering lock is engaged. This is so that the steering column will be locked in the same position when you come to refit the steering wheel later.

Expose the steering wheel retaining nut by removing the centre cover. (NB: NOT vehicles with an air bag.)

LATER MODELS

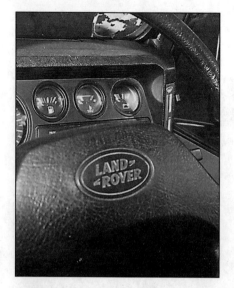

▲ *SWR1. Carefully lever the badge out from the centre of the wheel.*

EARLY MODELS

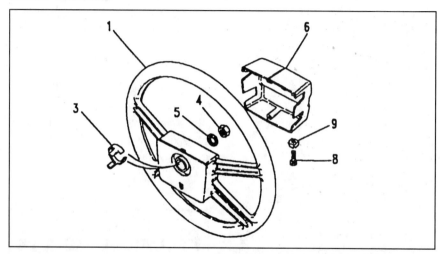

▲ *SWR2. Take out the retaining screw (8) and lift off the trim cover (6).*
(Illustration courtesy Land Rover)

On all vehicles, remove the steering wheel retaining nut (4) and washer (5), and mark the position of the steering wheel on the shaft so that it can be replaced in the same position and lift off the steering wheel.

If, as is likely, the wheel sticks on the splines, put the retaining nut back on by no more than one turn, pull hard towards you on the steering wheel, or hit the back of the rim with your hands. The retaining nut will stop the wheel from flying off into your face!

When refitting, note the following points:

i) Before refitting the wheel, make sure that the indicator cancelling ring (3) is in good condition – if not, replace it. Turn the ring so that the slots are vertical and the lug with the arrow points to the left, in the direction of the indicator switch.

ii) Make sure that the finisher attachment lug is at the bottom of the steering wheel when refitting it (early models) and make sure that the indicator cancelling forks are located properly in the cancelling ring slots.

iii) With the steering wheel back in place, and the shake-proof washer underneath the retaining nut, tighten the nut to the correct torque and refit the finisher.

STEERING COLUMN BEARING REPLACEMENT

A. Take off the circlip (d) from the lower end of the steering column and drift out the inner shaft (e) downwards, working from the top end of the column, complete with its lower bearing (b).

B. Drift out the roll-pin (f) from the bearing retaining collar (g) . . .

C. . . . and carefully tap the bearing (b) and collar (g) from the lower end of the inner shaft.

D. Remove the needle bearing (a) from the top end of the outer column.

E. Fit new bearings and refit the components in the reverse of the removal sequence but make sure that the new bearing at the top end of the outer column is fitted to a depth of 10mm from the end of the column, as shown.

STEERING LOCK-STOP ADJUSTMENT

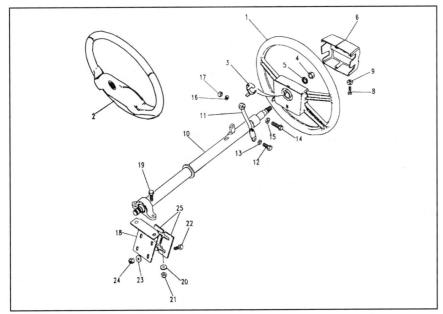

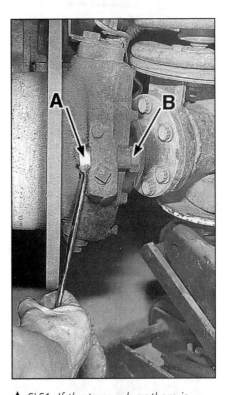

▲ *SLS1. If the tyres rub or there is insufficient lock on one side or the other, the steering lock in each direction is adjusted by slackening the lock-nut (A) and adjusting the position of this stop-bolt (B), before re-tightening the lock-nut. Simple but effective, in the Land Rover tradition!*

▲ *SCB1. If you have a lot of up and down play in the top of the steering column start by disconnecting/checking the upper steering column clamp (18) and checking that the rubber seal (25) beneath is intact. If the mounting is okay, and you need to replace the bearings, start by disconnecting the intermediate shaft and remove the steering wheel, as described in earlier sections. Take off the steering column shroud and disconnect all the electrical wiring from the switchgear. Disconnect the column from its lower bracket by taking out the mounting bolts (19) and disconnect from the upper brackets (11). Remove the column. (Illustration courtesy Land Rover)*

▶ *SCB2. Needle roller bearings are fitted to the top (a) and bottom (b) of the steering column (c) and if they are very badly worn, these bearings could break up and need replacement. If so, proceed as follows: (Illustration © Lindsay Porter)*

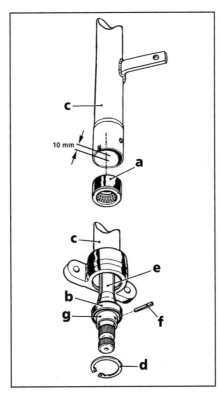

STEERING BOX REPLACEMENT

Refer to the illustration S5. (Page 171)

A. If the vehicle is fitted with power steering, clamp both hoses (in the flexible section!) near the steering box, so that a minimal amount of fluid is lost. Be prepared for the fluid that will be spilled and remove the feed and return pipes from the steering box.
B. On all models, disconnect the steering drop arm from the steering box and from the cross rod, as described in the section 'Track Rod and Cross Rod Ball Joint Replacement'.
C. From inside the engine bay, use typists' correction fluid to make an alignment mark between the universal joint on the intermediate steering column and the steering box pinion shaft (29). Take off the nut and pull out the clamp bolt which fix the UJ to the pinion.
D. Remove the nuts, bolts and washers holding the steering box tie-bar (11) to the steering box, and slacken (but do not remove) the lock-nut holding the tie-bar to its mounting.

E. ▲ SBR1. Remove the four mounting bolts (12) and the steering box can now be lifted away.

F. When refitting a steering box, reassembly is the reverse of the removal sequence but remember to use all new lock-nuts and also remember to correctly align the steering column UJ with the splined pinion on the steering box, using the marks you made when dismantling.
G. On vehicles with power steering, you will have to bleed the hydraulic system as described in a later section.

BLEEDING THE POWER STEERING SYSTEM

▲ BPS2. Push a length of clear plastic pipe onto the bleed nipple (see arrow) on top of the steering box, allowing it to drain excess fluid into a jar. Slacken the bleed screw and watch until a steady flow of fluid, free from air bubbles, comes out of the bleed screw, while your assistant tops up the reservoir as necessary.

Turn the steering to full left-lock, then full right-lock, holding it in each position from five to ten seconds. It is MOST IMPORTANT that the steering is not held at full-lock for more than 30 seconds at a time because otherwise the hydraulic system could be damaged.

Now check that there are no leaks anywhere in the hydraulic system and if all is clear, slacken the bleed screw once more to ensure that no more air will come out of the system. Remember to finish off by topping up the hydraulic fluid to the correct level.

▲ BPS1. Top-up the fluid reservoir to the MAXIMUM mark, have an assistant run the engine and be prepared to add more fluid very quickly if the level drops as the engine starts up. Once the level stabilises, turn the front wheels to the straight-ahead position. Now leave the engine running until it reaches its normal running temperature, allow it to run on tick-over and do not turn the steering.

POWER STEERING PUMP REPLACEMENT

▶ *PSP1. From beneath the vehicle, slacken the two adjustment clamp bolts and the pivot bolt (but do not remove them), release the tension from the belt and remove it. This is the type fitted with a supplementary tensioner pulley (3).*

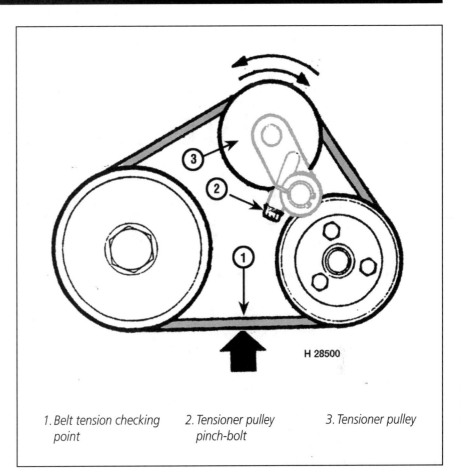

H 28500

1. Belt tension checking point
2. Tensioner pulley pinch-bolt
3. Tensioner pulley

▼ *PSP2. Clamp the flexible hydraulic hoses near to the pump (A) to minimise fluid loss but be prepared to catch such fluid as will be spilled. Disconnect the hydraulic hoses from the pump (B).*
(Illustration © Lindsay Porter)

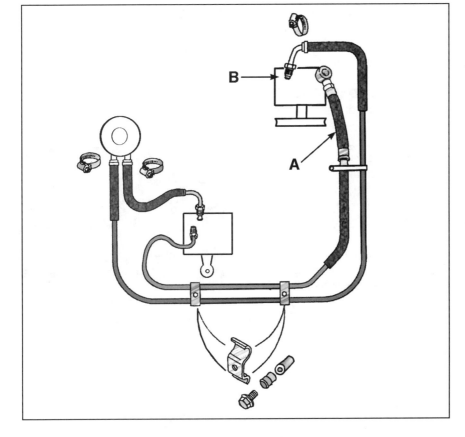

Now continue as follows:

A. Remove the tension/adjustment bolts slackened earlier and take off the pump complete with its adjustment plate and pulley.
B. Clean the surfaces then use paint, or something similar, to mark the position of the pump on the plate. Remove the four attachment bolts and separate the pump from the plate.
C. When refitting the pump, be sure to align the pump and adjustment plate as they were when previously fitted, and tension the drivebelt so that there is 12mm (½in) of deflection, using thumb pressure in the mid point of the belt run as shown in Figure PSP1.
It is IMPORTANT that you do not lever against the pump casing when tensioning the belt because this will easily damage and ruin the pump.
D. Top up and bleed the system.

Chapter 6

Electrical Equipment

In the old days, if a dynamo or a starter motor went wrong, most enthusiasts would have a go at repairing it themselves. Today, with solid-state circuitry, electronic modules and components that are difficult to obtain, things are not so clear cut. The easy solution is always to trade-in the faulty component for an exchange item, but that approach can also have its drawbacks. For one thing, there is a tendency for people to assume that a major component has failed when in fact the fault is a much more minor one, and a good deal of money can be wasted in this way. For another thing, there are still a number of areas where the enthusiast can carry out repairs without writing off the whole component.

In other words, it isn't practicable to completely rebuild your own alternator or distributor (if for no other reason than the fact that you can't buy all of the parts you would need), but it is entirely feasible to change worn alternator brushes or free off a seized distributor mechanism and, in so doing, save yourself a whole lot of money!

ALTERNATOR CHECKS
Alternators can be checked for a number of faults but there are several precautions to be taken. It is essential that good electrical connections are maintained at all times, including those at the battery. You should never disconnect battery cables or break any connections in the alternator control or charging circuits while the engine is running otherwise the alternator may well be irreparably damaged.

Whenever a rapid charger is used on the battery, it must be disconnected from the vehicle so as not to damage the alternator.

Battery voltages apply to the alternator even though the ignition is switched off. It is essential that the battery is disconnected before carrying out any work on the alternator, and also before carrying out any arc or MIG welding on the vehicle.

ELECTRICAL CONNECTIONS
Apparent alternator faults may be caused by no more than poor electrical connections. Disconnect, clean up and remake all of the charging and control circuit electrical connections, including the earth straps where they fit to the vehicle's chassis.

IGNITION WARNING LIGHT
Because the ignition warning light is connected in series with the alternator circuit, bulb failure will prevent the alternator from charging. DON'T replace the alternator, just for the price of a replacement bulb! Check the bulb first!

ON CHARGE!

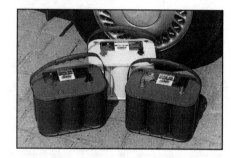

BAT1. These are quite different from conventional batteries. The plates are coiled and the acid is sealed-in gel. As a result, an Optima battery is smaller, more powerful and can be recharged in an hour without damaging it. It can be mounted at any angle – even upside down! Well, you never know…

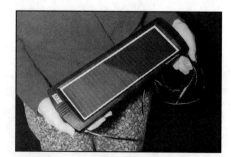

BAT2. When a car stands, its battery can quickly go flat which is irritating and shortens a battery's life. The Exide 12V Charger Battery Saver Plus provides a constant trickle charge from the sun – free and continuous!

LUCAS A115 AND A113 ALTERNATOR OVERHAUL

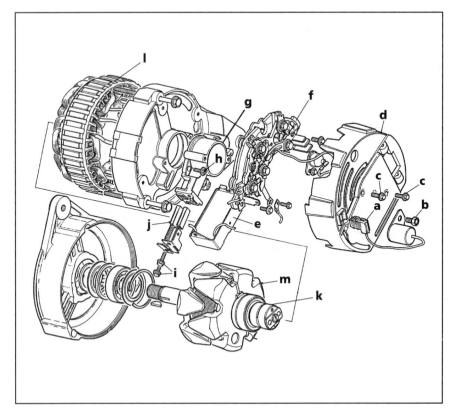

▲ AOA1. These are the components of these two alternator types. (Illustrations courtesy Lucas)

ELECTRICAL TESTS

ROTOR FIELD WINDING

▼ AOA2. Connect a battery operated ohmmeter between points A and B on the alternator slip ring. This enables you to check that there is continuity in the field winding (ie there are no breaks) and also that the resistance is about 3.2 ohms.

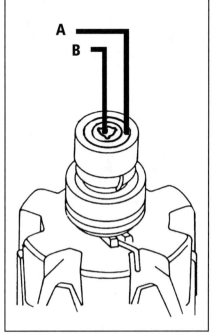

After disconnecting the battery, disconnect all of the electrical connections from the back of the alternator, making a careful note so that you know what goes where. Remove the alternator by slackening off all the pivot and tensioning nuts and bolts, taking the tension off the belt, removing the belt and then taking out all the bolts.

i) Pull out the wiring plug (a), take out the interference suppression capacitor screw (b) and remove the suppressor.
ii) Take out the two screws (c) and remove the cover (d).
iii) Make a careful written note of the positions of all the wires to the regulator (e), the rectifier (f) and the brush box components (g).
iv) Disconnect the wires from the rectifier and the regulator, then take out the

screws holding the regulator in place and remove it.
Note that one of the brush mounting plates is also held in position by one of the screws.
v) The two screws (h) holding the brush box in place can be taken out and the brush box (g) removed.
vi) Take out the two screws (i) and lift out the brush set from the brushes box. If the carbon part of a brush is less than 5mm (0.20in), they should be renewed.
vii) The slip rings, on which the brushes bear, can be wiped clean with a spot of solvent on a rag. If they are very heavily covered in deposits, use very fine glass paper to clean them before wiping clean with solvent.
viii) When reassembling the components, make absolutely sure that the brushes can move freely in the brush box.

STATOR WINDINGS

Because of the very low resistance of the stator windings, specialist equipment is needed to check them. However, if you see obvious signs of the varnish on the stator windings (see illustration AOA1, part l) the stator assembly is ripe for renewal – and this is probably a good indicator that you need an exchange alternator.

BEARINGS

If there are any signs of rubbing between the rotor (m) and the stator windings (l), it is fairly certain that the bearings are worn and you will need an exchange overhauled alternator.

No other checks can be carried out on the alternator without specialist equipment.

LUCAS A127 ALTERNATOR OVERHAUL

▶ *AOB1. Remove the alternator as described in the previous section. These are the component parts of a typical A127 alternator.*
(Illustrations courtesy Lucas)

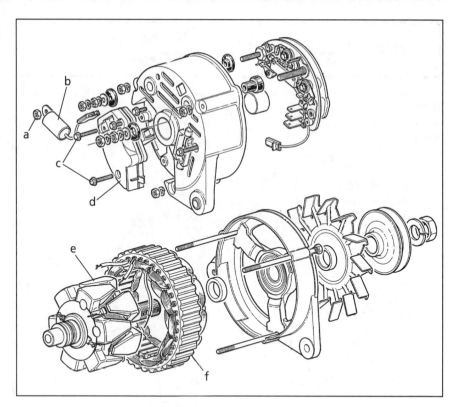

i) Remove the nuts and washers (a) holding the suppressors (b) – there are two rectangular units fitted to some models – and then remove the suppressors after pulling the electrical plugs out of their sockets in the back of the alternator.

ii) Remove the three bolts (c) holding the voltage regulator/brush box assembly (d) to the back of the alternator, tip the outside edge of the assembly upwards and remove it.

▼ *AOB2. You will now be able to see the protrusion of the brushes (A) which should be 5mm (0.20in) or more. If not, the brushes by themselves cannot be changed and the voltage regulator/brush box assembly must be replaced as a unit. Clean up the slip rings as described in the previous section.*

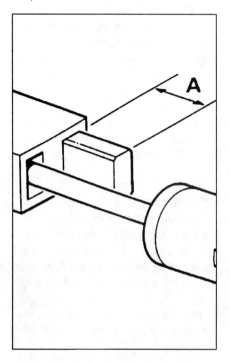

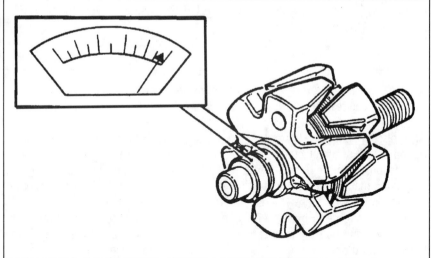

ROTOR FIELD WINDINGS

▲ *AOB3. Connect a battery-operated ohmmeter to the slip rings as shown. If there is no reading, there is a break in the wiring. You can also check for excessive resistance – you should obtain a reading of 3.2 ohms.*

STATOR WINDINGS

See illustration AOB1, part f. If the stator windings are burned or damaged, the stator will need to be replaced, which is usually a sure sign that the alternator should be exchanged for an overhauled replacement.

BEARINGS

If there are any signs of rubbing between the rotor (e) and the stator windings (f), it is fairly certain that the bearings are worn and you will need an exchange overhauled alternator.

No other checks can be carried out on the alternator without specialist knowledge or equipment.

STARTER MOTORS

There are many checks you can carry out to a starter motor but the great majority of starter motor 'faults' fall into one of three categories:

A. Battery condition, leads and connections – ie, not starter motor faults at all! Very many starter motors are replaced every year even though the fault lies elsewhere. Check all the main terminals first, especially those at the battery and the main cables leading to earth. Check also that the earth from the engine to the chassis is sound and then check all the connections on the starter motor itself.

B. Solenoid faults. The simplest way to find out if the solenoid is working is to listen to it while an assistant operates the starter switch. If it is working, you should be able to here the click of the contacts closing. If you can't, it may be a faulty solenoid – but do check the wiring, as mentioned above.

C. Worn brushes. For the starter motor to be faulty because of worn

brushes, the brush length will have to be considerably less than the minimum shown in the specifications. Don't just replace the old brushes on a whim; a set of brushes will typically cost around one fifth the price of an exchange starter motor so only replace them if you think it will really help!

If the starter motor is faulty in any other way, you are probably better off cutting your losses and going for an exchange starter motor. Replacement bush sets are available and replacement is not too difficult (except on the V8 engine fitted with the Lucas M78R starter motor and the diesel engine Lucas 2M113 starter motor) so we do include it here. In practice, if the bushes are worn, the rest of the starter motor may also be badly worn.

FOUR-CYLINDER PETROL ENGINE LUCAS 2M100 STARTER MOTOR

SOLENOID REMOVAL

▼ *SMO1. Take off the nut (a) and spring washer and remove the connecting link that leads to the solenoid 'STA' terminal. Take out the nuts and bolts (b) holding the solenoid (c) to the end bracket (d). Take off the solenoid return spring from the lever (e) and lift the solenoid away. (Illustration, courtesy Lucas)*

BRUSHES REPLACEMENT

Take off the end cap seal (f) and use a screwdriver to lever away the clip-ring (g) or, if necessary, cut through it carefully with a sharp cold chisel. Unscrew the through bolts (h) and take off the end cover (i). Remember to take off the thrust washer from the end of the armature shaft after the end cover has been lifted away. With the end cover lifted away, slide the brushes (j) from their retainers (k). If the brushes are worn down to 9.5mm (⅜in) or less they should be renewed.

BEARING BUSHES

If replacement bushes are available, carefully drift out the old bushes (l) and press in the new replacements. You could use each of the old bushes, with a bolt running through its centre and a nut and washer on the other side of the end plate, to pull the new bush squarely into place.

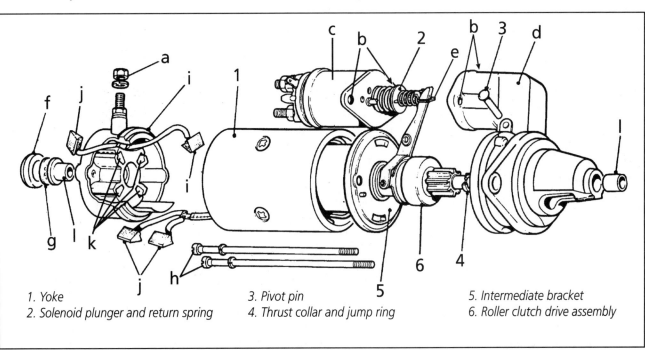

1. Yoke
2. Solenoid plunger and return spring
3. Pivot pin
4. Thrust collar and jump ring
5. Intermediate bracket
6. Roller clutch drive assembly

DIESEL ENGINE STARTER MOTOR LUCAS 2M113

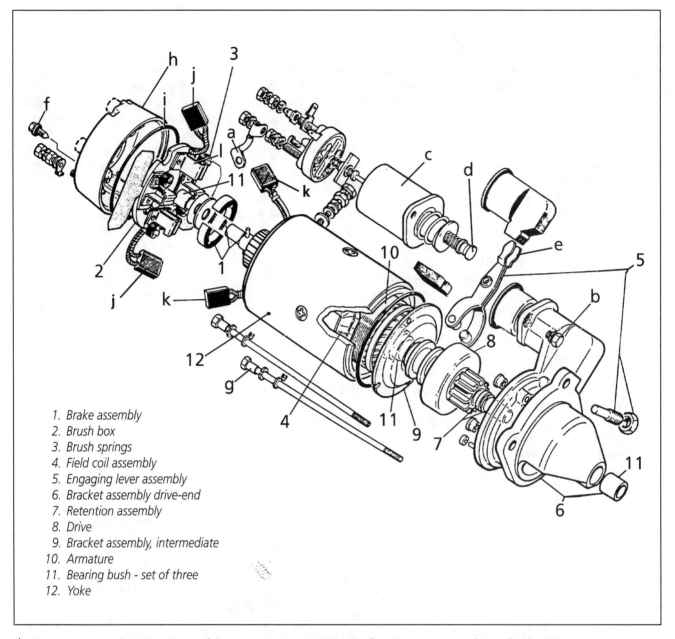

1. Brake assembly
2. Brush box
3. Brush springs
4. Field coil assembly
5. Engaging lever assembly
6. Bracket assembly drive-end
7. Retention assembly
8. Drive
9. Bracket assembly, intermediate
10. Armature
11. Bearing bush - set of three
12. Yoke

▲ SM02. These are the components of the Lucas 2M113 starter motor fitted to some 90 and 110 diesel engines. (Illustration courtesy Lucas)

SOLENOID REMOVAL

Disconnect the link to the starter motor (a), then take out the two hex-head screws (b) and withdraw the solenoid (c), lifting the front end of the plunger (d) to release it from the top of the engagement lever (e).

BRUSH REPLACEMENT

Take out the two brush box securing screws (f) and the two long through

bolts (g). The end plate (h) and seal (i) – if fitted – can now be removed. The brushes can now be seen and should be removed from under their spring clips. If the brushes have worn down to 8mm (⁵⁄₁₆in) or less, they should be replaced.

Wedge the earth brushes (j) in the open position in their housings (l) using the brush spring. Fit the field coil brushes (k) into position in the brush

box as it is offered back up into position. Now make sure that the brushes move freely in their holders. The rest of the reassembly process is the reverse of dismantling.

BEARING BUSHES

There are three bushes and replacement of the centre bush involves rather more dismantling on this type if the centre bearing is to be replaced.

TURBO DIESEL ENGINE (NOT 300 TDI) PARIS RHONE STARTER MOTOR

1. Solenoid
2. Solenoid plunger and spring
3. Drive-end bracket and bush
4. Reduction gear pinion
5. Reduction gear
6. Rubber pad
7. O-ring seal
8. Lever

9. Clutch-drive and pinion assembly
10. Rubber pad
11. Armature
12. Yoke
13. Roller bearing
14. Through-studs
15. Brush plate
16. Field coil brushes
17. Armature brushes

18. Brush plate cover
19. Reduction gear housing
20. Socket-headed screw
21. Terminal strap
22. Yoke location key

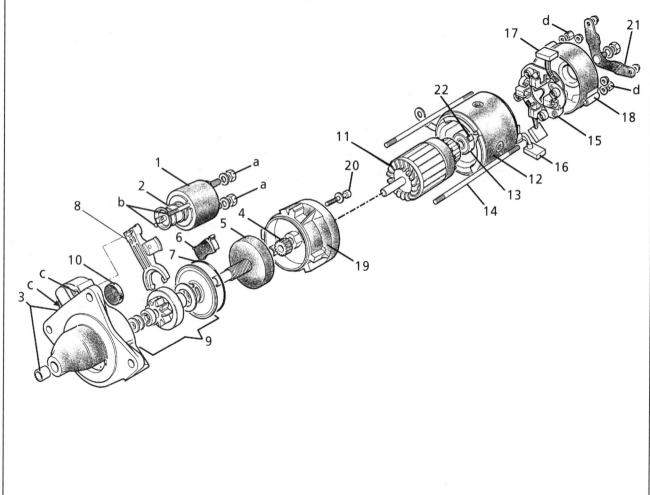

▲ SMO3. These are the components of the Paris Rhone starter motor. (Illustration © Lindsay Porter)

SOLENOID REMOVAL

Remove the lead which goes from the solenoid wiring connection (a) to the starter motor. Take off the two nuts from the mounting bolts (b) at position (c), and lift away the solenoid (1).

BRUSH REPLACEMENT

Take off the terminal strap (21), remove the two nuts (d) on the end of the through studs (14) and take off the brush plate cover (18). No information is available from Land Rover regarding the minimum length of the brushes. Refitting the brush box must be carried out in exactly the same sequence as described for the Lucas 2M113 starter motor. See previous section.

V8 ENGINE LUCAS M78R STARTER MOTOR

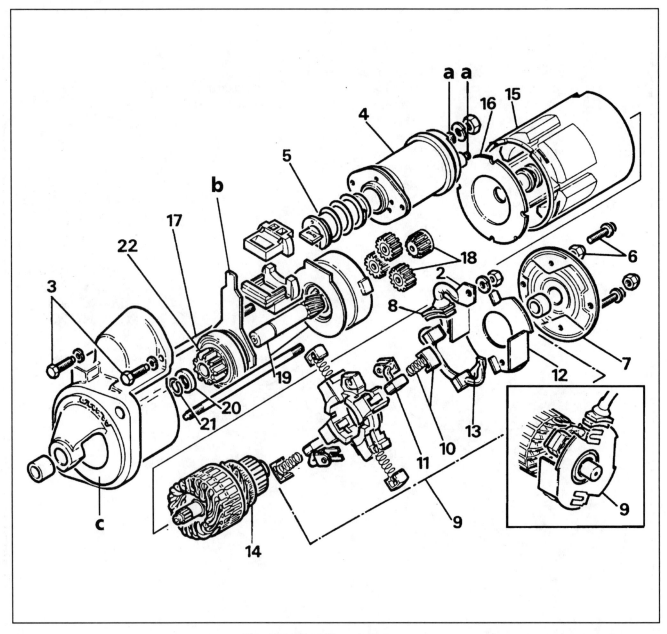

▲ SMO4. These are the components of the Lucas M78R starter motor. Its construction is rather more complex than the other starter motors featured here although brush replacement is, if anything, more straightforward. (Illustration courtesy Lucas)

SOLENOID REMOVAL
Take off the lead from the solenoid terminals (a) to the starter motor. Remove the fixing screws and washers (3) take away the solenoid (4), lifting and removing the solenoid plunger (5) from the lever (b).

BRUSHES REPLACEMENT
Remove the two screws and nuts (6) and take off the commutator end bracket (7). Pull out the grommet (8) holding the solenoid lead (2) in place and lift the brush box assembly (9) away.

To dismantle the brushes, start by removing the springs (10), then unclip and remove the earth brushes (11). After taking off the insulating plate (12), you can remove the armature brushes (11) complete with their connecting strap (13). If the brushes have worn down to 3.5mm (0.138in) or less, they should be replaced.

New brushes can be fitted without the need for any soldering.

Reassembly is the reverse of removal but make sure that the springs and clips (10) are not fitted until the armature brushes (11) are in place on the armature.

BEARING BUSH REPLACEMENT
The rear bearing bush can be fitted very simply, as described previously. The front bush can only be replaced with the drive end bracket (c) removed.

V8 ENGINE LUCAS 3M100PE STARTER MOTOR

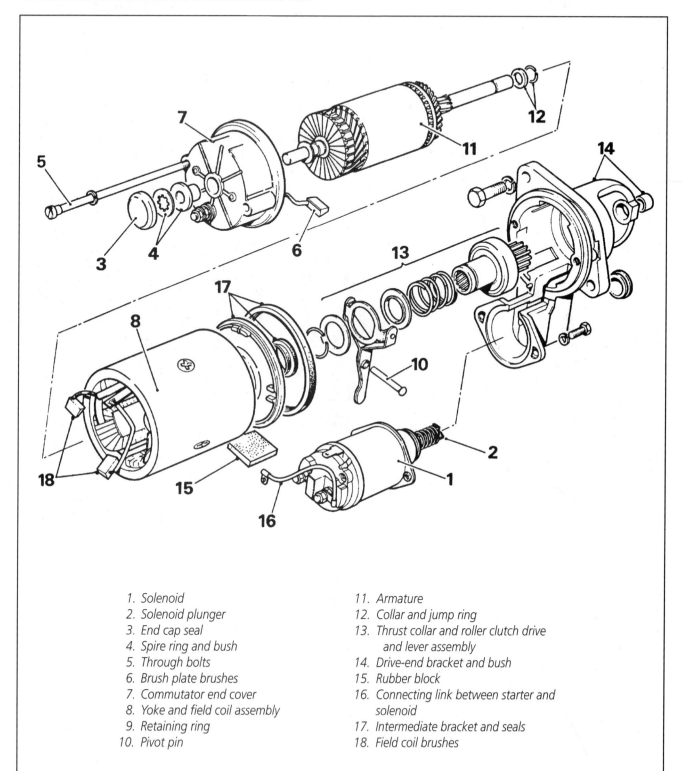

1. Solenoid
2. Solenoid plunger
3. End cap seal
4. Spire ring and bush
5. Through bolts
6. Brush plate brushes
7. Commutator end cover
8. Yoke and field coil assembly
9. Retaining ring
10. Pivot pin
11. Armature
12. Collar and jump ring
13. Thrust collar and roller clutch drive
   and lever assembly
14. Drive-end bracket and bush
15. Rubber block
16. Connecting link between starter and
   solenoid
17. Intermediate bracket and seals
18. Field coil brushes

▲ SM05. These are the components of the Lucas 3M100PE starter motor, which is essentially similar to the Lucas 2M100 unit described in an earlier section. If the brushes have worn down to 9.5mm (⅜in) or less, they should be replaced. (Illustration courtesy Lucas)

GLOW PLUG TESTING

When overhauling an engine, you will want to test the glow plugs and replace any that are not in perfect condition but faulty glow plugs will also lead to poor diesel engine starting and it is useful to know what to look for.

GLOW PLUGS OUT OF ENGINE

With the glow plugs unscrewed from the cylinder head, start by checking the glow plugs for their physical condition. If the tips have been burnt or eroded, the injectors should be checked for a bad injector spray pattern. If they are okay, hold the glow plug in a clamp or vice and apply a 12 volt current with jump leads from a 12 volt battery. If the glow plug is in good condition, it will start to glow red at the tip after about five seconds or so. If it starts glowing in the middle instead of the tip or if it takes much longer than five seconds to warm up, the glow plug is defective. Be sure to leave the glow plug for several minutes so that it cools down completely, before handling it. Do not apply current to the glow plug for more than about 20 seconds – especially if it fails to glow at all – because it is then probably faulty and there could be a short circuit. Do not apply 12 volts directly to the early series-wired glow plugs – see note below.

GLOW PLUGS IN VEHICLE

Early vehicles were fitted with glow plugs which were wired in series, which means that if one plug fails, the supply to all of the plugs will fail. It also means that if you apply 12 volts directly to one of these early series-wired glow plugs, it will burn out.

You can test the supply to the plugs by connecting a test light between the glow plug supply cable and a good earth on the bodywork or engine. With the 'ignition' turned on, the light should illuminate. You can test each individual glow plug by connecting a 12 volt test light in series with the glow plug, after first disconnecting it from its normal wiring connections. The connections would go:

12 volt feed to bulb; bulb to glow plug wiring connection; engine earth to battery earth. If the light illuminates, the plug is working. You may be able to rig up a 3 volt feed and a suitable bulb to test the early type of series-wired glow plug without burning it out.

If you still suspect glow plugs of inadequate performance, remove them from the vehicle and take them to a diesel engine specialist who will be able to test them properly and pronounce them well, ill or dead, at a very moderate charge.

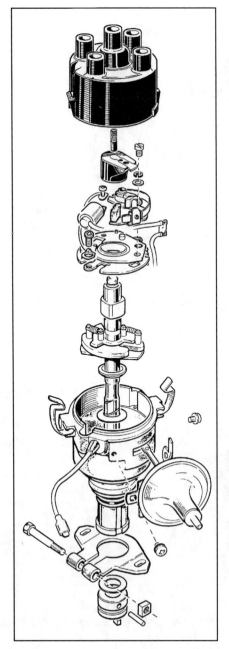

DISTRIBUTOR MAINTENANCE AND OVERHAUL

See the Safety chapter at the start of this book before carrying out any work on the ignition system.

Start off by removing the distributor from the vehicle – see Chapter 4 – and then tip and shake the distributor to see if there is any petrol slopping around in the vacuum unit. There should not be!

◀ *DMO1. This is a Lucas distributor fitted to the four-cylinder engines. It is typical of all the distributors fitted to 90, 110 and Defender Land Rovers. Although the Ducellier distributor which is also fitted to the four-cylinder engine, and the V8 engine's distributor are different in detail, their basic principles are exactly the same.*
(Illustration courtesy Lucas)

It is IMPORTANT to note that later electronic ignition distributors – ones which do not have a disc-shaped vacuum unit fitted to them – are not covered here and should not be stripped down or overhauled.

▶ *DMO2. The early Lucas electronic ignition distributor fitted to the V8 engines, can be checked in some respects, but not in others. Play in the rotor shaft bearings cannot be checked without removing the base plate assembly. It is* most important *that the electronic\pick-up components mounted on the base plate are not disassembled or opened up, for important health and safety reasons.*
(Illustration courtesy Lucas)

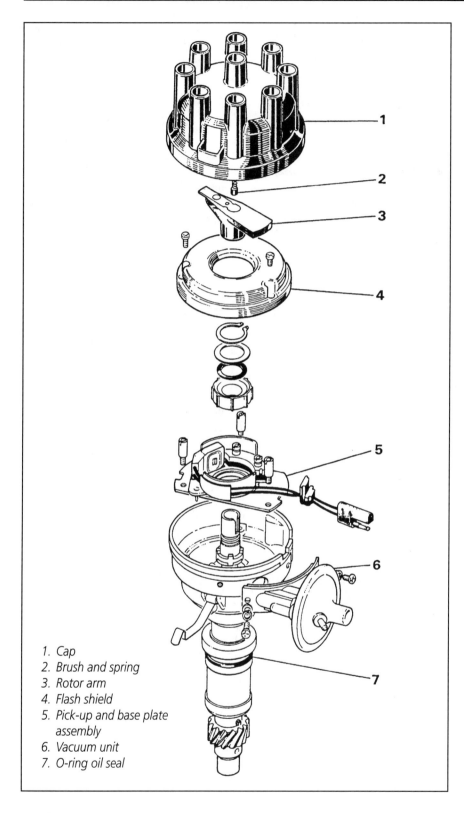

1. Cap
2. Brush and spring
3. Rotor arm
4. Flash shield
5. Pick-up and base plate assembly
6. Vacuum unit
7. O-ring oil seal

to a fluctuating dwell angle and poor engine inefficiency. Bearings cannot be fitted without specialist equipment (and cannot usually be purchased in any case) and such wear points to the need for an exchange replacement distributor. You might also find that a badly worn distributor lets your engine fail its annual emission tests.

B. Suck on the vacuum unit connection – the one that leads to the manifold – and you should be able to pull the distributor base plate around as you mimic the effect of the air depression in the manifold. When you let go, the base plate should return to its original position with a click. If it doesn't move, or if it sticks and is reluctant to return, you may find that the internal mechanism has seized through lack of lubrication. If, on the other hand, you find yourself against nothing, the vacuum unit will have ruptured internally and the only solution will be an exchange distributor. If the mechanism has seized, you may be lucky – see next check.

C. As well as the vacuum ignition advance system, which operated when you put your foot down hard, there is also a centrifugal advance which is operated by weights which fly out against the pressure of springs inside the distributor. The faster the engine goes, the more the weights are forced out and the more the ignition is advanced. The only way to check is to remove the distributor base plate and see if everything inside is nice and free. While you are in there, apply some lubrication to the springs and the pivots, as well as the pivot points for the vacuum advance mechanism.

It is a useful tip to squirt a *very* small amount of aerosol releasing fluid under the base plate, or to place a few drops of very light machine oil down the side of the rotor shaft, every time the engine is serviced.

The following checks can be carried out on most distributors:

A. With the body of the distributor held carefully but firmly in the vice (so as not to damage it) and the distributor cap and rotor arm removed, see if there is any movement at the top of the rotor shaft. If there is, the distributor bearings are worn and this will lead

HEADLIGHT REPLACEMENT

1988 MODEL YEAR ONWARDS

The plastic bezel has to be removed on these models, unlike the early models for which the instructions for removing the plastic bezel can be ignored.

1. Take out the screws and remove the side light lens . . .
2. . . . followed by the flasher lens.
3. Take out the three screws and detach the side light unit from the wing . . .
4. . . . and do the same for the indicator light unit.
5. Take out the two screws holding the plastic bezel to the wing and, with the two light units eased forwards as far as they will go, move the bezel to one side so that you can get at the headlight retaining screws.

EARLY MODELS

The plastic bezel is held in place only by the six screws which are taken out to allow the bezel to be removed.

ALL MODELS

6. Take out the three headlight rim screws and take off the rim.
7. Take out the light unit and remove the electrical connector from the rear.
8. The headlight bulb can now be accessed from underneath the rubber grommet, or the headlight backing components can be accessed from the vehicle.

HEADLIGHTS WITH REMOTE LEVELLING

An actuator is located behind the wing and the actuator arm passes through the wing and adjusts the headlight position. The end of the arm must be disconnected when dismantling the headlights. The actuator is connected via a loom to the headlight levelling switch mounted inside the vehicle.

DASHBOARD LIGHTS

In its typically thorough way, Land Rover ensure that warning lights and instrument lights can be replaced very easily.

IMPORTANT! Before attempting to replace any of the warning lights, disconnect the battery.

To replace warning lights, you simply take out the two screws and remove the warning light module from the front of the instrument panel. The plug connector is detached from the back of the module and this gives access to the warning light bulbs. Each bulb is twisted and then withdrawn from its socket.

The instrument panel is easily accessed after removing the four screws holding the panel in place, after which the panel is pulled forwards to give access to the bulb.

You may need to disconnect the drive cable from the back of the speedometer to allow you to pull the panel sufficiently far forwards.

WIPER MOTOR OVERHAUL

The wiper motor is a simple but effective mechanism which is very easily dismantled and checked. The drivegear needs to be properly lubricated and undamaged and the motor brushes need to be in a usable condition. The motor can only be dismantled once it has been removed from the vehicle.

▼ *WMO1. After removing the screws, the cover plate can be removed. Lever off the circlip (3) and washer which holds the connecting rod (4) in place. Take off the connecting rod and the washer from beneath it (5).*
(Illustration courtesy Lucas)

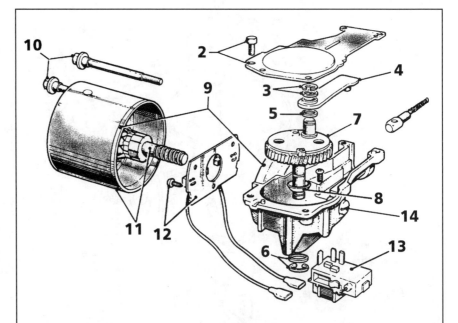

1. *Flexible drive*
2. *Gearbox cover*
3. *Connecting-rod retaining washer and circlip*
4. *Connecting-rod*
5. *Flat washer*
6. *Gear shaft retaining washer and circlip*
7. *Drive gear*
8. *Dished washer*
9. *Alignment marks – yoke to body*
10. *Yoke securing bolts*
11. *Armature and yoke*
12. *Brush gear assembly*
13. *Limit switch*
14. *Armature shaft adjuster screw*

Turn the unit over and take off the circlip and washer (6) from the gear shaft, then turn it back again and lift out the gear shaft and the dished washer (8).

Make alignment marks on the yoke and on the gear body (9) so that they can be reassembled in exactly the same location. Take out the yoke securing bolts (10) and remove the yoke and armature assembly. The screws holding the brush gear assembly (12) can be taken from the gear drive body.

Remove the brushes and if they are worn to 4.8mm (0.19in) or less, fit new brushes.

When reassembling the motor, be sure to thoroughly soak the yoke bearing felt washer with oil. When fitting the brushes, be sure to push the brushes apart so that they will fit over the armature. Reassemble the armature and yoke to the gearbox, using the alignment marks made earlier, and re-tighten the bolts. If a new armature has been fitted, slacken the thrust screw (14) before tightening the bolts.

Lubricate metal bearing surfaces in the conventional way, but be sure to only lubricate the gearwheel teeth, the armature shaft wormgear, the connecting rod and pin, cable rack and wheel box gearwheel with lubricant which is suitable for plastic. Land Rover recommend Ragosine Listate grease. If a new armature shaft has been fitted, hold the unit so that the armature shaft is in a vertical position with the adjuster screw (14) uppermost. Turn the adjuster screw inwards carefully until resistance is just felt, then unscrew it by a quarter of a turn.

Land Rover recommend that the motor should run (within one minute of being started from cold) at from 42 to 48rpm (low speed) and between 62 and 68rpm (high speed) although they do not state whether this is loaded or unloaded. Do not allow the windscreen wipers to rub across a dry screen.

WIRING TIPS

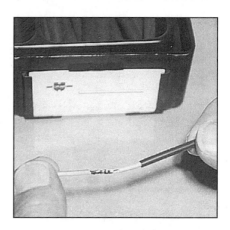

You must ALWAYS use the correct grade of wire for the application. Take a section of the piece you want to replace (or consult your Land Rover specialist) when buying replacement cable.

▶ *WT1. In addition, you should ALWAYS properly solder wiring joins. Insulation tape is not adequate. This is Wurth shrink-fit tube, which is pushed over the join . . .*

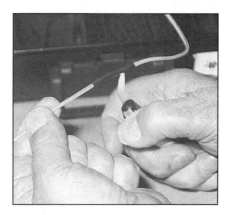

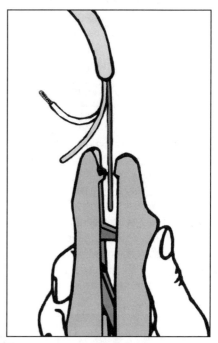

▲ *WT2. . . . and shrinks tightly in place when heated. Superb!*

▶ *WT3. For stripping wire, either use a purpose-made wire stripper which guarantees the result every time . . .* (Illustration courtesy Wurth)

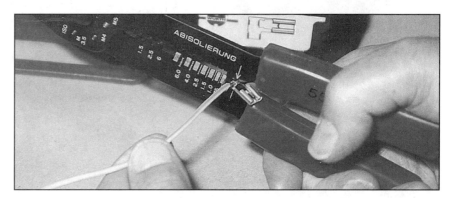

▲ *WT4. . . . or use a multi-purpose tool which is a touch slower to use but can cut wire or crimp connections, as shown here.*

Chapter 7

Interior

For details of door trim removal, see Chapter 3, Bodywork.

FRONT SEATS – REMOVAL AND REFIT

There are several types of front seat fitted to 90s, 110s and Defenders and although the removal procedures are similar, there are differences.

There is a very basic type of seat, very similar to those fitted to earlier Land Rovers. The seat base simply lifts up, after disengaging the leather strap at the front. The seat back is also held with a leather strap at the top and fixed at the hinge point with a pair of bolts.

▲ FSR1. The far more common – and more sophisticated type – has a seat base which pulls upwards off its clips. It is then a matter of removing the nuts and bolts holding the seat frame to the seat base in each of its four corners. With the seat cushion out of the way, the access plate from beneath the cushion is removed and you then have access to the separate nuts (when appropriate) inside the seat base. Some types have two bolts at the front location shown here.

REAR SEATS, FRONT FACING – REMOVAL AND REFIT

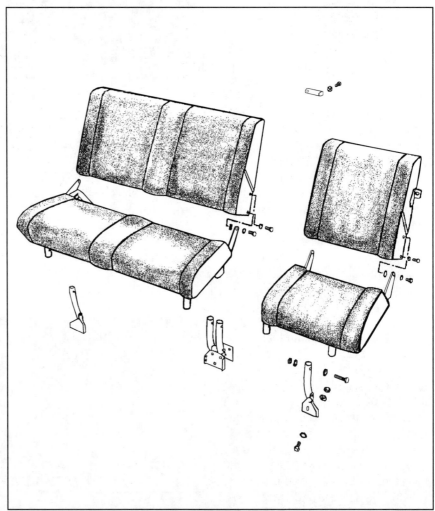

▲ RSF1. All rear seats are simple bolt-on, bolt-off affairs. With front-facing seats, the front brackets are bolted to the interior body, while the seat bases are bolted to the tops of the brackets. The hinged seat backs are held to brackets on the backs of the seat bases with nuts, bolts and washers. The removal and replacement sequence is all very straightforward, with no hidden tricks. (Illustration © Lindsay Porter)

REAR SEATS, SIDE FACING – REMOVAL AND REFIT

SEAT RE-COVERING

▶ RSS1. The basic type of side facing rear seat is bolted to the bodywork and is similar to the type of seat fitted to earlier Land Rovers. The seat base is fitted with bolts, nuts and washers which simply pass through the seat base, but it does need two people to lock the bolt heads while removing the nuts and washers from beneath the vehicle.

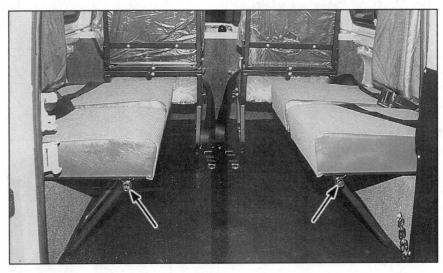

▲ RSS2. The individual type of inward facing rear seat has its own integral support bracket and these brackets do not have to be removed from the seat-pivot and mounting points shown here. The method of fixing the bases and rear supports is intrinsically similar to that of the type shown in illustration RRS1 – simple bolts, nuts and washers holding the frame and its mounting brackets to the vehicle's bodywork.

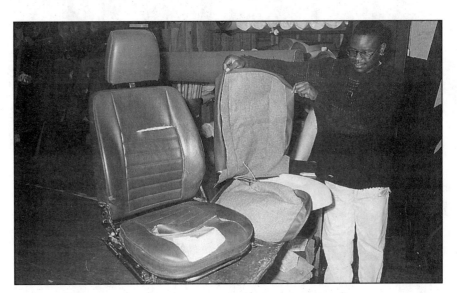

When it comes to re-covering your Land Rover's seats, there are two options (apart from the prohibitively expensive one of buying new replacement parts from Land Rover). You can re-cover your own seats as shown here, or you can take them to a specialist who will be able to undertake the job for you. Whichever route you choose, you will end up with seats that are as good as new and in whatever type of trim pattern you fancy. The re-covering process is demonstrated here by PWB Replacement Motor Parts Ltd, manufacturers of a huge range of top-quality Land Rover body, chassis and trim parts. As manufacturers, PWB don't supply private individuals so we were privileged to have this inside-view of how the job should be carried out.

PWB's trimmer, Nick Atkinson, makes the important point that you should never try to force anything when re-covering seats. Old covers should be carefully eased away, where they are glued to the foam. Clips should be bent back or eased away with care. And when refitting, be prepared to take as long as necessary to encourage each piece of trim and each fixing into place, firmly but carefully.

If you intend re-covering more than one seat, do them one at a time, so that the other can always be used as a point of reference.

◀ PWB1. Here, on the left, is a seat that has been brought in for re-covering with typical Land Rover wear and damage. Nick holds up the new covers that are going to be fitted and, on the bench next to him, is the new seat base foam which, in this case, will be needed. Small areas of foam damage can be repaired and any small missing chunks can be replaced with new material, although you would then probably have to glue a piece of thin foam over the surface to make it smooth again. See your local trim supplier if you need any additional parts such as these.

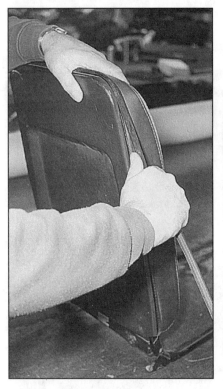

▲ PWB2. Now it's over to PWB's John Ross who demonstrates what to do with the backrest on a very early type of seat, the one with a hard plastic back. The first job is to peel off the rubber strip which holds the back to the frame . . .

▲ PWB4. Use a screwdriver to lever off the two clips holding the flap from the front cover, which has been passed underneath the base. Through the outer edge of this flap is a steel rod which must now be removed and retained for use with the new cover.

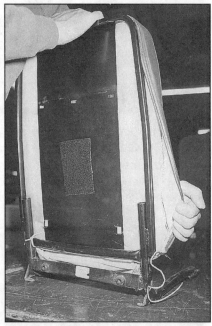

▲ PWB5. Undo the strings holding the bottom of the seat cover in place and pull the edges of the seat cover out of the channel around the frame. The principle is very similar to that for the seat base, which is shown later. When replacing the covers, the edges are eased into the channel, just as you would with a seat base, and then the strings are tied as you can see, still in place here bottom left.

▲ PWB3. . . . and lever off the back, taking very great care not to damage it.

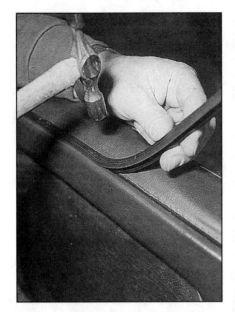

▲ PWB6. With the new cover in place and the seat back clipped on again, the rubber strip is hammered back into the channel, holding both the back and the seat cover in place. If you don't have John's skill and familiarity with the job, you would be well advised to use a soft-faced mallet so that you don't leave marks on the rubber strip.

▲ PWB7. Now John demonstrates how to re-cover the seat back on the far more numerous later-model seat types. The backrest clips are removed . . .

▲ PWB8. . . . and then a craft knife is used to cut right through the seat back, all the way round, exposing the frame.

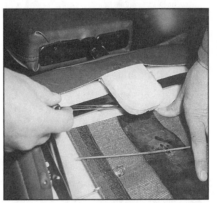

▲ PWB9. Now the headrest can be removed. There is a spring clip which must be depressed . . .

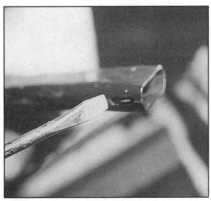

▲ PWB10. . . . more clearly demonstrated here, with the headrest removed.

▲ PWB11. John and Nick collaborate to slide out the steel bar which passes, on some models, through eyes mounted in the backrest foam. The bar – when fitted – holds the backrest foam firmly in position.

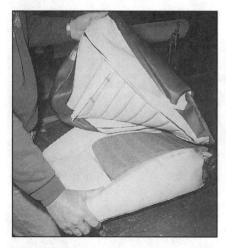

▲ PWB12. John lies the backrest down on the bench and pulls off the old cover.

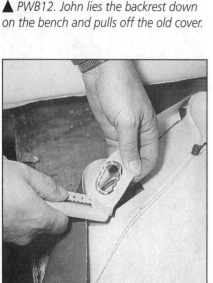

▲ PWB13. Before throwing the old cover away, it is important that you retrieve the trim ring from the top of it.

▲ PWB14. You have to lever up the tabs, take off the retaining ring and then you can remove and throw away the last piece of trim.

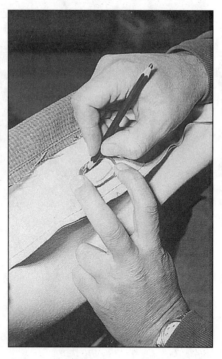

▲ PWB15. Use the trim ring to mark the position of the headrest aperture on the inside of the new cover, in the centre at the top. Draw around the inside of the trim ring and very carefully cut out with a sharp craft knife.

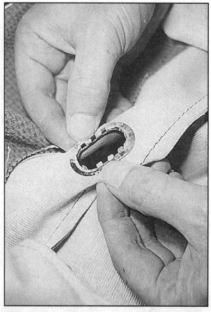

▲ PWB16. Note that here, the backrest trim is still inside-out. The trim ring, with claws, is pushed through the hole you have just cut from the outer side of the trim, the plain trim ring is pushed over the claws from above (the inner-side) . . .

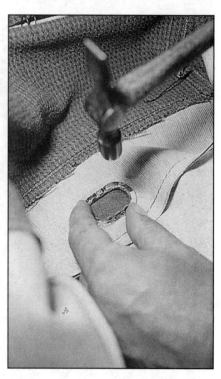

▲ PWB17. . . . and then the claws are very carefully hammered down. But don't hammer too hard, otherwise the claws will break off.

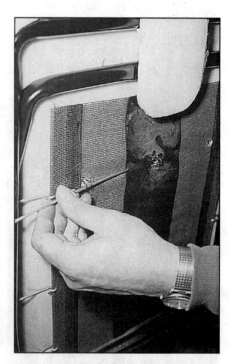

▲ PWB18. The backrest foam can, if necessary, now be replaced and this involves pushing the retainers through the backrest support and sliding the steel rod back into position again.

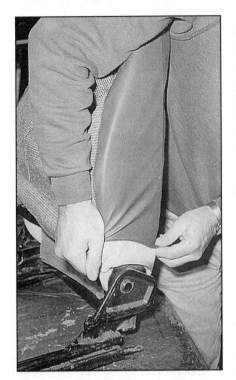

▲ PWB19. John now slides the new backrest cover over the foam. If you find this difficult to do, an old trick is to slide a suitable size plastic bag over the backrest so that the cover doesn't 'bind' on the foam.

▲ PWB21. Here you can see the flap folded around the bottom of the seat – viewed from the other side, now – and the back panel being introduced to the flap, where the two edges are overlapped and held down with the Velcro strip which PWB very thoughtfully fit.

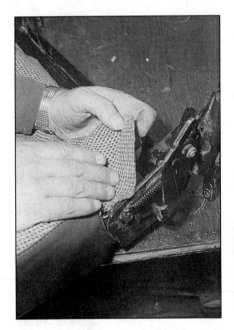

▲ PWB20. With the backrest lying down on the bench once again, John folds the outer edges of the flap, so that there are no raw edges showing, and passes the flap through the bottom of the seat.

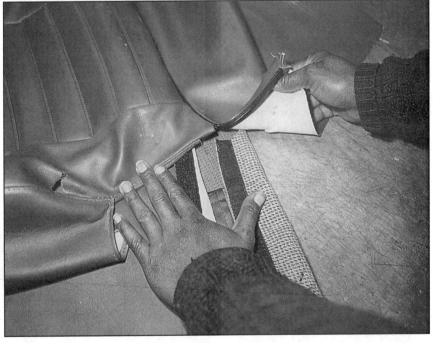

▲ PWB22. Here is the way that Land Rover originally did it – a long, push-on plastic clip which would be unnecessarily expensive to replicate and is undoubtedly more difficult to fit.

▲ PWB23. And here John demonstrates the superb looking and completed backrest.

▲ PWB26. The cover is also held with a number of plastic pegs which have to be very carefully levered out. Nick demonstrates that by levering from behind the trim, not from behind the head of the peg, the peg will come out without damage. Be sure to hang on to all of the pegs!

▲ PWB24. If John is the seat-back man, Nick is the seat-base man! The seat base is turned over and the two clips levered away with a screwdriver, after which Nick slides out the steel rod over which the clips were hooked.

▲ PWB25. Nick now pulls out the rubber strip which holds the seat base cover into the channel around the edge of the frame.

▲ PWB27. The edge of the trim is now easily pulled out from the channel and taken off the seat base.

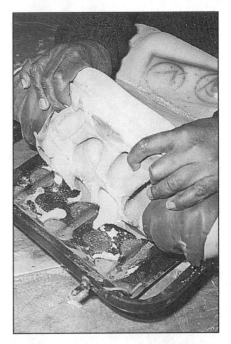

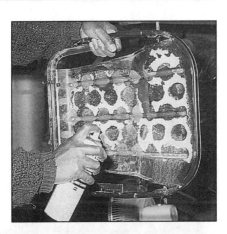

▶ PWB30. Here Nick applies aerosol adhesive to the cleaned-off seat base, and more adhesive is applied to the base of the foam.

▼ PWB31. The foam is placed in position on the steel seat base – and here you can see what the two strips of vinyl were for! They cover the (scarcely visible) gap between the pressed steel base and the edges of the seat frame. The surplus vinyl can now be cut away, back to the edge of the seat frame.

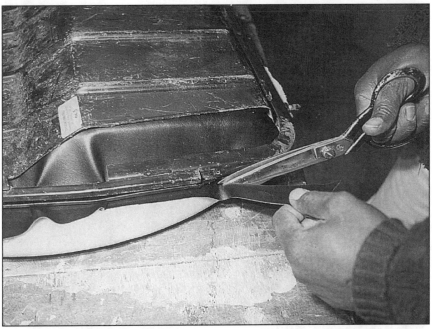

▲ PWB28. The old foam can be pulled away, but if it is to be re-used, take very great care to leave as little as possible behind on the seat base.

▼ PWB29. The seat base foam is far more prone to wear than the backrest and this one was deemed unsuitable for re-use. Before fitting the foam to the base, Nick fits the two pieces of vinyl trim which PWB supply with the kit, gluing it down to the edges of the underside of the foam.

▲ PWB32. Nick starts fitting the new seat base cover by pulling the back corners of the cover over the shoulders of the foam and pulling it down tight.

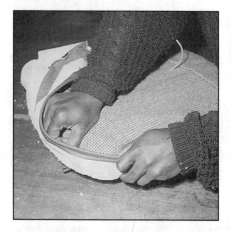

▲ PWB33. He then moves on to the front, and eases the front corners of the cover into place.

▲ PWB34. Taking very great care not to cause any damage, Nick uses a blunt screwdriver to ease the edges of the cover into the channel around the edge of the frame . . .

▲ PWB35. . . . and then hammers the rubber retaining strip into the channel, holding the trim in place. Once again, you may be well advised to use a soft-faced mallet rather than a hammer, to avoid any risk of marking the rubber strip.

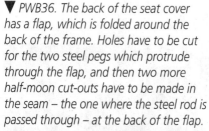

▼ PWB36. The back of the seat cover has a flap, which is folded around the back of the frame. Holes have to be cut for the two steel pegs which protrude through the flap, and then two more half-moon cut-outs have to be made in the seam – the one where the steel rod is passed through – at the back of the flap.

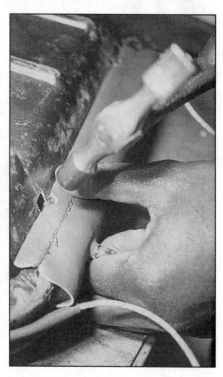

▲ PWB37. This is so that, after pushing the steel rod into the seam, and hooking the rod over the metal tongs which were levered open earlier, the tongs can be pushed behind the metal rod and then hammered down, holding the back of the seat cover in place.

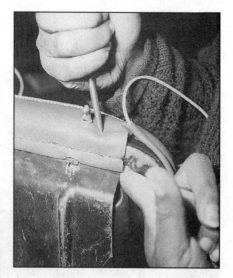

▲ PWB38. Now, here's the only slightly tricky bit. Nick uses the forefinger of his left hand to feel for the position of the hole in the steel frame, while using an awl to push a hole, very carefully, in the vinyl at the exact position of the hole in the steel.

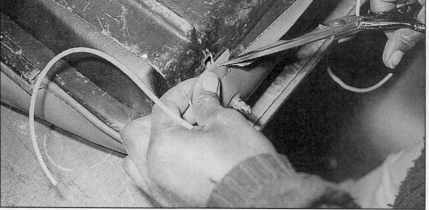

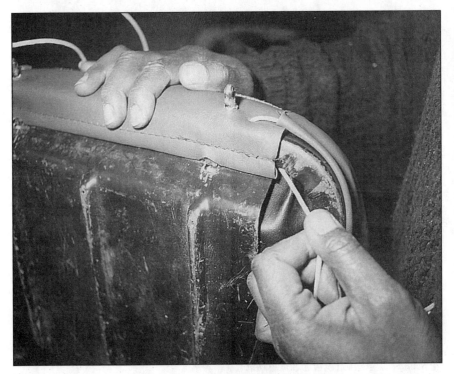

▲ PWB39. The string which emerges from the seam in the edges of the trim – the edge which has been held in the channel all the way around the edge of the seat – is pushed through the holes in the vinyl and the seat frame and pulled reasonably tight – but not so tight that you risk breaking it.

▲ PWB42. Now, there's just the headrest to attend to. After removing the trim plate screws and taking off the trim plate . . .

▲ PWB40. With the string held taut, the plastic peg that was removed earlier from this position is reintroduced and hammered down into the hole. This grips the string and prevents it from moving. Nick points out that if you break the string at this stage, the whole trim will have to be removed, a new string fitted, and all the weary work done all over again. So take great care!

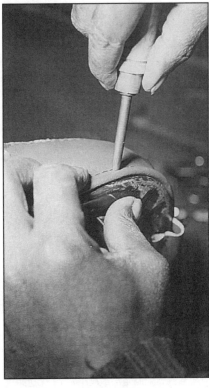

▲ PWB41. The awl is used to make holes for the other peg positions and the plastic pegs are re-fitted.

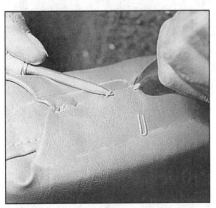

▲ PWB43. . . . the staples holding the trim in place are levered out.

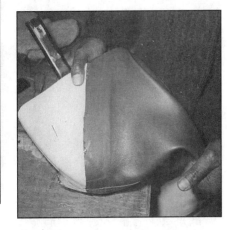

▲ PWB44. The old headrest cover can now be pulled off.

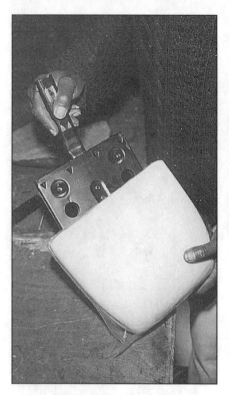

▲ PWB45. The steel arm which supports the headrest is then pulled out from the foam.

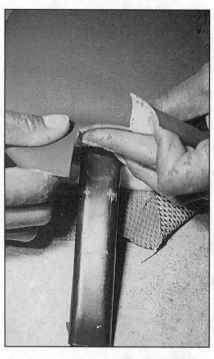

▲ PWB47. The new cover is pulled down over the headrest and two cuts made, directly in line with the supporting bar. The centre flap is tucked underneath, presenting a neat, folded edge . . .

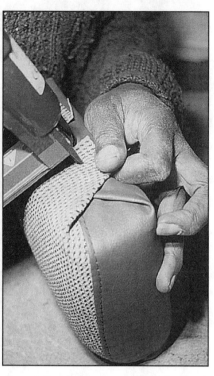

▲ PWB49. The flap created by the front piece of trim is treated in the same way and then the trim plate and screws are fitted back into place.

▲ PWB46. Nick slides a plastic bag over the foam, tucking the open end of the bag into the slot into which the supporting arm is slid back into place.

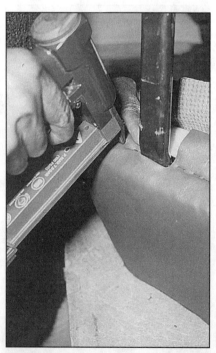

▲ PWB48. . . . and the back panel is stapled into place. You could of course use upholstery tacks just as well. Any surplus material can now be trimmed off with scissors.

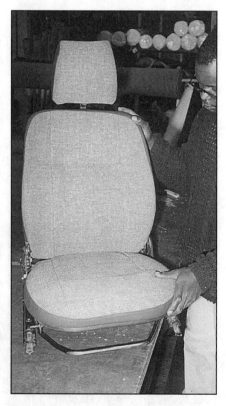

▲ PWB50. Nick displays the completed as-new Land Rover seat.

FITTING CARPETS

▲ FCS1. Carpet sets can be purchased from independent specialists – but beware! They rarely, if ever, drop straight in, and often need quite a lot of careful cutting and flapping to fit correctly.

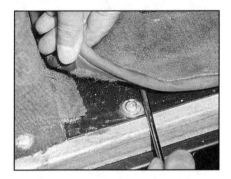

▲ FCS2. Carpets clip down with press-studs, which need to be fitted to the new carpet – with packing pieces if sound-proofing is added.

▲ FCS3. In some places, carpet as well as sound-proofing, is stuck down with contact adhesive. Use the scrape-on type rather than aerosol if you don't want to have glue squirting around the inside of the cab!

▲ FCS4. Sound-proofing the bonnet makes a big difference. (Oh please – we know it goes on the inside!)

FITTING A SOUND-PROOFING KIT

Land Rovers have many wonderful qualities, but one thing you can't accuse them of is quietness!

BJ Acoustics are among the best known manufacturers of sound-proofing kits for Land Rovers and claim that their kit will reduce engine, transmission and road noise by up to 50 per cent. Obviously, a County with its own sound-proofing will see a smaller reduction than this but the difference will be very noticeable – and very worthwhile! As *Land Rover Owner* magazine said after they fitted a kit to one of their vehicles, 'We were pleasantly surprised at how dramatically the engine and road noise had been reduced'.

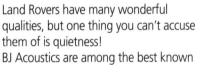

▲ BJ1. When the DIY kit is delivered to your door, it comes complete with a grumbling postman. Two of the parcels are very large and very heavy!

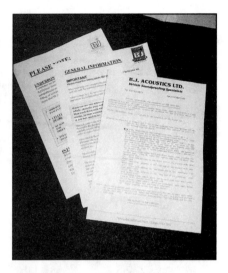

▲ BJ2. The kit will mean nothing to you unless you follow the enclosed instructions carefully.

▲ BJ3. The first job is to unpack all of the kits and spread the parts around. Go through the fitting instructions and identify each individual part so that you can see where it is to be placed. We recommend that you go to your local paint factors and buy a tin of panel wipe. Most of the BJ Acoustics kit has a self-adhesive backing and all the surfaces you will be fitting it to will need to be cleaned scrupulously. You may need degreasing agent to first shift any heavy deposits and you would be well advised to apply paint where bare metal is revealed, allowing the paint to dry for 24 hours before fitting the sound-proofing kit.

▲ BJ4. The lead-lined engine and bulkhead blanket consists of heat-resistant quilting around a heavy lead sandwich.

▲ BJ5. The removable plastic clips supplied are used to fix the blanket across the top of the engine and with the part nearest the camera folded between the rear of the engine and the bulkhead. The difference this makes to diesel engine clatter has to be heard to be believed! The addition of the BJ Acoustics lead-lined bellhousing blanket makes a tremendous difference to engine and transmission noise.

▲ BJ6. Each individual sound-proofing pad has a number written on the back of it. When you cross-refer this number to the instructions list you will see that Part 21 is adhered to the rear end of the driver's side rear wheelarch, while 23 goes on the passenger side rear wheelarch.

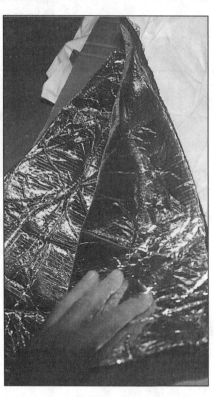

▲ BJ7. The sound-proofing mat for fitting to the engine bulkhead has to be cut, where appropriate. Note that the side facing the engine is silver-foil finished so that it also reflects heat away from your feet.

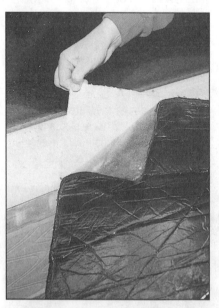

▲ BJ8. As with so many of the sound-proofing pads, the bulkhead section is self-adhesive. Whatever you do, don't peel off the backing paper until the pad has been cut out to fit and is ready to go on!

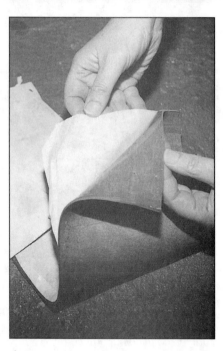

▲ BJ9. There is a set of mastic door pads included with the full kit. These are placed on the inside of each door skin, in the centre. They don't have to cover the whole of the inside of the door skin but have the highly desirable effect of cutting out the drumming that is created there. One pad can be fitted to the fuel tank.

Fitting a B J Acoustics sound-proofing kit is certainly not a five-minute job but the difference it will make to the enjoyment of your Land Rover will be immense. The company offers two excellent services. One is that they will travel to your premises and fit the kit for you (prices on application), or they're perfectly happy to 'hold your hand' and provide you with as much advice and assistance via the telephone as you may need. Bob and Jennifer, the eponymous husband and wife team behind the company, pride themselves on the standards of service they provide for their customers.

However, if you think you might need that sort of assistance, you may be best leaving the job until you've got a couple of days off in the normal working week – because I don't think their service extends to talking you through the job halfway through a Sunday afternoon!

DASH PANEL REMOVAL AND REFIT

After disconnecting the battery, remove the steering wheel, the steering column switches, the instrument panel and the switch panel.

Remove the radio/cassette player.

Remove the fusebox cover.

Take out the two screws from the base of the grab handle on the passenger side, lever out the badge from the top of the handle and remove the screw from beneath it. The grab handle can now be lifted up and away.

Take off the lower cover panel from the passenger side after removing the three retaining screws.

Take off the knobs from the heater and ventilation control levers after removing the small screws which pass through the side of them.

Take out the retaining screws holding the trim cover in place.

Two screws hold the cover to the heater and ventilation controls. When removing the cover and the screws, be sure to hang on to the spacers fitted between the cover and the control levers.

If you want to completely remove the controls, the cables will have to be detached.

The top panel is held in place by the screws which pass through the vent covers.

The front of the storage compartment has a trim rail which is also held in place with retaining screws.

The vent cover panel on the rear of the storage compartment is held in place with clips which are best levered out with a forked tool to prevent damage. If any retaining screws are fitted, remove them and then lift off the duct trim cover and the duct.

You can now lift out the insert from the storage compartment.

Unscrew the heater outlet ducts from the base of the dash panel.

The lower dash assembly can now be removed from the vehicle after taking

out all the retaining screws, not forgetting the two screws situated on the edge of the storage compartment. As the panel is removed, note the location of the foam seals from the ventilation housing inlets.

SEAT BELTS REMOVAL AND REFIT

In all cases, the seat belts are simple to remove – once you know how to get at them! All seat belt mountings are tightened to captive nuts in the bodywork. It is essential that all spacers and spring washers are replaced in exactly the correct order when seat belts are being refitted.

The top seat belt mounting is accessed by unclipping the top of the trim cover and hinging it forwards.

If the seat belt webbing and connector has to be passed through the aperture finisher, it will have to be levered out of position, taking care not to cause any damage.

The lower mounting (sometimes using the same mounting point as the inertia reel mounting) is similarly and simply unscrewed.

Seat belt stalks and centre belt mountings are covered with trim caps which are first levered off before undoing the mountings.

Rear seat belt mountings may be of the inertia reel or fixed type and their mounting brackets are a combination of the types also used at the front.

B-POST TRIM – 110 MODELS FROM 1988–ON

After removing the top seat belt mounting as described earlier, use a forked tool to lever out the plastic button. You can now remove the trim. When refitting, the button is carefully pushed back in.

▲ *DPR1. When reassembling, take great care not to trap or in any way damage any of the wiring, ensure that the ducting is securely in position and that the foam seals are correctly located.*

REAR QUARTER LIGHT TRIM

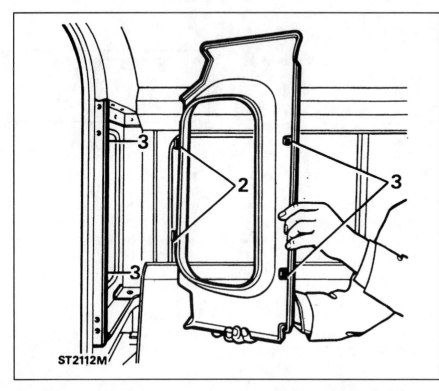

ST2112M

▲ RQL1. The trim is a single plastic piece which is clipped into place. Grasp the trim panel towards its top and bottom at the door aperture and pull it towards yourself to release the spring clips (3). As you pull it away, the two metal lugs in the corner of the vehicle will free themselves from the side trim clips (2).

When refitting, make sure that the two metal lugs are located behind the side trim and then bang the two spring clips on to the vertical rail adjacent to the door opening, using your hand. (Illustration courtesy Land Rover)

REAR SIDE WINDOW TRIM – STATION WAGONS FROM 1988–ON

You must first remove the rear seat and frame, the upper and lower seat belt anchorage bolts and the upper seat belt aperture finisher from the trim panel. You must also remove the rear quarter light trim. All of these are described in earlier sections.

Remove the front lower fixing, which consists of a Phillips head machine screw, two washers and a nut. . .

. . . and remove the centre and rear fixings, which consist of a Phillips head machine screw, single washer and a nut welded to a plate. As the screw is removed, the nut/plate will fall into the box section.

Three spring clips hold the top edge of the trim to the bodywork. Strike the trim upwards to release it.

Feed the seat belt through its aperture and the trim can now be removed from the vehicle.

Refitting is the reverse of removal, but note that on 90 models, the front-most bushed hole in the trim – the one nearest the B-post – is not used.

GRAB HANDLES

Two fixing screws are easily removed from each end of the grab handle once the plastic finisher has been lifted away.

UPPER TRIM PANEL – 110 MODELS

In order to remove this piece of trim, the B-post trim and the grab handle must first be removed, as described in earlier sections.

The top of the trim is held by clips and is removed by banging upwards, just as for the rear side window trim.

Appendix

CLUBS

Club addresses and officials (or at least, some of them!) change faster than we can reprint this book. See your favourite Land Rover magazine for details of the many hundreds of Land Rover clubs around the world.

SPECIALISTS

Clarke International
Hemnall Street, Epping, Essex.
CM16 4LG.
Tel: 01992 565300
www.clarkeinternational.com

**Noisekiller Acoustics (UK) Ltd
(formerly BJ Acoustics)**
103 Denbydale Way,
Royton,
Oldham, OL2 5UK.
Tel: 0161 652 7080
www.noisekiller.co.uk
E-mail: steve@noisekiller.co.uk

Ryder Towing Equipment Ltd
Alvanley House,
Alvanley Industrial Estate,
Stockport Road East,
Bredbury, Stockport,
Cheshire SK6 2DJ.
Tel: 0161 430 1120
www.rydertowing.co.uk

Sykes Pickavant Ltd
Full range of excellent DIY and professional panel beating tools. See local DIY and accessory shops.
Tel: 01922 702 222
www.sptools.co.uk

Witter Towbars
6-11 Drome Road,
Deeside Industrial Park,
Deeside CH5 2NY.
Tel: 01244 284500
www.witter-towbars.co.uk

Wurth UK Ltd
1 Centurion Way, Erith, Kent,
DA18 4AF. Tel: 0181 319 6000
www.wurth.co.uk

MAGAZINES

Land Rover Owner
Media House,
Lynchwood,
Peterborough PE2 6EA.
Tel: 01733 468582
www.lro.com

Land Rover Monthly
2 Brickfield Business Park,
Woolpit, Suffolk
IP30 9QS.
Tel: 01359 240066
www.lrm.co.uk
Lindsay Porter is the Technical Editor of this highly regarded magazine. Naturally, it has a large technical content each month.

Land Rover World
Kelsey Publishing Ltd,
Cudham Tithe Barn,
Berry's Hill,
Cudham,
Kent TN16 3AG.
Tel: 01959 541444
www.landroverworld.co.uk

Land Rover Enthusiast
PO Box 178,
Wallingford DO,
Oxfordshire OX10 8PD.
www.landroverenthusiast.com

Haynes
Restoration Manuals

Haynes **Restoration Manual** MGB (2nd Edition)

History, Buying, Specification, Bodywork, Mechanics, Interior, Electrics, Modifications

Lindsay Porter

For more information on books please contact: Customer Services,
Haynes Publishing, Sparkford, Yeovil, Somerset BA22 7JJ, UK
Tel. **01963 442030** Fax: **01963 440001**
Int. tel: **+44 1963 442030** Fax: **+44 1963 440001**
E-mail: **sales@haynes.co.uk** Website: **www.haynes.co.uk**